Synopt e

Sarah K on R

Philip Allan Updates
Market Place
Deddington
Oxfordshire
OX15 0SE

tel: 01869 338652
fax: 01869 337590
e-mail: sales@philipallan.co.uk
www.philipallan.co.uk

ISBN 0 86003 762 2

Designed by Neil Fozzard
Printed by Raithby, Lawrence & Co Ltd, Leicester

20 0400 3394

P00183

Contents

Introduction v

Chapter 1   Philosophy of Religion and Religious Ethics
             Religious language and ethical language 1

Chapter 2   Philosophy of Religion and Religious Ethics
             Human freedom and the existence of God 12

Chapter 3   Philosophy of Religion and Religious Ethics
             Religious experience 24

Chapter 4   Philosophy of Religion and Biblical Studies
             Religious experience 35

Chapter 5   Philosophy of Religion and New Testament
             Life after death 45

Chapter 6   World Religions (Islam) and Christian Belief
             Life after death 56

Chapter 7   Philosophy of Religion and New Testament
             Miracles 66

Chapter 8   Philosophy of Religion and World Religions (Judaism and Buddhism)
             Evil and suffering 79

Chapter 9   Old Testament/Jewish Bible and Christian Belief
             The nature of God 95

Chapter 10 Old Testament/Jewish Bible and World Religions (Judaism)
      Significant people 105

Chapter 11 New Testament and World Religions (Islam)
      Significant people 116

Chapter 12 Religious Ethics and New Testament
      Ethical theory and applied ethics 128

Chapter 13 Religious Ethics and Christian Belief
      Ethical theory and applied ethics 137

Chapter 14 Philosophy of Religion and Christian Belief
      Feminist theology 146

Chapter 15 Philosophy of Religion and Religious Ethics
      Concepts of authority 156

Bibliography 167

Introduction

The synoptic, or connections, paper in Religious Studies has caused considerable anxiety to both teachers and students since it was introduced in the specifications for A2. This is a great pity, since it is designed to give you an excellent opportunity to demonstrate your analytical skills and your understanding of how the different areas of the specification you have studied make fundamental links with each other. We have become too nervous of acknowledging these links in the past, which may explain the anxiety that sets in when faced with the prospect of answering a question which tests this specifically. It goes against the grain for philosophers to look seriously at the miracles of the New Testament, or for biblical scholars to confront the critical claims of philosophical analysis. Nevertheless, Religious Studies and Theology offer something that many other subjects do not, and that is the opportunity for truly multidisciplinary study. An undergraduate course in the subject will inevitably cover a wide range of options, including linguistic, historical, literary and philosophical study, so it is not unreasonable to approach our studies in a similar way at A-level.

The fear of the task should be dispelled if we first establish a systematic way of identifying connections. Initially it may seem forced and artificial, but once you get used to finding associations it will soon become second nature. And it's exciting when this happens, opening up new areas of the subject which may not previously have occurred to you. The process is made easier by mapping out the different disciplines you are required to study before tracing the links between them, building up an increasingly complex web, from which you then need to identify the most important connections.

This book is designed to help you learn this process and for it to become increasingly automatic for you to do so. It covers a range of synoptic tasks common to all the major specifications, including sample answers and subject-related notes. You will find different styles and approaches in the various chapters, but what is common to them all is the vital skill of *synopticity*. Most importantly, you should come away from reading this book with a stronger sense of how to establish connections and an understanding of *why* they are important. If you accomplish this, then you are equipped to tackle any question you may be asked. The examination boards do try to make things relatively straightforward, in so far as the areas that you are required to study are specified clearly. While you may not know the exact question in advance, or be able to take materials into the exam, you will be equipped with a fair amount of information ahead of the day. Broadly speaking, each of the options you are studying is united by a common concept, for example:

- The nature or purpose of miracles, religious experience, or life after death is relevant to both Philosophy of Religion *and* New Testament studies (as well as to other combinations). The way in which the biblical writers reveal their understanding of the nature of God is pertinent to both Old Testament/Jewish Scriptures and the New Testament.
- Issues of religious authority apply to any of the world religions and to the potential conflict between the authoritative claims of science and religion.
- The roles of key figures in any of the world religions present obvious connections, as do the contributions of significant people in the Old and New Testaments with those in later periods of church history.
- Moral and ethical teaching is relevant to all periods of religious history, to the teaching within sacred texts, and interconnects very closely with the broader processes of philosophical analysis.

These key areas, and many others in which there are obvious interconnections, have already been identified by the examination boards and these are sure to provide you with plenty of material to draw upon. You will never have to struggle to find these connections if you have prepared in advance. You can approach this preparation in four key stages, as follows.

1 Understanding, learning and consolidating the material in each of the units or modules you have studied

If your two modules/units are, for example, Islam and Ethics, then before you can make meaningful connections between them you must have a solid grasp of the material as it is relevant to the individual units. A study of religious experience within Islam, for example, must be firmly based on a foundation laid by an understanding of:

- the philosophical, psychological and conceptual issues raised by religious experience in general
- the nature of God as understood in Islam
- a knowledge and understanding of the key figures within the history of the faith

Only then can the different topics be brought together in a truly meaningful way.

2 Getting into the habit of finding connections

This is a skill best established at the beginning of your course but, since the synoptic or connections paper is an A2 examination, you might not be encouraged to do so at the early stages. However, whether you are in the first months or the final weeks of your Religious Studies A-level, you should start doing it now. Think about the different modules you are taking and make a list of areas that overlap. For example:

Philosophy of Religion → *Arguments for the existence of God* → *Cosmological Argument (universe as grounds for existence of God)* → *Design Argument (specific feature of the universe as grounds for existence of God)* → *Problem of 'bad design'; flaws in the natural order* → *Problem of natural evil* → *Challenges to belief in God; atheism* → *Responses to the challenge of natural evil (theodicies)* → *Universe with natural evil a better universe than one without (a toy world, no responsibility)* → *God at an epistemic distance, but can and does intervene at times* → *Miracles* → **New Testament accounts** → *Definitions: Hume, Aquinas, Holland* → *Necessary and sufficient conditions* → *Does God intervene to close the epistemic distance?* → *An interventionist God* → *Miracles as arbitrary* → *New Testament writers see them as proof of existence of God and person of Jesus* → *Credibility of New Testament accounts* → *Reliability of modern-day accounts* → *Problems of verification*

Think of this as an exercise in the association of ideas; you can practise it in class or with a partner. One of you names a topic and each of you follows with the related idea that immediately occurs to you. Start by doing this for one unit or module — as in the case above, which revolves around a few key areas in the Philosophy of Religion — but gradually build up to include ideas from your other modules too. Feel comfortable with the idea that there are no forbidden areas and make connections between as many topics as you can. Only then should you examine them to see if they will provide you with something really substantial or if they are too peripheral to pursue.

3 Evaluating connections

Once you have built up your confidence to make connections between your units, start to consider how well they support each other. For example, one of the reasons why philosophers are sceptical of accounts of miracles from religious believers is because they think that the occurrence of miracles is highly unlikely on all sorts of philosophical grounds. Does this therefore make it impossible to use accounts of miracles to justify philosophically the likelihood of their occurring? Would you be able to argue this convincingly, or is it possible that some accounts of miracles might well be true, despite logical argument against them?

If you are attempting to make connections between significant people in different religious traditions or across historical periods, devise criteria for assessing the similarities and differences between them. These might include: historical context; personal influences; distinctive doctrines; perennial significance; personality; manner of death, etc. Having done this, ask the all-important question *WHY?* Why is this important? Why am I including it in my essay? Why am I leaving it out? Why might someone challenge me on this point? Why might I defend my argument? A third or more of your marks are for evaluating the connections between the topics you are studying, so get used to doing this in the early stages of preparation.

4 Practising writing the essay

Although there is a lot to be said for spontaneity, the exam is not the time to be spontaneous. The examiner knows this too, and will not be expecting to see flights of intellectual creativity thought up on the spur of the moment. In any case, as our friend and colleague Peter Cole said at a conference, if you think you've really come up with a new theory, don't waste it on the exam: keep it to yourself and wait to publish it in your own book! What the examiner does expect you to have done, however, is not only to have thought about connections before the day of the exam, but also to have practised writing about them. The synoptic unit is just like any other paper you will be sitting: you need to have established your timing and to have tested your revision. Because you may only be writing one essay, the exam will feel different from those in which you have to write two, and you will have to pace yourself differently. If you haven't tested this out prior to the day, you will not have established when you are likely to feel tired or identified those areas that are slower to come to the front of your brain once you are in the unique conditions of a real exam.

Practise several versions of a synoptic essay several times under timed conditions, and on the day the whole experience will feel familiar. Also, don't forget that the fact that you may be writing one essay in the time usually allocated for two tells you something about its length. It should be approximately twice the length of a standard exam essay. If you're not getting past the staples in the middle of the exam booklet, you haven't written enough.

Mind-mapping the synoptic task

Mind-mapping, spider diagrams and association-of-ideas flow charts are not a new tool for learning, planning or revision. However, they come into their own in your preparation for this unit. Brainstorming the individual topic areas that need to be connected gives you a basis for making the connections, and then uniting them into a separate mind map shows you exactly where they are. Use lots of colours, big sheets of paper (A3, not A4) and feel free to include any ideas that come into your brain. If you have too many, you can soon eliminate those that are less helpful. Let's take as an example the connecting theme of life after death in both New Testament and Philosophy of Religion. First, create a mind map or spider diagram of everything you can think of related to life after death in the New Testament. It doesn't have to be detailed, just key ideas that will remind you of what you need to develop as you write your essay (see opposite).

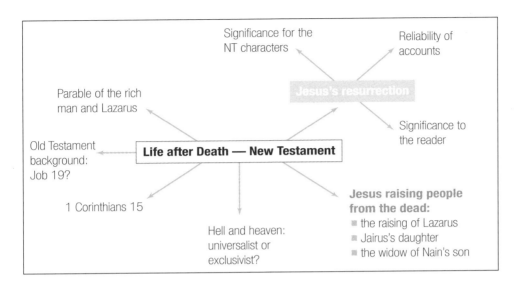

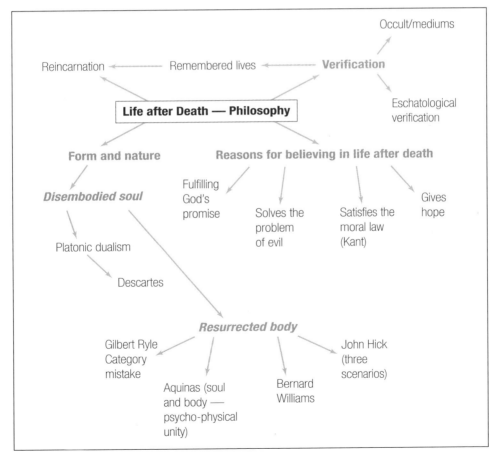

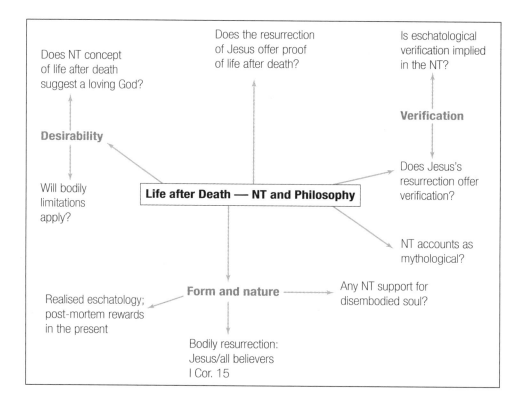

These models are, of course, incomplete and if you are familiar with these topics, you can find for yourself more ways of making links between the concept of life after death in Philosophy of Religion and in New Testament. The method should be clear, however, and by the time you are at the point of making links between the two units the relevant ideas will already have been explored in the individual mind maps. The more you come back to it, the more ideas will come to you and the more links you will see between your units.

Religious language and ethical language

Religious language

The problems of religious language

- Distinctive religious terminology — how do we understand it?
- How can we use everyday language to speak of God?
- Do we preserve God's difference from, or emphasise his similarity to, humanity?
- How do we avoid making religious language obscure?
- Is religious language meaningful?
- Is it subject to verification and/or falsification?
- Is religious language only understandable to the believer?
- Is religious language best used cognitively or non-cognitively?

The nature of religious language

- **Cognitive** — or **realist** — language makes factual assertions that can be proved true or false, e.g. statements that are believed by those who use them to contain meaningful, objective, factual content: 'God exists'; 'God loves us'; 'God will execute a final judgement'. The following are not: *'crypto-commands, expressions of wishes, disguised ejaculations, concealed ethics, or anything else but assertions'* (Anthony Flew, 1955). Cognitive claims assume a **correspondence theory of truth** between the language use and the concepts or objects to which that language refers.
- **Non-cognitive** — or **anti-realist** — language is used to make claims that are to be interpreted in some other way, perhaps as symbols, metaphors, ethical commands or other non-literal modes of expression. It is language that serves some function other than that of expressing factually, objectively true claims. Rather, it expresses the meaning that religious discourse has to an individual and the

community to which he or she belongs. Such language — which includes the use of symbol and myth — assumes a **coherence theory of truth**; truth or falsity is related to the other statements with which it is associated, rather than to objectively real situations.

Verification and falsification

The Vienna Circle derived a radical new theory of language, which was termed the **verification principle**. This stated that only assertions that were *in principle* verifiable by observation or experience could convey factual information, i.e. that the means by which it could be tested was known, even if it could not be tested in practice. Assertions that there could be no imaginable way of verifying must be either analytic (self-explanatory) or meaningless. Since statements about God are neither analytically true nor open to verification by observation, they were therefore rendered meaningless.

The falsification principle

The failure of the verification principle led to a new challenge: *'What would have to occur or to have occurred to constitute for you a disproof of the love of, or the existence of, God?'* (Flew, 1955). Rather than demand that an assertion be verifiable, the **falsification principle** demanded that the speaker must be able to say what would count, at least in principle, towards its falsification. Hence: *'In order to say something which may possibly be true, we must say something which may possibly be false'* (John Hick, 1966).

Flew used Wisdom's parable of the gardener to illustrate how believers were guilty of not allowing evidence that failed to prove the existence or love of God actually to count against their theological statements which *'die the death of a thousand qualifications'*.

Flew observed:
Now it often seems to people who are not religious as if there was no conceivable event…the occurrence of which would be admitted by sophisticated religious people to be a sufficient reason for conceding…'God does not really love us then'.

R. M. Hare proposed that a believer's statements were **bliks**: ways of regarding the world which are in principle neither verifiable nor falsifiable, but because they make a significant difference to his or her life, the believer's claims are not meaningless. Basil Mitchell claimed that believers do recognise challenges to faith without allowing them to be conclusively falsified.

Richard Swinburne (1979) argued that:
…there are plenty of examples of statements which some people judge to be factual which are

not apparently confirmable or disconfirmable through observation. For example: Some of the toys which to all appearances stay in the toy cupboard while people are asleep and no one is watching actually get up and dance in the middle of the night and then go back to the cupboard, leaving no traces of their activity.

Language games

Ludwig Wittgenstein was concerned only with the *use* of language rather than the meaning of it, since it is the context that defines its function. Certain terminology is applied in a way that is appropriate to one context and not to another, reflecting the way the speaker understands the world:

Suppose someone were a believer and said: 'I believe in a Last Judgement,' and I said, 'Well, I'm not so sure. Possibly', you would say that there was an enormous gulf between us. If he said, 'There is a German aeroplane overhead', and I said, 'Possibly, I'm not so sure,' you'd say we were fairly near.... Suppose someone is ill and he says: 'This is a punishment', and I say: 'If I'm ill, I don't think of punishment at all.' If you say, 'Don't you believe the opposite?' — you can call it believing the opposite, but it is entirely different from what we would normally call believing the opposite. I think differently, in a different way. I say different things to myself. I have a different picture. (Cited in Mitchell (ed.), 1971)

The two understandings of illness described in this conversation — one essentially religious and one not — reflect different forms of life, neither of which is necessarily right or wrong. The language is used in different ways and needs to be understood in that context. The concept of category mistake is helpful in comprehending this way of understanding language: to speak of a 'soul' and to try to see it as a physical object would lead to the kind of problems inherent in using religious language inappropriately.

Analogy

D. Burrell (cited in Coggins and Houlden (eds), 1990) observed:
Analogies are proportional similarities which also acknowledge dissimilar features.

David Hume (cited in Coggins and Houlden (eds), 1990) stated:
Wisdom, thought, design, knowledge — these we justly ascribe to him because those words are honourable among men, and we have no other language by which we can express our adoration of him.

Thomas Aquinas (cited in Hick (ed.), 1964) wrote:
Among beings there are some more and some less good, true, noble and the like. But more and less are predicated of different things according as they resemble in their different

ways something that is the maximum…so that there is something which is truest, something best, something noblest…. Therefore there must also be something which is to all beings the cause of their being, goodness, and every other perfection, and this we call God.

- Everything that is said of man belongs to God in a greater and more perfect way, although we know of man's qualities first and from him learn of God's.
- If we remove all creaturely concepts from a word and project what is left onto God, then we learn that God is without limit.
- **Analogy of proportion:** all good qualities belong proportionately to God and to man; thus we know that proportionately they must exist pre-eminently in God.
- **Analogy of attribution:** God is the cause of all good things in man and other beings and thus attributes to them what belongs to him first in a greater and higher sense.
- Analogy dispenses with the need to speak of God either **equivocally** (as completely different from man) or **univocally** (as exactly the same in his nature and character).

Aquinas wrote:

Hence from the knowledge of sensible things the whole power of God cannot be known; nor therefore can His essence be seen. But because they are His effects and depend on their cause, we can be led from them so far as to know of God whether He exists, and on to know of Him what must necessarily belong to Him, as the first cause of all things, exceeding all things caused by Him.
(Cited in Hick (ed.), 1964)

Symbol and myth

Symbol: *'a pattern or object which points to an invisible metaphysical reality and participates in it'* (Erika Dinker-von Schubert, cited in Halverson and Cohen (eds), 1960).

Symbols *identify* — point to the concept they are conveying — and *participate* — share in some way in the meaning of that concept. Symbols may be pictorial, abstract, verbal or active (a symbolic action). Symbols are therefore subtle modes of communication, which belong to high-level discourse. While they do not belong exclusively to religious language, symbols are of particular value to discourse that deals with issues that are beyond the factual and objective.

Rowan Williams wrote:

The development of symbolism in religious language is not a process of the encrustation of an original, simple idea with distracting and extraneous illustration or ornament. Like all other serious human discourse, religious language requires a symbolic foundation.
(Cited in Coggins and Houlden (eds), 1990)

Myth: *'a symbolic, approximate expression of truth which the human mind cannot perceive sharply and completely, but can only glimpse vaguely, and therefore cannot adequately or accurately express'* (Millar Burrows, 1946).

Myths embody and express claims that cannot be expressed in any other way, frequently making use of symbol, metaphor and imagery in a narrative context. In the nineteenth century D. F. Strauss wrote that modern readers needed to shift the focus of myth from the 'story of a *miraculous* occurrence to the *story* of a miraculous occurrence'. Rudolph Bultmann claimed:

It is impossible to use electric light and the wireless and to avail ourselves of modern medical and surgical discoveries and, at the same time, to believe in the New Testament world of demons and spirits.

(Cited in Green, McKnight and Marshall (eds), 1992)

Ethical language

Before we can begin to establish what constitutes good or bad moral or ethical behaviour, we need to consider whether we can define what morality *is*. A primary consideration is whether ethical language can be said to have any meaning, and to grasp the different implications behind ethical claims.

Absolutism: *never* take the life of another human being.

Relativism: it is *sometimes* right to take the life of another human being.

Subjectivism: *I think* it is right to take the life of this human being.

Objectivism: *the law* tells me that it is wrong to take the life of this human being.

Cognitivism: when I say that it is wrong to take the life of another human being I am *asserting this as a moral fact*.

Non-cognitivism: when I say that it is wrong to take the life of another human being I believe this to *cohere with other beliefs* I hold which are not necessarily factually true.

Naturalism: what is right or wrong can be defined with reference to things *in the world*.

The naturalistic fallacy: preserving life *is* a good thing and therefore you *ought* to preserve life. Is it legitimate to move from a **descriptive statement** (is) to a **prescriptive statement** (ought)?

Intuitionism: I do not know by definition whether it is wrong to take a human life, but by *intuition*.

Emotivism: when I say that taking a human life is wrong I am expressing my *opinion*.

Intuitionism

Proponents of intuitionism argue that ethical terms cannot be defined, since the properties ascribed to them, such as 'good' or 'ought', can also be defined in non-ethical terms. G. E. Moore (1993 edn) argued that 'good' can be defined no more successfully than 'yellow' since ethical values are self-evident and can be known only directly by intuition. Moore argued: *'If I am asked, "What is good?" my answer is that good is good, and that is the end of the matter.'*

Emotivism

In *Language, Truth and Logic* (1936), A. J. Ayer maintained that ethical claims were not designed to make factual claims but to invoke certain emotional responses in the hearer, and so what they *mean* is less important than what they *accomplish*:

Thus, if I say to someone, 'You acted wrongly in stealing that money', I am not stating anything more than if I had simply said, 'You stole that money'. In adding that this action is wrong, I am not making any further statement about it, I am simply evincing my moral disapproval of it. It is as if I had said, 'You stole that money' in a peculiar tone of horror, or written it with the addition of some special exclamation marks. The tone, or the exclamation marks, adds nothing to the literal meaning of the sentence. It merely serves to show that the expression of it is attended by certain feelings in the speaker.

It is worth mentioning that ethical terms do not serve only to express feeling. They are calculated also to arouse feeling and so to stimulate actions. Indeed, some of them are used in such a way as to give the sentences in which they occur the effect of commands. Thus, the sentence, 'It is your duty to tell the truth' may be regarded both as the expression of a certain sort of ethical feeling about truthfulness and as the expression of the command, 'tell the truth'. The sentence, 'You ought to tell the truth' also involves the command 'tell the truth', but here the tone of the command is less emphatic. In the sentence 'It is good to tell the truth', the command has become little more than a suggestion.

However...

- Ethical statements are not usually judged according to the response of the listener.
- If ethical claims were contingent on emotions, then they would be changeable.
- Moral statements are not validated by the weight of emotional force.
- Emotivism effectively prescribes complete freedom of action.
- How can we judge between two people's moral opinions?
- Emotions can isolate individuals and groups as much as unite them.

Synoptic question and answer

Question 1 Philosophy of Religion and Religious Ethics

> Compare and contrast the distinctive problems of religious and ethical language.

The problem of religious language has troubled philosophers since earliest times. How do we speak of a transcendent God, beyond direct human experience, infinitely more perfect in all ways than human beings, in the limited language that is available to us? At the same time, believers want to be able to speak of God so they have to find a way that expresses how God is different from all other things and beings, and yet is meaningful to them. Religious language is language that deals with God and other theological matters, including religious worship, practice, behaviour and doctrine. It includes terms which we ascribe only to God in their primary context (i.e. omnipotent) and words which are about distinctively religious beliefs (i.e. the Last Judgement). However, even when we speak of religious issues we invariably have to use language that is drawn from our common linguistic and lexical store, and this raises problems of a particular kind.

Ethical language poses peculiar problems too. Important ethical words — or, as A. J. Ayer called them, **ethical symbols in a proposition** — such as good, bad, right or wrong, are very difficult, if not impossible, to define. Similarly, there are considerable problems in determining what we consider to be an objectively true statement about a matter of morality and what is merely subjective opinion. Before we can begin to establish what constitutes good or bad moral or ethical behaviour we need to consider whether we can define what morality is. The branch of moral philosophy that is concerned with this issue is **meta-ethics**, which examines the issue of what we mean when we say that a thing or an action is good, bad, right, wrong, moral or immoral. A primary consideration is whether ethical language can be said to have any meaning. If we are unclear as to the meaning of basic ethical terms such as these, then how can we begin to make authoritative, or at least convincing, claims about the morality of particular actions? The statement 'Killing is wrong' is complicated enough, since we are immediately faced with a vast range of different situations in which not everyone would agree that killing was wrong, but if we are not even sure about what we mean by 'wrong', then ethical debate will be fraught with difficulties. There are many ways of approaching both this problem and that of religious language which can be considered, and in so doing their distinctive characteristics are exposed.

Perhaps the primary characteristic problem of religious language can be summarised as the problem of how to talk meaningfully about God. Aquinas observed that we could talk of two things as either completely different (equivocally) or as meaning exactly the same thing (univocally), but that neither of these approaches works for talking about God. If we use human language of God — saying that he is wise or loving, for example — we don't intend to say that he is exactly the same in his possession of wisdom or love as human beings are. If we did mean this, then we would be saying that God is no better than or different from humans, and so would he really be God at all? Would he be a god worthy of worship (assuming, perhaps wrongly, that God must be perfect to be worthy of worship)? At the same time, we don't mean that his love or wisdom is so different from man's that it is beyond our comprehension. We have some concept of what love means when applied to man and although we apply it to God differently, something of that original concept remains. Neither way is totally satisfactory, however, since it is effectively a compromise, and neither too could the principle of the *via negativa* — speaking of God in terms of what he is not — ever satisfy the believer who wants to make positive claims about him. Aquinas suggested, therefore, that analogy provided the means of speaking successfully about God, which preserved his difference, while allowing the relationship between man and God to be expressed. Hence, to say that John is wise and God is wise makes the connection clear because John's wisdom comes from God. There is still a difference, however, because we know that God, as the cause of wisdom, possesses it in a different and greater way.

This only deals, however, with cognitive statements about God — statements that are intended to be true or false. When a believer says that 'God is good' they intend it to be objectively true — that there is an objectively real being called God, who possesses in a real and objective way the quality we know as goodness. This exposes another characteristic problem of religious language — that it assumes that there is such an objective reality. Some philosophers have suggested that since this is a false assumption to make, then religious language cannot be meaningful. This was the argument of the **Logical Positivists**, who claimed that since it was impossible to verify or to falsify the existence of God, then all religious claims were meaningless, and that even to ask the question 'Does God exist?' was meaningless. A. J. Ayer claimed that religious language confused statements about empirical propositions (such as the claim that there is a regularity within nature) with metaphysical claims — for example, that such regularity within nature points to the existence of God. However, Ayer (1936) maintained, surely *'no religious man would admit that this was all he intended to assert in asserting the existence of God'* because *'in talking about God he was talking about a transcendent being who might be known through certain empirical manifestations, but certainly could not be defined in terms of those manifestations'*. On this basis, Ayer asserted, 'God' is therefore a metaphysical term and *'then it cannot be even probable that a god exists'*.

This was a very radical approach to religious language, growing out of a philosophical movement that made it impossible to discourse on anything that could not be verified or falsified using objective, mathematical or analytical criteria. And it is with this movement that we find a very important point of connection with ethical language. The Logical Positivists, and A. J. Ayer especially, argued that ethical language was meaningless if it were understood as intending to express a proposition that has factual content. Ethical statements could not have objective reality because they were nothing more than the expression of a subjective opinion. If someone claims 'Abortion is wrong', for example, they are not making an objectively true statement with which we are obliged to agree because it can be verified using the Positivists' criteria of meaning, but rather someone is just expressing what they *feel*. Feelings are not objective, but subjective, so cannot be relied upon, and hence the statement is meaningless.

Ayer used the example of the claim 'You acted wrongly in stealing that money', which he argued conveys no more information than the statement 'stealing money'. The ethical claim 'You acted wrongly' is an expression of moral disapproval but adds nothing to the literal meaning of the sentence. He suggested that simply adding exclamation marks to the statement — 'stealing money!!' — would serve just as well as 'You acted wrongly' and in both cases nothing was being said that could be true or false. Ayer (1936) wrote: *'Another man might disagree with me about the wrongness of stealing, in the sense that he might not have the same feelings about stealing as I have, and he may quarrel with me on account of any moral sentiments. But he cannot, strictly speaking, contradict me.... For neither of us is asserting a genuine proposition.'*

Ultimately, therefore, Ayer effectively dismissed the ability to make ethical and religious assertions on the same grounds, although he was later forced to acknowledge that his theories were in some ways too strict, and he allowed that some things might be verifiable in principle, and on those grounds would be meaningful. Not surprisingly, this approach has been challenged by many thinkers, who observe that those who make ethical and religious claims do, at least some of the time, understand what they say to have factual content, irrespective of whether those claims can be verified or falsified, or whether they have truly empirical status. Richard Swinburne (1979) argued that: *'there are plenty of examples of statements which some people judge to be factual which are not apparently confirmable or disconfirmable through observation. For example: Some of the toys which to all appearances stay in the toy cupboard while people are asleep and no one is watching actually get up and dance in the middle of the night and then go back to the cupboard, leaving no traces of their activity.'*

Hence, when we claim that God has an eschatological plan which he will fulfil, or that there are certain moral commands which humankind recognises as having some universal, real, value, then it is likely that in most, if not all, situations the speaker will be intending to express something they believe to be in some way literally true.

However, one way in which both religious thinkers and ethicists have tried to deal with these problems is to abandon the cognitive use of ethical and religious language altogether. This means that, in the case of religious language, when we make statements such as 'God is wise' we are not referring to an objectively real God to whom this description objectively applies, but to something which is anti-realist. Anti-realist language serves another function than that of making cognitive, objective statements which can be proved true or false. Such a function, for example, might be to express the sense of community that binds believers together, or to express the concept of God in descriptive terms that are drawn from symbolic and mythological language. 'God is our rock' or 'the Lord is my shepherd' are examples of claims about the nature of God which are not intended to be interpreted literally, but which still convey ways of understanding God that are very important to the believer. Such language assumes a coherence theory of truth in so far as the truth or falsity of a claim — or more precisely its value and application, or use — is related to the other statements with which it is associated, rather than to objectively real situations.

A classic anti-realist approach was offered by Ludwig Wittgenstein's theory of language games. He proposed that religious language is anti-realist, subject to rules, and expressing a form of life, without making statements that are true or false. Language can be used correctly or incorrectly within the rules of the game, but its primary purpose is not to make factual statements. Thus, it is non-cognitive. All forms of life have their own language and hence stand alone from each other. Wittgenstein was concerned only with the *use* of language, rather than the meaning of it, since it is the context that defines its function. Just as in a game of cricket certain terminology is applied in a way that is appropriate to that game and not to another, so too can religious language be used appropriately or inappropriately, reflecting the way the speaker understands the world. Wittgenstein used the example of the very different understandings of the world expressed by those who hold a religious view of the world and those who do not: *'Suppose someone were a believer and said: "I believe in a Last Judgement," and I said, "Well, I'm not so sure. Possibly", you would say that there was an enormous gulf between us.... Suppose someone is ill and he says: "This is a punishment", and I say: "If I'm ill, I don't think of punishment at all." If you say, "Don't you believe the opposite?" — you can call it believing the opposite, but it is entirely different from what we would normally call believing the opposite. I think differently, in a different way. I say different things to myself. I have a different picture'* (cited in Mitchell (ed.), 1971).

Is this the same of ethical language? If we say 'Stealing is wrong', are we saying something that we believe has objective truth or are we saying something that we think has a meaning for a specific moral community, but is not necessarily an objective fact which we expect everyone to agree with? This is a hard question to consider, since if it has objective truth we do need to consider where it originates from. If it originates from the Bible, then we need to ask whether the Bible is a reliable source of moral teaching, or whether it just expresses the opinions of a relatively small group of people who, while separated by several centuries, were nevertheless united by a shared belief. If it originates from God, then we are back to questions about God's existence and whether we can speak objectively of an objective lawgiver (God) giving objective laws. 'Stealing is wrong' may just be a consensus arising out of the experience of the community over many centuries, and has evolved into a moral law because it allows for society to operate more effectively — but this does not necessarily make it an absolute moral truth which would be logically impossible to deny.

If the religious believer has difficulty defining God in meaningful ways — i.e. what does it mean to say 'God is loving'? — then the ethicist also has difficulties defining ethical terms. What does it mean to say that something is *good*? Can we define *good* itself in terms of something else? G. E. Moore identified a real problem here, and claimed that we can no more define good than we can define yellow. An inner sense directs humans to know what is right or wrong, just as we simply 'know' what is yellow, but, as Moore (1993 edn) argued: *'If I am asked, "What is good?" my answer is that good is good, and that is the end of the matter.'* All attempts to define good result in us defining it in terms of something else — such as 'the greatest good for the greatest number' or 'that which distributes love most widely' or 'those actions which can be universalised'. This leads to the **naturalistic fallacy** — saying that because something ought to be the case, then it is: because more people ought to be made happy by action A rather than action B, then action A is morally good. In ethical terms, to say that something is good, and therefore prescribe it as a moral action we should be obliged to perform, is unconvincing to many. Why should we seek the happiness of the greatest number, do our duty or pursue the virtues? These may be good in some circumstances, or even most, but that alone is not sufficient to make them a matter of moral obligation.

In the same way, the religious believer has difficulty defining God in a way that is acceptable to everyone. Anselm claimed that God is *'that than which nothing greater can be conceived'*, but in reality not everyone will accept that description — even believers. Those who define God in terms of an objective reality — a being who is good, loving, omnipotent and omniscient, and who can be directly experienced in and through the world — may appear to be very far from someone who defines God as a transcendent supreme being or source of enlightenment, but who cannot be encountered in the physical world. However, both parties may claim to believe in God and resist the challenge of the other to redefine God. Ultimately, therefore, it is clear that both issues of morality and theology are infinitely complex, and language is too limited and too overlaid with presumptions to make it possible to speak of ethics or of God without a vast range of problems.

Human freedom and the existence of God

It is certainly the case that our concept of morality would have no point or application, and therefore no meaning outside of the context of a community of persons, who are normally and normatively capable of rational, autonomous action.   (Jean Porter, 1995)

What is freedom?

The notion of freedom needs to be clarified here. Human beings are definitely not free to do some things: to grow feathers, or to live in outer space without mechanical assistance, for example. Humans are also not free to make rational choices if coerced by means of force (**external constraint**) or because they are psychologically unable to make rational judgements (**internal constraint**). **Libertarians** (those who maintain that humans have free will) do not deny that there are certain predictable factors about the universe — the sun rises and sets, a year is 365 days, and summer follows spring. Libertarians do maintain, however, that at least some of our actions are performed without there being any immediately contributing causes, and we may choose to perform action A when we could *equally* have chosen to perform action B.

The relationship between human freedom — or the lack of it — and moral behaviour is a crucial one, since it is generally accepted that our freedom to perform a morally good action or to refrain from performing a bad one is a vital part of the way we evaluate that action. Immanuel Kant maintained that spontaneous moral actions could never be truly moral since they could not be the consequence of reflection, consideration and choice. Real morality, he claimed, was about struggling with a choice of two real options — whether to follow the **categorical imperative** (duty) or not. Truly moral choices cannot be those that are arbitrary and random since such actions cannot be morally responsible. If we believe that every action is *determined* by the totality of a person's experience, knowledge, genes, circumstances, pre-existing relationships, *and* the fact that there are laws of nature which govern everything in the world, then we cannot reasonably blame an individual for acting wrongly, or praise them for doing something good. However, some would argue that even if our actions were inevitable, it does not stop them being morally good or bad, and that it is still appropriate to praise or blame. There is something unsatisfactory about failing to punish criminal behaviour. Furthermore, there is something about the fact that we think we can reason with other human beings about their moral choices that leads us to believe that human moral behaviour is, to some extent at least, free, and that we can make significant choices about the way in which we behave. We also believe that this freedom is important in itself and our freedom, and that of other human beings, should not be violated by imposing upon our capacity to make reasoned choices about things that are of direct concern to us.

Reinhold Niebuhr observed that the distinguishing mark of history is that human beings impose their desires and goals upon nature and have freedom to do this because they are able to understand the way in which single events belong to a general pattern. He argued that since every event, once it has taken place, can be interpreted as an inevitable and determined consequence of a series of events, there is a temptation to be more deterministic in our view of human behaviour than may be appropriate. He cited the *endless variety and unpredictability of the historical drama'* as proof of the reality of human freedom, and noted that although the Bible assumes a divine providence over all human destiny, it does not violate human freedom but, rather, gives meaning to it.

What are the alternatives to freedom?

Fatalism, in its most general form, argues that future events cannot be altered and that all our actions and desires are pointless because they themselves are part of a sequence that only leads us to believe we are free. It does not explain why this pattern of events exists, but just states that it does. Fatalists maintain that whatever happens is bound to happen, whatever one might do to change it. **Determinism**, however, argues that everything is determined by prior causes and that everything requires a **sufficient reason** to occur as it does. In other words, things happen because of actions we take or because of the people we are. This view corresponds with a basic assumption of modern science, that with enough information we could predict with complete accuracy what will happen in the universe at any given future moment. This view is convincing, since we are aware that the universe is not a random series of events and we are able to predict and plan in the knowledge that certain laws (arguably) will hold firm. Similarly, human behaviour appears to exhibit freedom of choice, but that choice is determined by other causes which precede it, just as physical events are determined by prior causes, even if we had a choice of alternative courses of action.

Hard determinists claim that all freedom is illusory, although this is a difficult position to maintain with conviction. Whether we think of freedom primarily as *practical* freedom (freedom to do what one wishes) or *metaphysical* freedom (being responsible for one's choices), we can appeal to reason and counter the determinists' argument with the claim that we *feel* free. Furthermore, if we take hard determinism to its logical extreme, then we are forced to acknowledge that even holding a deterministic view is itself determined!

Soft determinism, or **compatibilism**, holds that there is still a clear difference between free and unfree actions, since we are free to perform an action as long as we are not coerced into doing it or prevented from doing it. It maintains that we are sometimes free even though all events are caused by those causes that exist prior to them. Such a position holds that we could have made a different choice from the one we made, had we chosen to do so. Nevertheless, this still implies that the choice made was influenced by factors which preceded it, and which presumably determined that choice rather than others.

The existence of God

Theological determinism maintains that the events in the world have been pre-ordained by God. John Calvin (1509–64) believed in the absolute sovereignty and omnipotence of God: God has total knowledge of everything that has happened and will happen in the world, and due to human sinfulness true knowledge of God can only be found in scripture. Theological determinism holds that only some of humankind will be saved and the death of Jesus was for some only. Calvin's theology could be supported by biblical text, although it is not without controversy. The biblical writers could not possibly conceive of anything happening independently of God and offer many examples of his omniscient determinism, despite the serious problems for sin and suffering that this raises. God's omniscience is generally understood to mean his complete and exhaustive knowledge of the universe, to the effect that God could not fail to have knowledge even of fictions or his perfect omniscience would be compromised. An omniscient God must know all true propositions and hold no false beliefs, although he must know what they would constitute. Arguably, many religious believers accept this view of God without fully appreciating the problems that it poses for God's other characteristics — his omnipotence and omnibenevolence.

The problem of God's omniscience

The problem of evil

The most overwhelming problem offered for God's omniscience is the inevitable claim that seems to derive from it: that God knows of all past, present and future events of evil and suffering, and has failed, and will continue to fail, to intervene to prevent their occurrence and, following on from this, to prevent the occurrence of the consequences of those events. This further questions God's omnipotence since if he could have made a world in which evil and suffering did not occur, then it is reasonable to ask why he did not do so; and if he could not have made such a world, then his sovereignty and power are compromised. Although the biblical writers seem to be comfortable with the view that God is, without contradiction, responsible for both good and evil — the great flood, the sufferings of Job or the death of the first-born — modern thinkers are less satisfied with this.

Salvation

If God has chosen some people to be saved and others to suffer eternal damnation, then what difference does it make how we behave, what choices we make and what influence others attempt to have on us? How can we justify the moral good-ness of those who do not believe in God, since what eschatological value can it have to them? If salvation is by faith and not works, does faith even have any meaning if God has determined that an individual should have faith?

Revisionist views of God's omniscience

The biblical perspective

It is possible that the biblical material can be interpreted as also offering a picture of a God who does not know all events in advance and who is able to regret his actions and to change his mind: *'And God saw the wickedness of man on earth and that all men were corrupt, and he repented that he had made man on earth and it grieved him in his heart'* (Genesis 6:5–6); *'And the Lord was sorry that he had made Saul king over Israel'* (1 Samuel 15:35).

The Bible also offers a universalist perspective on salvation as well as a determin-istic, exclusivist one: *'The Lord…is patient with you, not wanting anyone to perish, but everyone to come to repentance'* (2 Peter 3:9).

Furthermore, it may be claimed that salvation is not simply reserved for those who are chosen by God to be saved, but rather that all humankind — not just those within the Christian tradition — are able to respond to God's gift of grace at any time. Grace — God's undeserved and freely offered favour to humankind — is not just available in the future, according to whether an individual has been determined to receive it, but is something that is available in the present.

The problem of suffering

The view that God knows all events in advance has led to the assumption that such divine knowledge is somehow *causal* knowledge. However, if God's knowledge of future events is based on an inductive principle, much as our knowledge of the future is based on the principle that what happened in the past is likely to be a reliable guide to what will happen in the future, this does not require that he is responsible for bringing it about. After all, my knowledge — based on previous experience — that the sun will rise tomorrow does not cause it to rise. Its rising is an objective fact that will occur (or not occur) independent of my existence. It is possible that the relationship between God's perfect omniscience and the occurrence of events of evil and suffering may be similar, if it is conceivable that events can take place independently of a God who remains omniscient, omnipotent and perfectly good.

Removing the problem of omniscience

If God does not know all things, then the problem is resolved. The work of process theologians has been along these lines: God's knowledge is not fixed and complete, but, like humankind's, is developing. God learns more about his creation and about human beings and he is therefore able to suffer with them as he strives (although he may not always succeed) to bring about the best outcome. Jürgen Moltmann (2001 edn) argued that this process was exemplified in the Holocaust, during which time God identified with and experienced the suffering undergone by the Jews. He did not know of it in advance, however, or determine it, and is not responsible for it.

A rejection of God's omniscience

Anton Thorn questioned why anyone should accept belief in an omniscient God when *'this notion cannot be integrated with the facts of reality'*.

- For an omniscient being, knowledge cannot be the result of reason, as it is for human beings. Such a being would not be required to go through the long processes that humans have to face to gain new knowledge and to extrapolate from existing knowledge. Thorn called God's omniscience **unearned knowledge**; it is never the product of any mental effort. He argued that such knowledge is at odds with every other concept of knowledge that we have, and hence it is incomprehensible. The religious believer, he maintained, desires this unearned knowledge for themselves and seeks it through, for example, mystical experiences. In so doing, however, the theist surrenders all attempts to use reason and truth and highlights their own pursuit of unearned knowledge.

- What purpose would exhaustive knowledge serve? If God is immortal, everlasting and eternal, what need does he have of such knowledge? He does not need to deal with any problems of existence, since not only should he be able to overcome all problems, but he also cannot be said to face any.
- Thorn argued that since there is no reason for God to possess exhaustive knowledge or for the universe to require an omniscient God, then the claim that God is omniscient has simply been made by those who can influence others with the notion of an all-knowing God. Thorn claimed that the notion of a God who knows all things, however private, serves only to benefit those who would seek dominion over others through coercing them into certain behaviour patterns. None of the classical arguments for the existence of God demand his omniscience, and yet omniscience is postulated as an essential characteristic of the God of classical theism.

Synoptic question and answer

Question 2 Philosophy of Religion and Religious Ethics

If God did not exist, would humankind be more or less free?

It is certainly the case that our concept of morality would have no point or application, and therefore no meaning outside of the context of a community of persons, who are normally and normatively capable of rational, autonomous action. (Jean Porter, 1995)

Whether we assess morality from the perspective of religious belief or from a secular perspective, it is equally the case that we believe the freedom to act or to refrain from acting to be a crucial factor in determining the responsibility that a person should take for their actions. In law, a defendant may be considered to have 'diminished responsibility' if we think that his or her freedom was in some way limited or curtailed — by medical or psychological factors, by the exercise of force or constraint by others, or by limitations imposed on the person by the circumstances they were in. In such cases we would normally expect punishment to be less severe, or even to be withdrawn completely. We exercise rational judgement in such cases to ascertain how truly free the individual was before we determine whether they are in a position to be held responsible for their actions.

The nature of God, held by classical theists to be omnipotent, omniscient, eternal, unchanging and perfectly good, also has important implications for human morality and the responsibility that we expect an individual, and even humankind as a whole, to take for their actions. Such a God, with unlimited powers to engage in dealings with the universe and human beings, would surely impose considerably on human freedom. If God knows all events — past, present and future — and is able to do all things, then necessarily he must be causally involved in all events and in all actions. This view is known as theological determinism and was formulated by John Calvin in the sixteenth century. Theological determinism maintains that the events in the world have been preordained by God, who is absolutely sovereign and omnipotent and who has total knowledge of everything that has happened and will happen in the world. Due to human sinfulness, true knowledge of God can only be found in scripture, upon which humankind is dependent to discover God's will and purpose. Theological determinism has implications for salvation, since the view holds that only some of humankind will be saved and the death of Jesus was for some only — a limited atonement. Calvin's theology could be supported by biblical text, although it is not without controversy. The biblical writers could not possibly conceive of anything happening independently of God, and offer many examples of his omniscient determinism, despite the serious problems for sin and suffering that this raises. God's omniscience is generally under-stood to mean his complete and exhaustive knowledge of the universe, to the effect that God could not fail to have knowledge even of fictions or his perfect omniscience would be compromised. An omniscient God must know all true propositions and hold no false beliefs, although he must know what they would constitute. Arguably, many religious believers accept this view of God without fully appreciating the problems that it poses for God's other characteristics — his omnipotence and omnibenevolence.

In order to assess whether this view poses an unacceptable limitation on human free-dom, we need to consider what freedom is. Human beings are definitely not free to do some things: to grow feathers, or to live in outer space without mechanical assistance, for example. We are also not free to make rational choices if coerced by means of force (external constraint) or because we are psychologically unable to make rational judge-ments (internal constraint). Libertarians (those who maintain that humans have free will) do not deny that there are certain predictable factors about the universe — the sun rises and sets, a year is 365 days, and summer follows spring. Libertarians, however, maintain that at least some of our actions are performed without there being any immediately contributing causes and we may choose to perform action A when we could *equally* have chosen to perform action B. This is perhaps the closest to freedom we can get in a world that is governed by laws which we cannot avoid. The law of gravity, for example, works with such regularity that we do not expect to be free from its effects. The implications of a world in which it did not apply would be enormously difficult — we would be unable to plan or predict with any degree of accuracy, since we would be unable to rely on the dependency of natural laws. Hence, the freedom which a libertarian maintains that we have is freedom to make genuine choices *when others are available*. We do not have the choice whether to float above the ground or not, so it is not a limitation on our freedom not to be able to do so. However, it is a matter of choice for us whether we show compassion towards someone who is suffering, whether we steal or refrain from stealing, or whether we are prepared to perform acts of self-sacrifice in the face of danger to others and ourselves. What we need to consider is whether the existence of God serves to limit the freedom we have to make such choices — whether they are predetermined by him, or whether the very fact of his existence ensures that we act *as if we did not have a choice*, since if we act as if there were no choices even when there are, then our freedom is limited.

The relationship between human freedom — or the lack of it — and moral behaviour is a crucial one, since it is generally accepted that our freedom to perform a morally good action or to refrain from a bad one is a vital part of the way we evaluate that action. Kant maintained that spontaneous moral actions can never be truly moral since they cannot be the consequence of reflection, consideration and choice. Real morality, he claimed, is about struggling between two real options — to follow the categorical imperative (duty) or not. Truly moral choices cannot be those that are arbitrary and random since such actions cannot be morally responsible. If we believe that every action is *determined* by the totality of a person's experience, knowledge, genes, circumstances, pre-existing relationships, *and* the fact that there are laws of nature which govern everything in the world, then we cannot reasonably blame an individual for acting wrongly, or praise them for doing something good. However, some would argue that even if our actions were inevitable, it does not stop them being morally good or bad, and that it is still appropriate to praise or blame. There is something unsatisfactory about failing to punish criminal behaviour. Furthermore, there is something about the fact that we think we can reason with other human beings about their moral choices that leads us to believe that human moral behaviour is, to some extent at least, free, and that we can make significant choices about the way in which we behave. We also believe that this freedom is important in itself and our freedom and that of other human beings should not be violated by imposing upon our capacity to make reasoned choices about things that are of direct concern to us.

What are the alternatives to this freedom which we tend to presuppose belongs to all rational human beings? Fatalism, in its most general form, argues that future events cannot be altered and that all our actions and desires are pointless because they themselves are part of a sequence that only leads us to believe we are free. It does not explain why this pattern of events exists, but just states that it does. Fatalists maintain that whatever happens is bound to happen, whatever one might do to change it. Connected, but nevertheless distinct, is the view of determinists, who argue that everything is determined by prior causes, and that everything requires a sufficient reason to occur as it does. In other words, things happen because of actions we take or because of the people we are. This view corresponds with a basic assumption of modern science, that with enough information we could predict with complete accuracy what would happen in the universe at any given future moment. This view is convincing, since we are aware that the universe is not a random series of events, and we are able to predict and plan in the knowledge that certain laws (arguably) will hold firm. Similarly, human behaviour appears to exhibit freedom of choice, but that choice is determined by other causes which precede it, just as physical events are determined by prior causes, even if we had a choice of alternative courses of action.

Hard determinists claim that all freedom is illusory, although this is a difficult position to maintain with conviction. Whether we think of freedom primarily as *practical* freedom (freedom to do what one wishes) or *metaphysical* freedom (being responsible for one's choices), we can appeal to reason and counter the determinists' argument with the claim that we *feel* free. Furthermore, if we take hard determinism to its logical extreme, then we are forced to acknowledge that even holding a deterministic view is itself determined! Soft determinism, or compatibilism, holds that there is still a clear difference between free and unfree actions, since we are free to perform an action as long as we are not coerced into doing it or prevented from doing it. It maintains that we are sometimes free even though all events are caused by those causes that exist prior to them. Such a position holds that we could have made a different choice from the one we made had we chosen to do so. Nevertheless, this still implies that the choice made was influenced by factors which preceded it, and which presumably determined that choice rather than others.

So, where does God fit into all this? Theological determinism falls somewhere between fatalism and determinism, since if God is omniscient and omnipotent, sovereignly determining all events that are to take place in the history of the universe, then there is no point in beginning to challenge them. Any struggle that humankind makes to free itself from divine determinism is doomed to failure and that struggle is, itself, determined. What implications does this have for human behaviour? Does the existence of God limit the choices we make?

The view that since God omnisciently knows all future events, then human freedom is limited implies that God's knowledge is causal knowledge. This may be the case for various reasons. Firstly, and most conservatively, it could be because there is, literally, no event outside his knowledge. Timeless, eternal, perfect and omnipotent, there is nothing that God cannot know or else his perfection would be limited. Since he is not bound by time, as human beings are, then nothing can be outside God's knowledge because it hasn't yet happened, since we only fail to know what has not yet occurred because we are limited by time and can only know what has happened in the past and what is happening in the present. If God's omniscience is of this nature, are we committed to saying that he causes the events which he omnisciently knows? If so, it is because we are also committed to certain other beliefs about God — that his creative power is absolute and continuing, and so no event *can* happen without his direct involvement. To speak of an event taking place without God's direct causal intervention would be a limitation on his power.

There may be a legitimate way around this, however. Peter Cole makes the useful analogy that we might sit on the top of a hill, giving us a clear view of the road below. From this position we can see the traffic approaching from several miles in either direction. As we see two vehicles approaching from opposite directions we can see whether they are heading on a collision course or whether they will pass each other safely. However, our perspective — which is above that of those who are actually on the road — has no causal implications for what will happen. The fact that we can see that two cars are headed for collision does not in any way *cause* the collision. Our knowledge is not causal knowledge. In the same way, God may see all events in time, from the beginning of the world to its end, while not actually causing them. Although God's knowledge of future events is infinitely greater than the knowledge we have from our position on the top of the hill, analogously we can still understand it as not being causal, even while being truly omniscient.

This position is useful when considering the difficult relationship between the omniscience of God and the evidential problem of evil. After all, my knowledge, based on previous experience, that the sun will rise tomorrow, does not cause it to rise. Its rising is an objective fact that will occur (or not occur) independent of my existence. The cars heading for collision on the road will collide whether or not I am on the top of the hill to see them collide. It is possible that the relationship between God's perfect omniscience and the occurrence of events of evil and suffering may be similar if it is conceivable that events can take place independently of a God who remains omniscient, omnipotent and perfectly good.

A more liberal view of God's omniscience again has parallels with human knowledge of future events. When we come to know someone well we begin to anticipate and predict the way in which they will act. We know their preferences and habits, and the things they say and do in particular circumstances. In fact, we come to expect them to act in the same way and when they act out of character we are surprised and look for an explanation for why they have acted in this way. If we can come to know people so well, then how much better must God know his creation? God's omniscient knowledge of our future actions may be derived from the intimate knowledge he has of how each person acts, based on their psychological, emotional, intellectual, social and spiritual characteristics. Arguably, of course, we could say that as God has created them in this particular way he has in fact determined them to act in a predictable fashion, but we are not compelled to this view since we still have freedom to act differently. David Hume (1975 edn) observed rather quaintly: *'A person of an obliging disposition gives a peevish answer. But he has the toothache or has not dined. A stupid fellow discovers an uncommon alacrity in his carriage. But he has met with a sudden piece of good luck. Or even when an action, as sometimes happens, cannot be particularly accounted for, either by the person himself or by others, we know, in general that the characters of men are, to a certain degree, inconstant and irregular.'*

Thus, we can have intimate knowledge of a person's characteristics, leading us to be able to make reasonably accurate predictions of how they will behave, but there still remains open the possibility that they may behave differently, and we account for this because we know that human nature is inconsistent. Similarly, God's creation of human beings allows for human liberty and freedom, which ensures that all their actions are not completely determined.

Moreover, it is worth considering whether there are good grounds for viewing God's total omniscience as essential to classical theism. It is possible that the biblical material can be interpreted as *also* offering a picture of a God who does not know all events in advance and who is able to regret his actions and to change his mind: *'And God saw the wickedness of man on earth and that all men were corrupt, and he repented that he had made man on earth and it grieved him in his heart'* (Genesis 6:5–6); *'And the Lord was sorry that he had made Saul king over Israel'* (1 Samuel 15:35). The Bible also offers a universalist perspective on salvation as well as a deterministic, exclusivist one: *'The Lord…is patient with you, not wanting anyone to perish, but everyone to come to repentance'* (2 Peter 3:9).

Furthermore, it may be claimed that salvation is not simply reserved for those who are chosen by God to be saved, but rather that all humankind — not just those within the Christian tradition — are able to respond to God's gift of grace at any time. Grace — God's undeserved and freely offered favour to humankind — is not just available in the future, according to whether an individual has been determined to receive it, but is something that is available in the present.

Ultimately, if God does not know all things, then the problem is resolved. The work of process theologians has been along these lines: God's knowledge is not fixed and complete, but, like humankind's, is developing. God learns more about his creation and about human beings and he is able therefore to suffer with them as he strives (although he may not always succeed) to bring about the best outcome. Jürgen Moltmann (2001 edn) argued that this process is exemplified in the Holocaust, during which time God identified with and experienced the suffering undergone by the Jews. He did not know of it in advance, however, or determine it, and is not responsible for it.

Nevertheless, there are still important questions to be considered. Is God the creator of morality? This is an old dilemma going back at least as far as Plato's Euthyphro

Dilemma: does God command that which is good, or is something good because God commands it? What is the relationship between God and morality? Aquinas maintained that God's natural moral law was observable by all humankind simply through observing what was within nature. The application of reason to experience would show humankind what was right. Other perspectives on God and morality emphasise the need for a personal moral commander to give morality meaning but do not necessarily provide answers to difficult questions, such as whether Abraham was free to obey or disobey when God told him to sacrifice Isaac. It is conceivable, however, that the link between an omniscient moral commander and human morality is contrived; Anton Thorn questioned why anyone should accept belief in an omniscient God when 'this notion cannot be integrated with the facts of reality', and offers an argument as to why a belief in God's omniscience has been encouraged at the expense of human freedom.

First, for an omniscient being, knowledge cannot be the result of reason, as it is for human beings. Such a being would not be required to go through the long processes that humans have to face to gain new knowledge and to extrapolate from existing knowledge. Thorn called God's omniscience 'unearned knowledge', claiming it is never the product of any mental effort. He argued that such knowledge is at odds with every other concept of knowledge that we have, and hence is incomprehensible. The religious believer, he maintained, desires this unearned knowledge for themselves and seeks it through, for example, mystical experiences. In so doing, however, the theist surrenders all attempts to use reason and truth and highlights their own pursuit of unearned knowledge.

Second, what purpose would exhaustive knowledge serve? If God is immortal, everlasting and eternal, what need does he have of such knowledge? He does not need to deal with any problems of existence, since not only should he be able to overcome all problems, but he also cannot be said to face any. Thorn argued that since there is no reason for God to possess exhaustive knowledge or for the universe to require an omniscient God, then the claim that God is omniscient has simply been made by those who can influence others with the notion of an all-knowing God. Thorn claimed that the notion of a God who knows all things, however private, serves only to benefit those who would seek dominion over others through coercing them into certain behaviour patterns. None of the classical arguments for the existence of God demand his omniscience, and yet, for the purposes of limiting human freedom, omniscience is postulated as an essential characteristic of the God of classical theism.

Religious experience

Mysticism in the philosophy of religion

What is mysticism?

Mysticism: a religious experience in which one is overwhelmingly aware of the ultimate; utterly swept up in the presence of God: intensely personal, other-worldly and transcendent; the recipient touches and communicates with the divine and with levels of reality beyond the spatiotemporal world.

The Christian mystic is regarded as one who has been raised to a high degree of contemplative prayer. The mystical experience consists in a conscious, deep, and intimate union of the soul with God…while the soul, on its part, has prepared itself, normally according to an accepted pattern of asceticism.
(Clifton Wolters, 1998 edn)

The mystic's lifestyle, relationship with God and mode of preparation are part of receiving a mystical experience. There are three steps of preparation:

- **Purgation** — ridding the soul of tendencies that prevent it from paying attention.
- **Illumination** — preliminary disclosures which focus attention.
- **Contemplation** — the stage in which the presence of the divine penetrates the believer.

Mystical experiences are enormously wide-ranging, but there appear to be several common features: a profound sense of union and unity with the divine; time is transcended; it is a **noetic** experience (William James) — not just subjective, but something is clearly revealed to the experient; a deep sense of joy and well-being. Rudolph Otto coined the term **numinous** to describe the event, tracing it back to the *mysterium tremendem et fascinans*, which he said was the origin of religion. In mystical experiences the individual was both attracted and repelled by a sense of awe and wonder: *'Depart from me, for I am a sinful man, O Lord'* (Luke 5:8); *'Woe is* *me! For I am lost; for I am a man of unclean lips, and I dwell in the midst of a people of unclean lips; for my eyes have seen the King, the Lord of hosts'* (Isaiah 6:5).

In the **early church**, mystical experiences appear to have been universally available (Acts 2, 1 Corinthians 12–14) until taken over by a spiritual élite and by ascetics. Mysticism flowered during the **English Middle Ages**, encouraged by:

- a more personal approach to religion — emphasis on the suffering Christ, the cult of the Virgin Mary and the swing away from institutional religion which challenged the role of the clergy as the means of intercession
- the **Anchorite** tradition, which was closely associated with mysticism. A recluse, or solitary, would enter the service of enclosure. He or she spent time in prayer and devotions but also offered spiritual direction to the local community

Female mysticism

Mysticism was more central in female religiosity and in female claims to sanctity than in men's, and paramystical phenomena...were far more common in women's mysticism.... Women's devotion was more marked by penitential asceticism...extreme fasting and illness borne with patience.

(Caroline Walker Bynum, cited in Parsons 2002)

Julian of Norwich received 16 'showings' on 8 May 1373 during a time of dire sickness. Although she describes herself as 'uneducated', her evaluations of these showings are insightful and profound:

Our Lord showed me a little thing, the quantity of a hazelnut, in the palm of my hand; and it was as round as a ball. I looked thereupon with the eye of my understanding, and thought: 'What may this be?' And it was answered generally thus: 'It is all that is made'.... In this Little Thing I saw three properties. The first is that God made it, the second that God loveth it, the third that God keepeth it.

(Julian of Norwich, cited in Wolters, 1998 edn)

Only if we deny any possibility of divine communication can Julian's claims be completely ruled out.

(Clifton Wolters, 1998 edn)

The Spanish Catholic Reformation

The institutional church was nervous because if carried to its logical extreme, personal faith of the mystical kind did away with the need for priests, sacraments and the authority of the church as the guide to an individual's faith and doctrine. Teresa of Avila, a Carmelite nun, experienced ecstatic visions of hell and the Holy Spirit, and direct and personal experiences of the love of God, which she described as a 'mystical marriage'. Nicola Slee observed:

It is not difficult to see how these emphases represent a kind of compensatory channelling of women's spirituality into permissible forms. Denied liturgical office, authority had to come from supernatural sources rather than institutional ones...denied overt expression, women's sexuality found shape in erotic devotion to Christ; denied official religious power, women could assume control over their bodies...and thus tacitly transcend patriarchal rule.

(Cited in Parsons, 2002)

Teresa used her experiences to institute practical reform of the Carmelite order. There was greater emphasis on the expression of personal, biblical faith, the ultimate goal being to lose oneself in the presence of God, rather than the scholarly emphasis on reason and intellectualism within religious belief.

Problems of mysticism

- *'Sir, the pretending to extraordinary revelations and gifts of the Holy Ghost is a horrid thing, a very horrid thing'* (Bishop Butler to John Wesley, cited in Wolters, 1998 edn).
- Spiritual élitism (gnosticism).
- Rejection of the church and the sacraments as the ministers of God's grace.
- Opposed to ethical and eschatological doctrines.
- Problems of testing the validity of mystics and their experiences: *'Levitations, ecstasies, trances and the like...prove nothing — not even the holiness of the entrances'* (Clifton Wolters, 1998).

However...

As long as it flourishes, it constitutes a continual challenge to what William James calls 'a premature closing of accounts with reality' in terms of an exclusively ethical, institutional, theological or intellectual presentation of religion.... The mystic's witness to the accessibility of the living presence...in the hearts of contemporary men and women has been an enormous encouragement to the religious yearnings of men.

(Douglas V. Steere, cited in Halverson and Cohen (eds), 1960)

Moral decision making

Approaching moral decision making

- Why make moral decisions? A range of choices is available — no single solution is immediately evident. We need to weigh and balance the available and possible solutions.
- What influences moral decision making?
  - **Consequences** — teleological approaches to ethical dilemmas, based on the likely or probable outcomes.
  - **Motives** — consequences are less important than the means of reaching them.

- ❖ **Absolute values** — are there absolute rules and laws that should apply in every case?
- ❖ **Situationist approaches** — should laws be laid aside in the interests of a compassionate or relative approach to the dilemma?

- Objective or subjective? Does the situation deal with issues that are truly independent of our opinions, feelings or even our very existence (objective)? Does it deal with issues that depend on the way we relate to them and how they cohere with other religious or moral beliefs we hold (subjective)? *'Moral argument tries to appeal to a capacity for impartial motivation which is supposed to be present in all of us'* (Thomas Nagel, 1987). Is it possible to be impartial, or are we always influenced by personal prejudices or convictions?

- Are we more influenced in moral decision making by institutional authority or by personal experience? What are the problems of each? Who makes the rules? Who evaluates experience? How do we verify experience?

- How useful are ethical theories in moral decision making? Can any ethical theory solve all moral dilemmas?

- *'It remains true…that a man must in the moment of decision do what he thinks is right. He cannot do otherwise. This does not mean that what he does will be right or even that he will not be worthy of blame or punishment. He simply has no choice, for he cannot at that moment see any discrepancy between what is right and what he thinks is right'* (William K. Frankena, 1973).

The relationship between God and morality

Then tell me, what do you say the holy is? And what is the unholy? For consider, is the holy loved by the gods because it is holy? Or is it holy because it is loved by the gods?

(Plato, *Euthyphro*, fourth century BCE)

The nature of the relationship between God and morality — indeed, if there is one at all — is a vital one for religious believers to resolve. If at least part of what it means to believe in God is to live in obedience to his will and his law, then the way in which God makes moral commands is crucial to understanding how humans should respond to them.

R. B. Braithwaite observed that to be religious and to make religious claims is to be committed to a set of moral values, e.g. a religious conversion includes a reorientation of the will in line with that of God. Of course, it is not necessarily the case that God, even if he exists, should be the sole arbiter of morality, but for those who believe in an omnipotent God, the classic problem was concisely expressed by Plato in the Euthyphro Dilemma: *Is something good because God commands it? OR Does God command that which is good?*

Is morality subject to divine command?

Is the fact that God commands morality sufficient to make it good? Or does God command that which is good independent of his judgement? How do we deal with situations in which God has not expressly given a command? Does any command given by God acquire a moral status? Can non-believers access God's morality? Is obedience to God's moral command motivated by fear? If so, is that true goodness? Is God greater than morality, or is it greater than him? Is humankind free to disobey God's commands?

Søren Kierkegaard

We should not confuse ethics or morality with doing the will of God. For example, God's command to Abraham to sacrifice Isaac (Genesis 22) is clearly something that was not moral, according to usual human standards. In this case, however, Abraham was being called to obedience that went beyond human understanding of morality, and being bound to the moral law of society would have been a hindrance to the fulfilling of God's will.

Conscience

There is a principle of reflection in men, by which they distinguish between and disapprove of their own actions.
(Joseph Butler)

A Christian view of the conscience would claim that it is universal whether humankind believes in God or not, and that it is God-given (Romans 2:12ff.). Humankind's conscience has been affected by the fall, however, and thus is corrupted and imperfect (Genesis 3), but it can be redeemed by Jesus Christ, whose death cleanses our unhealthy conscience and enables us to retune our conscience with the divine will (Romans 3:21–22). J. V. Langmead Casserly wrote: *'A well trained conscience remains a factor of the utmost importance in the moral life'* (cited in Halverson and Cohen, 1960).

What influences the conscience?

Do upbringing and environment shape the conscience? Does education? What about religious background, teaching and influence? Is a 'good conscience' dependent on being able to communicate with God? Can the conscience be overridden in crisis situations or by fear? If so, is this a good thing? Is the exercise of conscience essential for an ordered society? For a religious believer, is conscience more or less important than God or is it to be identified with him? Can conscience be explained psychologically?

Synoptic question and answer

Question 3 Philosophy of Religion and Religious Ethics

'Mystical experiences might appear to be common phenomena, but how "mystical" is interpreted will vary considerably between those who use the term.'

(a) Explain ways in which the term 'mystical' might be used in the context of religious experience.

(b) Explain and evaluate the challenges which may be made to the value and credibility of mystical experience.

(a) Mysticism is a special category within the broader context of religious experience in which the experient is brought into a heightened, even overwhelming, awareness of the ultimate. The mystic's experience is characterised in many ways, but most commonly it is described as being intensely personal, transcendent and other-worldly, enabling the experient to communicate with the divine on a level of reality far beyond the spatio-temporal world. There are elements of mysticism in almost all the major world religions — the Islamic Sufi tradition and the Jewish Kabbalah, for example — but this essay will focus on the understanding of the Christian mystical tradition.

Mysticism seems to have had a particular appeal for philosophers of religion and has encouraged the development of special terminology in an attempt to describe it. This is perhaps quite significant, suggesting as it does that the mystical experience is ineffable — beyond regular language. If this is the case, then we should immediately be wary, perhaps, of the limits of mysticism. If we are hoping to find special revelations within the mystical experience, then the problems we may have in communicating them are not insignificant. Mystical experiences are not always fully clear to the person who directly experiences them, and it is likely that they will remain to some degree shrouded in mystery even to them. Their impact is, however, very significant. Rudolph Otto coined the term 'numinous' to describe mystical experiences, tracing them back to the overwhelming sense of mystery and wonder which he believed was at the heart of religion. William James called them 'noetic' experiences, which clearly revealed something to the experient while filling them with a deep sense of joy and well-being.

The reaction of the experient to mystical experiences tells us a good deal about their nature. Mystical experiences seem to have been prevalent in both the Old and New Testaments. In the temple, Isaiah sees a vision of God high up on a throne, surrounded by cherubim, and even though he responds to the calling he perceives in the vision, he is overwhelmed with a sense of his own unworthiness: *'Woe is me! For I am lost; for I am a man of unclean lips, and I dwell in the midst of a people of unclean lips; for my eyes have seen the King, the Lord of hosts'* (Isaiah 6:5). When Peter meets Jesus for the first time, and is blessed with a remarkable catch of fish simply by following his instructions, his reaction is similar: *'Depart from me, for I am a sinful man, O Lord'* (Luke 5:8). Even though his experience is far more public, it seems, than Isaiah's, he is overwhelmed by the presence of the divine, realising that he has been given an opportunity to transcend the physical world. This opportunity compels him even while he attempts to withdraw from it.

Paul's church at Corinth seems to have been highly attracted to the mystical, to the extent that Paul feels obliged to reorientate the church members' minds on more prosaic issues — keeping order within worship, ensuring that the poor and less spiritually gifted are not left out from proceedings, and generating an attitude within church that will not alienate those to whom it is new. On the day of Pentecost the 12 inner-circle apostles experience being filled with the Holy Spirit and the charismatic gift of tongues that comes with it, and it is clear that it was not intended to be their prerogative only. However, although in the early church experiences appear to have been universally available, they were eventually taken over by a spiritual élite, many of whom were ascetics or solitaries. Clifton Wolters (1998) wrote: *'The Christian mystic is regarded as one who has been raised to a high degree of contemplative prayer. The mystical experience consists in a conscious, deep, and intimate union of the soul with God…while the soul, on its part, has prepared itself, normally according to an accepted pattern of asceticism.'*

Although not all the biblical characters who receive mystical experiences seem to have been engaged in a long period of prior preparation, for some (e.g. Ezekiel or possibly the writer of Revelation) their whole life is devoted to the kind of intense spiritual exercise that gives them a spiritual perspective on their existence and the world. During the English Middle Ages the mystical tradition flourished among anchorites, many of whom were women. Caroline Walker Bynum observed: *'Mysticism was more central in female religiosity and in female claims to sanctity than in men's, and paramystical phenomena…were far more common in women's mysticism…. Women's devotion was more marked by penitential asceticism…extreme fasting and illness borne with patience'* (cited in Parsons, 2002).

Among these anchorites was Julian of Norwich, who, in May 1373, received 16 mystical revelations while she was seriously ill. She spent subsequent years evaluating them in detail, and although they are at times obscure, Clifton Wolters commented that: *'Only if we deny any possibility of divine communication can Julian's claims be completely ruled out.'*

Mysticism seems to have influenced a more personal and less institutional view of religion, encouraging the individual to approach God directly, without the need for priests, sacraments or other ecclesiastical authorities. Nicola Slee suggested that it is therefore *'not difficult to see how these emphases represent a kind of compensatory channelling of women's spirituality into permissible forms. Denied liturgical office, authority had to come from supernatural sources rather than institutional ones...denied official religious power, women could assume control over their bodies...and thus tacitly transcend patriarchal rule'* (cited in Parsons, 2002). Teresa of Avila, the most famous of the Spanish mystics, used her experiences to institute practical reform of the Carmelite order and to encourage an emphasis on the expressions of personal, biblical faith rather than on reason and intellectualism, which seems to run counter to the tradition of mysticism.

(b) If mystical experiences are able to endow individuals with a special spiritual authority which might otherwise have been denied them, it is very important to consider how reliable such experiences are. While the possibility of direct, personal communication with God has long been considered a vital part of the Christian experience, the role of ecclesiastical authority, the teaching of the Bible and the weight of tradition passed down from generations of believers has also been considered to be vital. Recipients of mystical experiences who use them as the basis for authorising a new revelation need to rest on secure foundations, or risk being marginalised as charlatans or deceivers. During the Spanish Catholic Reformation the institutional church was unsurprisingly nervous, since if carried to its logical extreme, personal faith of the mystical kind could be seen as the only sure guide to revelation. Christian history is littered with messianic pretenders, founders of religions and itinerant preachers who have claimed special revelation of the mystical kind and who have drawn many followers as a result.

Although mysticism encourages the individual to examine and value his or her personal relationship with God, it has been criticised for encouraging a spiritual élitism (one of Paul's major concerns) and for opposing ethical and eschatological doctrines. If an individual's faith and relationship with God rests entirely on the circumstances and content of their personal encounter with him, it is clearly not subject to any external, objective testing but can be claimed to be beyond any other, more universal, and hence less 'special', revelation. Any religious experience is deeply personal and subjective, open to levels of interpretation that only the experient can truly appreciate. Nevertheless, some form of evaluation should be necessary if the experient is to use it to authenticate further moral or religious teaching.

First, we know that accounts of mystical experiences are no sure guide to their authenticity. Bishop Butler observed to John Wesley that: *'the pretending to extraordinary revelations and gifts of the Holy Ghost is a horrid thing'* (cited in Wolters, 1998 edn) and Clifton Wolters (1998) wrote: *'Levitations, ecstasies, trances and the like...prove nothing — not even the holiness of the entrances'*. Many claimants to mystical experiences have subsequently been revealed to be frauds, even if, in some cases, they continue to have an enormous following.

But more important is the question of whether mystical experiences should be the grounds on which life-changing decisions are made, moral theories re-evaluated and religious teaching reconsidered. We make moral decisions as a matter of course every day, some weightier than others, but always against a background of many potential influences. It is because we find ourselves torn between a reluctance to lay aside all moral absolutes and a paradoxical fear and attraction of the consequences of our actions that moral dilemmas are just that — dilemmas. The possibilities are enormous: do we decide on the basis of consequences or motives? Do we believe that there are moral absolutes, objective standards that exist independently of our own opinions, to which we must subscribe, or, rather, that moral decisions should be made situationally? In the mid-1960s, Episcopalian theologian Joseph Fletcher proposed that the only legitimate way to make ethical decisions was on the situational basis of agape, that quality of love which was exemplified in Jesus's ministry. His approach was subject to considerable criticism from fellow Christian writers, even though he was essentially basing it on a not illegitimate reading of the New Testament. How much more are we likely to be wary of the claims made on the basis of an utterly unverifiable experience? Thomas Nagel (1987) observed that *'moral argument tries to appeal to a capacity for impartial motivation which is supposed to be present in all of us'* and yet it is clear that we do not always approach moral decision making in an impartial manner.

Those who would ask serious questions about the value and credibility of mystical experience may do so on the basis that it appears to reject tradition and history in favour of what seems to be a new revelation. J. S. Whale (1957) observed: *'Mysticism often pays a heavy price for its tendency to belittle the historical and the factual.... Even the most nebulous mysticism which contends that no events or facts are vital for religion, forgets that mystics themselves are not the individualists they think they are; they too belong to a continuous tradition of religious experience.'* Nevertheless, the power of a personal revelation and the charisma of the experient can have a very significant impact on religious history. In 1820 Joseph Smith allegedly received several visions that led to the founding of the Mormon Church, a sect which Josh McDowell claims now baptises a third of a million people each year. Smith claimed that God spoke to him in ways that he had spoken to no one before, sometimes through the angel Moroni, and revealed to him that all the Christian churches were wrong in their understanding of key doctrinal issues. An analysis of Smith's visions and prophecies is thought to reveal several key problems, and the Mormon Church is based on extra-biblical revelation, incorporated in three further publications, which in itself poses problems. Christianity teaches that the Bible is the sole, authoritative source of God's revelation, eternally valid and enduring. Furthermore, Smith's revelations led to a new translation of the Bible for use within the Mormon Church, which, like other translations produced by sects and cults, was designed to affirm in some way the new revelations given to Smith. Leadership within the church is given the highest authority, and the Living Prophet (the most important figure in present-day Mormonism) is considered to be more vital than any previous revelations. In 1945, the official magazine of the church, *Improvement Era*, claimed: *'When our leaders speak, the thinking has been done. When they propose a plan — it is God's plan. When they point the way, there is no other which is safe. When they give directions it should mark the end of the controversy.'* In other words, any new revelation is considered to be more important than any that has preceded it, and the voice of the church leaders has ultimate authority. Thus, any teaching the church offers its members — not only on matters of doctrine, but on marriage, medical treatment and other lifestyle matters — is considered to have ultimate authority and final sanction.

How does this work if we apply it to moral decision making? Does God's word provide the final word on morality or is it subject to further revelation or the ravages of time? Plato's *Euthyphro* exposed this dilemma in the fourth century BCE: *'Then tell me...is the holy loved by the gods because it is holy? Or is it holy because it is loved by the gods?'* The nature of the relationship between God and morality — indeed, if there is one at all — is a vital one for religious believers to resolve. If at least part of what it means to believe in God is to live in obedience to his will and his law, then the way in which God makes moral commands is crucial to understanding how humankind should respond to them. R. B. Braithwaite claimed that to be religious and to make religious claims is to be committed to a set of moral values, in the way, for example, that a religious conversion includes a reorientation of the will in line with that of God. Of course, it is not necessarily the case that God, even if he exists, should be the sole arbiter of morality, but for those who believe in an omnipotent God the classic problem is whether something is good because God commands it or whether God commands it because it is good.

It seems that the safest position for Christians to occupy is the former. If God's word does not make moral law, then moral law is subject to something other than God and God himself must be subject to it. For many, the omnipotent God of classical theism cannot be subject to anything and *his* word — not that of humankind or some other higher being — is, on all things, final. Nonetheless, the question still remains as to how we access God's word. If we are dependent on it being revealed through humankind, we are back to the same problem — how can we be sure of the accuracy of the revelation? Do we therefore rely only on the Bible? If so, how do we deal with making moral decisions on matters that are not discussed explicitly in the Bible — abortion, say, or drug-dealing? And what of humankind's freedom? What are the implications of freely choosing to disobey God? Would we, like Abraham, have obeyed God's command to kill Isaac, and would it have been 'immoral' to do so? Kierkegaard argued that we should not confuse morality with doing the will of God and that Abraham was called to an obedience that went beyond human understanding of morality. This solution, however, cuts little ice with those who argue that God's morality must be meaningful to those who are called to be obedient to it.

Mystical experiences are clearly open to much criticism, but they do offer the chance for God's voice to break through into a culture that has become entrenched in a tradition which has stagnated. Douglas V. Steere observed: '*As long as it flourishes, it constitutes a continual challenge to what William James calls "a premature closing of accounts with reality" in terms of an exclusively ethical, institutional, theological or intellectual presentation of religion*' (cited in Halverson and Cohen, 1960). When making moral decisions, however, perhaps neither mystical experience nor formalised ethical theory can provide a solution that is beyond question.

It remains true…that a man must in the moment of decision do what he thinks is right.… This does not mean that what he does will be right.… He simply has no choice, for he cannot at that moment see any discrepancy between what is right and what he thinks is right.

(William K. Frankena, 1973)

Religious experience

Religious experience in the philosophy of religion

Human beings enjoy a wide variety of different experiences: physical experiences, emotional experiences, intellectual and aesthetic experiences. Religious experiences are beyond ordinary, worldly explanation and usually take place within a context of religious expectancy and hope. Religious experiences may be individual — where someone is made aware of a transcendent reality — or corporate — where a gathering of people, usually already focused on the divine, appear to be influenced by powers beyond normal control and understanding.

Schleiermacher defined religious experience as one that yielded a sense of the ultimate, an awareness of wholeness, a consciousness of infiniteness and finiteness, an absolute dependence and a sharp sense of contingency. William James observed that religious experience draws on the common store of emotions — happiness, fear and wonder — but is directed at something divine. The result of such an experience will be reverence, a joyful desire to belong to God and a renewed approach to life. Such symptoms will be testimony to the reality of the experience. For the religious believer whose life is lived in a state of 'God consciousness', all things have the potential to be a religious experience: the beauty of the natural order, their daily experiences and the way they believe that they fit into the plans and purposes of God.

Richard Swinburne (1996) observed:
An omnipotent and perfectly good creator will seek to interact with his creatures and, in particular, with human persons capable of knowing him.

Paul Tillich identified a feeling of 'ultimate concern' as being characteristic of religious experience, since it demands a firm decision from the person receiving it. He identified two types of religious experience:

- sharing the life of the religious community and being governed by its 'ultimate concern'
- suddenly grasping as critical a concern that has previously been regarded as unimportant or illusory. This is essentially what takes place in a conversion experience

Swinburne's **principle of testimony** is also helpful. He described it thus (1979): *'In the absence of special considerations the experiences of others are (probably) as they report them.'*

We cannot work on the basis that we constantly doubt people's accounts of religious experiences any more than we doubt basic facts about the world that we have not directly experienced ourselves. Swinburne identified three types of evidence which may well give us grounds for saying that a person's experience is not as they report it:

- The circumstances surrounding the experience render the resultant perceptions unreliable, e.g. hallucinatory drugs.
- There is particular evidence that the person is not telling the truth, e.g. they were not in the place they say they were when they had the experience.
- There is evidence that the experience was not caused by God, e.g. someone believes they have experienced God because they had a fever.

According to Swinburne, however, most religious experiences do not take place under the influence of drugs; evidence that things are not as they reported would have to be decisive, not merely ambiguous; and the fact that a fever may contribute to the experience does not mean it is a complete explanation for it.

Religious experience in the Bible

All types of religious experience are found in the Bible, which provides a useful source of case studies for a comparison of religious experiences and an examination of their nature and purpose. Some biblical experiences have become textbook cases: in the Old Testament Moses sees a burning bush and hears a voice calling him to a particular mission (Exodus 3); Elijah experiences a great storm, followed by a 'still small voice' and a command to continue his prophetic activity (1 Kings 19); Isaiah sees the Lord lifted up high in the temple and hears a voice telling him to take God's message to his people (Isaiah 6). In all these cases the person sees and hears outward phenomena that acquire a special, symbolic significance, and at the same time they believe that they are called to a special task.

In the New Testament, Jesus's disciples experience the Transfiguration (Mark 9:2–13). On the road to Emmaus (Luke 24:13–26) two disciples meet the risen Jesus but fail to recognise him until they witness him breaking bread, a moment of revelation that causes them to interpret their walk on the road with him as a religious experience. Paul receives a blinding vision on the road to Damascus, which changes his whole life. As with the Old Testament experiences, visual and verbal symbols are given a special interpretation and demand a response from the person receiving the experience. It is not something they can ignore. These experiences are received by people who are called to be part of God's ongoing purpose. They require the person receiving them to engage in God's work, sometimes in great conflicts, such as those that Moses and Paul are forced to confront. The crucial test of the integrity of a religious experience is the response that the individual makes to it.

Moses

Moses was the great leader and lawgiver of the people of Israel, who led them out of slavery in Egypt and made them into a holy nation of God's people. God spoke to him through a burning bush, telling him that he had chosen him to lead the Israelites out of slavery and into freedom. Subsequently, led by Moses and under God's guidance, the Israelites wandered for 40 years (the Exodus), during which time they encountered many trials and tribulations which united them as one people. The climax of the story occurred at Mount Sinai, where God gave the people the Law, including the Ten Commandments (Exodus 20). Finally, the people reached the land of Canaan. His work complete, Moses died before he entered the Promised Land.

Moses is, arguably, the greatest figure in the Old Testament. He was a strong, caring leader — the people continually failed to obey God during the Exodus, yet he constantly interceded with God on their behalf and pleaded with the people to remain steadfast in their faith (Numbers 14). His experience of God had given him a deep personal relationship with God (Exodus 24:18) and, as a result, God was able to renew the covenant with his people. Moses became the model for all the later prophets and the forerunner of the Messiah (Deuteronomy 18:18). His role in the history of the Israelites is therefore of paramount importance: it was through him that the people escaped from slavery to freedom and, in his role as mediator, he was able to bring the law of God to the people and enable them to understand the nature and significance of their relationship with God.

Paul

Paul and his companions had set off on the road to Damascus when suddenly a bright light from heaven shone down and the risen Christ challenged Paul, saying *'Saul, Saul, why do you persecute me?'* (Acts 9:4). Paul was blinded and his life changed for ever. He was taken to Damascus, unable to see and overwhelmed by his experiences. He could not eat or drink until Ananias, a Christian living in Damascus, visited him and restored his sight through the power of God. Paul was converted to Christianity by his experience and went on to teach the message of Jesus Christ throughout the known world, and to establish the Christian Church.

The ministry of Paul was not bounded by the limits of a life. It influenced decisively all European history, and through European history the history of the whole modern world. Paul's was the most significant human life ever lived. (E. M. Blaiklock, 1959)

How do modern believers experience God?

The Bible speaks of God in personal terms. He is described as loving and trustworthy and as having a personal relationship with those who love him, rather like a parent and child. It suggests a God with whom humans can have a relationship — reflecting their own relationships with each other. Worship is humankind's response to God. It may be through silence, stillness, wonder, praise or dedication. God himself is at the heart of Christian worship. True worship requires two elements: revelation, through which God shows himself, and humankind's response to God. God makes himself known in a number of ways — through creation, his written word and through Jesus Christ and the Holy Spirit. Worship depends on revelation and, from this, knowledge of God.

Prayer enables the believer to communicate with God in worship. God is personal and seeks a loving relationship with humankind, made possible through the ministry of Jesus Christ. Prayer allows the believer to relate to God and to change things in God's world.

Although many religious experiences have a deeply personal significance, many are reported as happening within a corporate gathering. Luke describes one of the most important corporate religious experiences in the Christian tradition:
When the day of Pentecost had come, they were all together in one place. Suddenly a sound like the blowing of a violent wind came from heaven and filled the whole house where they were sitting. They saw what seemed to be tongues of fire that separated and came to rest on each of them. All of them were filled with the Holy Spirit and began to speak in other tongues as the Spirit enabled them. (Acts 2:1–4)

This kind of religious experience is familiar to many Christians today. Indeed, in the 1990s many churches reported a wave of corporate experiences such as this, which became known as the **Toronto Blessing**. Such corporate religious experiences have a very powerful effect on many of those present. Some Christians, however, remain sceptical about the validity of such experiences, arguing that in a crowd of like-minded individuals it can be easy to be swept along in a tide of religious fervour and emotion.

There can be no certain answer as to the validity of religious experiences. They remain very much in the realm of personal belief and faith. Yet the evidence remains compelling, as Swinburne (1996) observed:

The only way to defeat the claims of religious experience will be to show that the strong balance of evidence is that there is no God. In the absence of that strong balance, religious experience provides significant further evidence that there is a God.

Synoptic question and answer

Question 4 Philosophy of Religion and Biblical Studies

'Key figures in the Bible often become influential because of their religious experience.'

(a) Consider how a person might decide whether or not an experience they have had is a religious one.

(b) Examine the lives of two people from the Bible where this could be said to be the case and evaluate their contribution to the development of their religious tradition.

(a) Human beings enjoy a wide variety of different experiences: physical, emotional, intellectual and aesthetic. Religious experiences are beyond ordinary, worldly explanation and usually take place within a context of religious expectancy and hope. They may be individual — where someone is made aware of a transcendent reality — or corporate — where a gathering of people, usually already focused on the divine, appear to be influenced by powers beyond normal control and understanding.

The Bible speaks of God in personal terms, describing him as loving and trustworthy and as having a personal relationship with those who love him, rather like a parent and child. It suggests a God with whom humans can have a relationship, which reflects their own relationships with each other. God makes himself known in a number of ways — through creation, his written word and through Jesus Christ and the Holy Spirit. Worship depends on revelation and from this comes knowledge of God. Worship is humankind's response to God. It may be through silence, stillness, wonder, praise or dedication. God himself is at the heart of Christian worship. True worship requires two elements: revelation, through which God shows himself, and humankind's response to God. Prayer is communicating with God in worship. God is personal and seeks a loving relationship with humankind, made possible through the ministry of Jesus Christ. Prayer allows the believer to relate to God and to change things in God's world.

Many scholarly suggestions have been made as to what precisely characterises a religious experience. Schleiermacher defined it as an experience that bestows a sense of the ultimate, an awareness of wholeness, a consciousness of infiniteness and finiteness, an absolute dependence and a sharp sense of contingency. William James observed that religious experience draws on the common store of emotions — happiness, fear and wonder — but is directed at something divine. The result of such an experience will be reverence, a joyful desire to belong to God and a renewed approach to life. Such symptoms testify to the reality of the experience.

Paul Tillich identified a feeling of 'ultimate concern' as being characteristic of religious experience, since it demands a firm decision from the person receiving it. He identified two types of religious experience: sharing the life of the religious community and being governed by its 'ultimate concern', and suddenly grasping as critical a concern that has previously been regarded as unimportant or illusory. This is essentially what takes place in a conversion experience.

Although many religious experiences have a deeply personal significance, many are reported as happening within a corporate gathering. In the Acts of the Apostles, Luke describes one of the most important corporate religious experiences in the Christian tradition: *'When the day of Pentecost had come, they were all together in one place. Suddenly a sound like the blowing of a violent wind came from heaven and filled the whole house where they were sitting. They saw what seemed to be tongues of fire that separated and came to rest on each of them. All of them were filled with the Holy Spirit and began to speak in other tongues as the Spirit enabled them'* (Acts 2:1–4).

Interestingly, this kind of religious experience is familiar to many Christians today. In the 1990s, many churches reported a wave of corporate experiences such as this, which became known as the 'Toronto Blessing'. Such corporate religious experiences have a very powerful effect on many of those present. However, religious experiences need not simply be thought of in terms of a specific event. In a sense, all believers live in closeness to God, or 'God consciousness', and for them all things have the potential to be a religious experience — for instance, the beauty of nature or seeing God at work in their lives. Other individual experiences have a vivid personal significance and lead to a complete transformation of life and outlook. Nicky Cruz, the leader of the Mau Maus, a violent street gang in 1950s New York, described his experience of God (1968): *'All my fear was gone. All my anxieties were gone. My hatred was gone. I was in love with God...with Jesus Christ...and with all those around me. I even loved myself.'* There was no doubt for him that his experience was unambiguously one of God and his interpretation would lend weight to the view of Richard Swinburne (1996) that: *'An omnipotent and perfectly good creator will seek to interact with his creatures and, in particular, with human persons capable of knowing him.'*

Nevertheless, however powerful an individual's experience might be, whether a third party finds it so is another question. Swinburne's 'principle of testimony' is helpful here. He described it thus (1979): *'In the absence of special considerations the experiences of others are (probably) as they report them.'* We cannot work on the basis that we constantly doubt people's accounts of religious experiences any more than we doubt basic facts about the world that we have not directly experienced ourselves. Swinburne identified three types of evidence which may well give us grounds for saying that a person's experience is not as they report it:

- The circumstances surrounding the experience render the resultant perceptions unreliable, e.g. hallucinatory drugs.
- There is particular evidence that the person was not telling the truth, e.g. they were not in the place they say they were when they had the experience.
- There is evidence that God did not cause the experience, e.g. someone experienced God because they had a fever.

As Swinburne said, however, most religious experiences do not take place under the influence of drugs; evidence that things are not as they are reported would have to be decisive, not merely ambiguous; and the fact that a fever may contribute to the experience does not mean that it is a complete explanation for it. His argument, therefore, is that if an experience has appeared to someone to be religious, then it is more reasonable to accept this as the best explanation than to maintain that their account is unreliable.

There can be no certain answer as to whether or not a person has had a religious experience. Religious experiences remain very much in the realm of personal belief and faith. Yet the evidence remains compelling, as Swinburne (1996) observed: *'The only way to defeat the claims of religious experience will be to show that the strong balance of evidence is that there is no God. In the absence of that strong balance, religious experience provides significant further evidence that there is a God.'*

(b) All types of religious experience are found in the Bible and many have become textbook cases. In the Old Testament Moses hears God speak through a burning bush, calling him to a particular mission (Exodus 3); Elijah experiences a great storm, followed by a 'still small voice' and a command to continue his prophetic activity (1 Kings 19); and Isaiah sees the Lord lifted up high in the temple and hears a voice telling him to take God's message to his people (Isaiah 6). In all these cases, the people concerned have seen and heard outward phenomena that acquire a special, symbolic significance, and at the same time they believe that they have been called by God to undertake a special task.

In the New Testament Jesus's disciples see Moses and Elijah at the Transfiguration (Mark 9:2–13). On the road to Emmaus (Luke 24:13–26) two disciples meet the risen Jesus, but fail to recognise him until they witness him breaking bread, a moment of revelation which causes them to interpret their walk on the road with him as a religious experience. Perhaps most famously, Paul receives a blinding vision on the road to Damascus, which changes his whole life. As with the Old Testament experiences, people see and hear what they believe to be God; they are required to respond and undertake God's commission to them. It is not something they can ignore.

These experiences are clearly dramatic and are received by people called to be part of God's divine plan. They require the person receiving them to engage in God's work, sometimes in situations of conflict and often at considerable personal risk to themselves. These dramatic experiences act as points of reference — they mark a great change in the person, perhaps a conversion experience, and the event remains an inspiration, both to the experient and to those who follow them. The crucial test of the integrity of a religious experience is the response that the individual makes to it. This is shown in the example of two important biblical figures — Moses and Paul. In both these cases the individual receives a dramatic and vivid experience of God, which changes not only their lives but the course of world history. The experiences are not only inspirational, but they also carry great authority both in terms of the giver of the experience (God) and the task given to the experient. The experiences testify that God called Moses and Paul and this gives their teaching and work the authority it needs to succeed in the hearts and minds of those who follow.

Moses is the great leader and lawgiver of the people of Israel, who leads them out of slavery in Egypt and makes them into a holy nation of God's people. His religious experience is indeed dramatic. God speaks to him through a burning bush, telling him that he has chosen him to lead the Israelites out of slavery and into freedom. The story has interesting features — God speaks to Moses in a direct and personal way and even tells Moses his name — which in those days was particularly important since to know the name of God was to have a personal relationship with him: *'God said to Moses, "I AM WHO I AM". This is what you are to say to the Israelites. I AM has sent me to you'* (Exodus 3:14).

Subsequently, led by Moses and under God's guidance, the Israelites are led out of Egypt (the Exodus) and wander for 40 years in the wilderness, during which time the people encounter many trials and tribulations which unite them as a nation. The climax of the story occurs at Mount Sinai, where God gives the people the Law, including the Ten Commandments (Exodus 20). Finally, the people reach the land of Canaan, although Moses dies before he enters the Promised Land.

Moses is, arguably, the greatest figure in the Old Testament. He lived around 1300BCE and was a strong, caring leader: although the people continually fail to obey God during the Exodus, he constantly intercedes with God on their behalf and pleads with the people to remain steadfast in their faith (Numbers 14). His religious experience of God has given him a deep personal relationship with God (Exodus 24:8) and, as a result, God is able to renew the covenant with his people. Moses becomes the model for all the later prophets and the forerunner of the Messiah (Deuteronomy 18:18).

Moses' contribution to the history of the Israelites (and, subsequently, the Western world) is of enormous importance. It is through him that the people escape from slavery to freedom. More than this, he is able to renew the covenant and he gives the people God's law, which became known as the Law of Moses. It is through the Law and the covenant that his people are able to establish a sense of national identity. Moses enables his people to understand the nature and significance of their relationship with God.

Paul was a Jew and a Roman citizen, born about 6BCE. As a learned Pharisee and a man of authority within Judaism at that time, he would clearly have believed that God had a special relationship with his people and that, one day, God would send his Messiah to drive away their enemies and establish God's kingdom on earth. In common with many Pharisees at the time, he holds the followers of Jesus Christ, the crucified Messiah, in contempt. He is present at the stoning to death of the first Christian martyr, Stephen, and soon after he willingly undertakes a mission to bring the new Christians back to Jerusalem for trial and judgement. He and his companions are on the road to Damascus, en route to persecute the Christian community there, when suddenly a bright light from heaven shines down and the risen Christ challenges Paul, saying: *'Saul, Saul, why do you persecute me?'* (Acts 9:4).

Paul is blinded and his life is changed for ever. He is taken to Damascus, unable to see and overwhelmed by his experiences. He cannot eat or drink until Ananias, a Christian living in the town, visits him and restores his sight through the power of God. He becomes a follower of Christ and over the ensuing years is responsible for the establishment of the early church throughout the Roman world. It is through this religious experience that Paul is able to develop his teaching about Christ and the manner in which he sees his mission. A. N. Wilson (1998) observed: *'The essential things — the certainty of human unworthiness before the perfection of God, the atoning sacrifice of Christ on the Cross, the glorious promise of the resurrection and everlasting life — these are the core of Paul's religion. And, above all, the knowledge that Christ, the drama of his passion, death and resurrection, but also the continuing presence in the world are in us. That is the winning formula.'*

Paul became known as the Apostle to the Gentiles and there is no doubt that his work changed the lives and culture of everyone in the western world from that time onwards. E. M. Blaiklock (1959) described it thus: *'The ministry of Paul was not bounded by the limits of a life. It influenced decisively all European history, and through European history the history of the whole modern world. Paul's was the most significant human life ever lived.'*

Moses and Paul are both exceptional people, both of whom had dramatic religious experiences. Their contribution to their religious tradition and to human history is exceptional. Yet it must be remembered that the majority of people who claim to have had religious experiences do not have dramatic ones. They may hear the 'still small voice of God' within themselves, or see God's hand at work through answered prayer. Their experiences may not be as dramatic as Moses' and Paul's, but that makes them no less valid or decisive in their lives and the lives of others. It is experiences of this kind that keep religious traditions alive, even if it is the experiences of the type made known to Moses and Paul that make the history books.

Life after death

Life after death: philosophical issues

Why is the concept of an afterlife important?

- We find it hard to accept that this life is all that there is and that a God who created human beings for a relationship with him would limit it to the physical realm. *'If the human potential is to be fulfilled in the lives of individuals, these lives must be prolonged far beyond the limits of our present bodily existence'* (John Hick, 1966).
- The moral law needs to be balanced, with good rewarded and evil punished.
- We place high value on human life and it is hard to conceive of something of such high value ending, even if its continuation demands that we postulate some alternative mode of existence.
- *'Ordinary people seem not to realise that those who really apply themselves in the proper way to philosophy are directly and of their own accord preparing themselves for death and dying'* (Plato, *Phaedo* 63e–64a).

Is life after death a meaningful concept?

According to Antony Flew, the notion of life after death is incoherent because death and life are two mutually exclusive categories, and pronouns and proper nouns refer to real, living human beings, and not to postmortem beings to whom you cannot ascribe personal identity. However, if the phrase 'surviving death' is meaningful and not misleading to those who hear it — i.e. people who understand its context — then it is a legitimate way of speaking.

Can life after death be verified?

Since it is logically impossible for a person to verify their own postmortem existence prior to death, then in this life the concept remains unverifiable. It will be eschatologically verifiable, however. Near-death experiences (NDEs), psychic experiences, occult activity and the apparent evidence of remembered lives could point to the existence of an afterlife.

Postmortem existence and personal identity

What survives: body? Or mind/soul? Or both? The physical body can be seen and identified as a matter of fact, but the mind/soul is a person/thing that cannot be analysed in the same way. There are two main strands of thought regarding this issue:

Dualism: humans have composite natures — material (the physical body) and non-material (mind/soul). Descartes maintained that: *'My essence consists solely in the fact that I am a thinking thing (or a substance whose whole essence or nature is to think).'*

Materialism, or **behaviourism:** mental events are really physical events occurring to physical objects. Gilbert Ryle described dualism as proposing a *'ghost in a machine'*, and rejected as a **category mistake** the notion that body and mind are separate entities.

The disembodied spirit/soul

The traditional Greek view, expressed by Socrates as he faced death, is that the death of the body can have no real and lasting effect on the soul. Plato conceived that humankind has an immortal, pre-existent soul, which has encountered these forms before becoming effectively imprisoned in the physical body. Death will bring about the final separation of body and soul when the soul will re-enter the eternal realm from which it came.

Criticisms of this view

Thomas Aquinas stated:
Since, therefore, the natural condition of the soul is to be united to the body...it has a natural desire for union with the body, hence the will cannot be perfectly at rest until the soul is again joined to a body.   (Cited in Hick (ed.), 1964)

Bryan Magee (1997) claimed:
The human body is single entity, one subject of behaviour and experience with a single history.

The resurrected body

John Hick argued for the strength of the resurrected body position in his illust-ration of a Mr X, who disappears from a learned gathering on one side of the world and reappears on the other, without apparently having traversed time and space. A similar scenario is proposed: Mr X dies in New York but a replica of him appears in London, complete in every way. Hick argued that if we can accept that these strange scenarios are in some way logically possible, then it is also logically possible for Mr X to die and a replica of him to appear in some place inhabited by resurrected beings:

Mr X then dies. A Mr X replica, complete with the set of memory traces which Mr X had at the last moment before his death, comes into existence. It is composed of other material than physical matter, and is located in a resurrection world which does not stand in a spatial relationship with the physical world.

(Hick, 1966)

The doctrine of bodily resurrection suggests that resurrection and eternal life depend on an act of God's divine love. The New Testament writers suggest that Jesus appeared to his disciples in bodily form, talked and ate with them; they could touch him and they saw his scars. Yet he was different: he appeared and disappeared and was beyond death: *'Look at my hands and my feet…touch me and see; a ghost does not have flesh and bones as you see I have'* (Luke 24:39).

Eschatological verification

Ultimately, however, we are still left with the problem of whether any kind of post-mortem existence can be verified. John Hick resolved this with the principle of **eschatological verification**. He envisaged two travellers walking down a road, one of whom believes it leads to the celestial city and one who believes that there is no final destination. Which one of them is right will not be verified until they reach the end of the road, although their particular positions will have a vital influence on the way they experience and interpret what happens to them on the road. Nevertheless, their respective positions will be either verified or falsified, although it is not possible to do so during the course of their earthly existence.

Life after death in the New Testament

The raising of Lazarus (John 11:1–44)

The raising of Lazarus takes place among people who believe in Jesus and love Lazarus, a friend and follower of Christ. Lazarus has been dead and buried for 4 days before Jesus arrives, but Lazarus's sister, Martha, seems to believe that Jesus can still do something: *'But I know that even now God will give you whatever you ask'* (John 11:22). She does not really understand the power of Christ, however, probably thinking that Jesus will be able do something for Lazarus in the life to come — she mentions the *'resurrection at the last day'* (John 11:24) — but not in the present instance. Yet this **futuristic eschatology** is about to be overtaken by a **realised eschatology** of the present as Jesus declares that he is *'the resurrection and the life'* (John 11:25). Martha declares her belief that Jesus is *'the Christ, the Son of God'* (John 11:27).

Jesus's resurrection

In the Synoptic Gospels, Jesus predicts his death and resurrection three times (Mark 8:31, 9:31, 10:34 & //s), and after the Transfiguration he warns the disciples to *'tell no one until the Son of Man should have risen from the dead'* (Mark 9:9). None of the predictions attempts to explain *how* Jesus's resurrection will be accomplished. The evangelists were not concerned with the mechanics of God's miraculous activity, but rather with the reality of it, and the gospel accounts of the Resurrection do not attempt a description or analysis of what happened. The Resurrection is not narrated, but proclaimed. Although all four accounts are quite distinctive, enabling the evangelists to make use of the narrative to emphasise key themes that have run throughout their gospels, there are significant links between them. All the gospel accounts include:

- the fact of the empty tomb
- the visit of women (in John's case Mary Magdalene only) to the tomb
- information that Jesus has risen from the dead conveyed by angels or by a mysterious stranger
- motifs of surprise, lack of recognition and disbelief
- instructions or commissioning by Jesus

Not all the gospel accounts can be said, strictly speaking, to include a resurrection appearance and in the Marcan account (the shortest, and possibly most reliable, one) the news that Jesus had been raised from the dead is not immediately believed by the disciples, male or female, although interestingly the women are more receptive than the men. The appearances of Jesus in Matthew and in John 21 appear to be of a figure that is of a more mystical and spiritual nature than in the other accounts where, for example, Thomas is invited to touch him, or where he eats broiled fish.

Paul's teaching (1 Corinthians 15:3–9)

Paul's teaching on the Resurrection and its significance for all Christian believers is based on his conviction that *'If Christ be not risen, then your faith is in vain'* (1 Corinthians 15:17). His is the earliest resurrection tradition, written at least

10 years before the earliest gospel account. It can be summarised in four key stages:

- Christ dies for our sins in accordance with the scriptures (1 Corinthians 15:3b).
- He is buried (1 Corinthians 15:4a).
- He is raised on the third day in accordance with the scriptures (1 Corinthians 15:4b).
- Then he appears to various people (1 Corinthians 15:5–9).

The list of appearances that follows seems to validate the first three points, which are presented by Paul as both historical and theological certainties; taken together, the four formulae are offered as the grounds on which the believer can be absolutely certain of the future hope of their own resurrection.

R. H. Fuller (1972) wrote:

The presupposition of Paul's argument is that there is a constitutive and organic relationship between the resurrection and the future resurrection of believers.... Christ's resurrection was the beginning of the eschatological process of resurrection.... When, therefore, Paul goes on to define the nature of resurrected existence, what he says about it will apply equally to Christ.

Paul clearly seems to use the appearances — to Peter (Cephas), the Twelve (interestingly, since Judas would be dead by then), to *'more than 500 brothers and sisters'*, to James, to *'all the apostles'*, and *'last of all...to me'* — to prove the Resurrection. Rudolph Bultmann claimed that this was a fatal step that leads to the further attempt to historicise it in the gospels, and ultimately in the highly imaginative accounts of the apocryphal gospels.

The resurrection of all believers

Paul's teaching (1 Corinthians 15:12–57)

R. H. Fuller suggested that Paul's readership in Corinth was anticipating not a bodily resurrection like Christ's, but simply the opening up of a new existence made possible by their baptism — a present state, but not accompanied by any concept of future hope. Paul writes to them to correct this picture. The resurrection of believers will, like Christ's resurrection, involve the resurrection and recreation of a *body*. However, the corruptible and perishable flesh will be transformed into something incorruptible, something that can only be created by God in the miracle of the Resurrection.

Eternal life

In the Fourth Gospel, the emphasis on salvation as a present experience overshadows the idea of future salvation and bodily resurrection. John teaches that as soon as a person makes this decision they enter into eternal life. The transition from death to life has already taken place, and thus Jesus can say: *'I am the resurrection and the life; he who believes in me, though he die, yet shall he live, and whoever lives and believes in me shall never die'* (John 11:25–26). Eternal life transcends physical death and nothing can separate humankind from the communion it has with God: *'I give them eternal life, and they will never perish. No one will snatch them out of my hand. What my Father has given me is greater than all else, and no one can snatch it out of the Father's hand'* (John 10:28–29).

Robert Kysar called this the **preserver theory**. He claimed that the evangelist includes some futurist references in order to preserve the traditional view alongside his own present perspective, even though they are contradictory; arguably, the evangelist feels that the futurist perspective is no longer meaningful.

Interpreting the resurrection accounts

Rudolph Bultmann claimed that the *'real meaning of the resurrection message was not that an incredible event took place on Easter Sunday, but the cross is permanently available to us in the church's preaching as the saving act of God'* (cited in Fuller, 1972). Martin Dibelius observed that even the most sceptical historians acknowledge that something happened, but we cannot know the precise nature of this event, even though the New Testament writers believed it to be unambiguous.

It is the task of the systematic theologian to wrestle with the scientific, philosophical, and theological problems posed by the New Testament message of Christ's resurrection, but it is the task of the New Testament scholar to probe the historical basis of this proclamation.

(R. H. Fuller, 1972)

Synoptic question and answer

Question 5 **Philosophy of Religion and New Testament**

How useful is the New Testament in proving or disproving life after death?

The question asked presupposes that there are issues about life after death that are open to question, and this is clearly evident from the perspective of both the philosopher and the biblical scholar. The concept of life after death is one which, by definition, requires the scholar to think about issues that are not restricted to those of earthly life and hence are essentially beyond investigation, only being open to speculation. Nevertheless, this does not prevent thinkers from postulating the nature of postmortem existence, its timing, its character, its desirability and the language that may be used to describe it. There is no doubt that life after death is central to the teachings of the New Testament, and within the realms of philosophy it occupies a key place in discussions concerning personal identity and the relationship between the mind and the body. The New Testament writers, however, have a focus to their discussions that does not necessarily interest the philosopher in the same way: the resurrection of Jesus. R. H. Fuller (1972) observed: *'It is the task of the systematic theologian to wrestle with the scientific, philosophical, and theological problems posed by the New Testament message of Christ's resurrection, but it is the task of the New Testament scholar to probe the historical basis of this proclamation.'*

The New Testament teaching on the resurrection of Jesus and on the hope of resurrection for all who believe in him could provide the philosopher with important material to inform an investigation. However, it is not inconceivable that a belief in the logical possibility of life after death need not include belief in the historical resurrection of Jesus. If life after death is a logical possibility, then in philosophical terms it need not depend on the resurrection of Jesus, although from the perspective of the New Testament writers — Paul in particular — the resurrection of Jesus serves as the guarantor of the resurrection of all who believe in him. Again, R. H. Fuller (1972) wrote: *'The presupposition of Paul's argument is that there is a constitutive and organic relationship between the resurrection and the future resurrection of believers.... Christ's resurrection was the beginning of the eschatological process of resurrection.... When, therefore, Paul goes on to define the nature of resurrected existence, what he says about it will apply equally to Christ.'*

What, then, is the difference between establishing the logical possibility of life after death and the historical fact of the resurrection of Jesus? John Hick's famous replica theory (1966) attempts to demonstrate that life after death is a concept that may be logically conceivable without necessarily making reference to the resurrection of Jesus. He proposes that we consider the case of Mr X, who disappears from a learned gathering on one side of the world and reappears on the other, without apparently having traversed time and space. A similar scenario is proposed: Mr X dies in New York but a replica of him appears in London, complete in every way. Hick argued that if we can accept that these strange scenarios are in some way logically possible, then it is also logically possible for Mr X to die and a replica of him to appear in some place inhabited by resurrected beings: *'Mr X then dies. A Mr X replica, complete with the set of memory traces which Mr X had at the last moment before his death, comes into existence. It is composed of other material than physical matter, and is located in a resurrection world which does not stand in a spatial relationship with the physical world.'*

Hick's argument appears to be that life after death — in the form of a replicated body — is not inconceivable, but this is a far cry from the concerns of the New Testament writers, who are much less interested in attempting to explain how Jesus's resurrection came about, or how to conceive of the process of passing from earthly life to postmortem existence. The evangelists were concerned not with the mechanics of God's miraculous activity but rather with the reality of it, and the gospel accounts of the Resurrection themselves do not attempt a description or analysis of what happened. The Resurrection is not narrated, but proclaimed. It is accepted as an accomplished fact and not rationalised. Readers are not invited to test the claims but rather, in 1 Corinthians 15, Paul expresses some exasperation with the Corinthians for their reluctance to accept that the resurrection of Jesus — a historical fact, verified by appearances to individuals and to crowds — ensures their own resurrection.

At first glance, the New Testament writers appear to be clear on the nature of resurrection as well as its reality. With the exception of the most reliable Marcan manuscripts, the evangelists describe the appearances of Jesus in highly physical terms. In John 20:27, Thomas is invited to place his fingers in the marks of the nails and the spear in Jesus's hands and side. In Luke 24:39–43 the disciples are given the opportunity to touch Jesus's flesh and he eats fish before them, proving that he is not a ghost. Paul makes clear to the Corinthians that the resurrection body will be just that — a body. It will be a spiritual body, transformed from contingent corruptibility to imperishable incorruptibility (1 Corinthians 15:52), and as different from the physical body as a seed is from the plant into which it grows (1 Corinthians 15:37, 42–44) but, nevertheless, Paul clearly finds the term 'body' to be the most appropriate to describe the form it is to take.

There is a tension, however, between the fleshly body that the risen Jesus seems to have in the Lucan and Johannine passages above, and the rather more mystical form he has in the Matthean account — the disciples, both men and women, *worship* him rather than attempt to cling to his physical form — and in John 20:17 when Jesus instructs Mary not to hold on to him before he has ascended to *'my Father and your Father, my God and your God'*. The physical and the spiritual resurrection body of Jesus present different challenges to those who see him, a body that can pass through locked doors, and yet can also eat.

This tension is a key element in the problems that face the philosopher in attempting to clarify the nature of life after death. Aquinas claimed that: *'Elements that are by nature destined for union naturally desire to be united with each other; for any being seeks what is suited to it by nature. Since, therefore, the natural condition of the soul is to be united to the body...it has a natural desire for union with the body, hence the will cannot be perfectly at rest until the soul is again joined to a body. When this takes place, man rises from the dead.'*

However, the dualist tradition — to which Plato and, later, Descartes belonged — argued rather for the separation of body and soul or spirit. Descartes wrote: *'Our soul is of a nature entirely independent of the body, and consequently…it is not bound to die with it. And since we cannot see any other causes that destroy the soul, we are naturally led to conclude that it is immortal.'*

Plato conceived that humankind has an immortal, pre-existent soul, which has encountered true reality before becoming effectively imprisoned in the physical body. At birth the soul forgets its previous life, but through philosophy we can be reminded of the nature of true reality and recall this lost knowledge. This process is known as **anamnesis** — literally, 'non-forgetting'. The soul, like the Forms, is immortal and immutable, unlike the body, which is a physical entity and so is changeable and imperfect. Plato believed that humankind should seek to rise above the inconvenient limitations of the body and its needs and desires, and instead seek to be identified once more with our immortal soul and be united with the unchanging Forms. Death will bring about the final separation of body and soul when the soul will re-enter the eternal realm from which it came.

In the *Phaedo*, Plato argued that: *'Ordinary people seem not to realise that those who really apply themselves in the proper way to philosophy are directly and of their own accord preparing themselves for death and dying.'* While the means of preparation that Plato envisaged is a far cry from the kind of preparation that Paul or John had in mind — belief in and acceptance of Jesus as God — there is a common chord. The New Testament writers are clear that this life is the realm in which humankind prepares for the next. A person's actions and decisions have a bearing on their eschatological future, and the most important decision is whether or not to believe that Jesus is the only way to eternal life and postmortem existence. The believer is not embracing an abstract philosophy but, the New Testament writers would claim, is entering into a relationship with a real, living presence, which in turn will reveal the reality of postmortem existence. The Fourth Evangelist teaches that as soon as a person makes that decision, they enter into eternal life. The transition from death to life has already taken place, and thus Jesus can say: *'I am the resurrection and the life; he who believes in me, though he die, yet shall he live, and whoever lives and believes in me shall never die'* (John 11:25–26). Eternal life transcends physical death and nothing can separate humankind from the communion it has with God: *'I give them eternal life, and they will never perish. No one will snatch them out of my hand. What my Father has given me is greater than all else, and no one can snatch it out of the Father's hand'* (John 10:28–29).

The New Testament writers make clear why life after death, rooted in a relationship with Jesus, is a desirable goal — it is the only way that humankind can avoid the inevitable consequences of sin and separation from God. For the philosopher, however, it may be necessary to find some other reason to justify postmortem existence. If it is, as discussed, possible to conceive of the logical possibility of life after death without belief in the resurrection of Jesus, then life after death need not acquire its significance from Jesus's resurrection either. For the philosopher, life after death might be desirable simply because it is hard to accept that this earthly existence is all that there is — there must be something beyond earthly life which gives meaning to it. Furthermore, we place such a high value on life that it is hard to conceive of it ending, even if its continuation demands that we postulate some alternative mode of existence. Human potential is rarely completely fulfilled in this life and Hick suggested that: *'If the human potential is to be fulfilled in the lives of individuals, these lives must be prolonged far beyond the limits of our present bodily existence'*. Our comprehension of morality, too, may demand that an afterlife is necessary to redress the balance of good and evil, to reward the virtuous and punish the evil.

However, while these notions do not depend on the resurrection of Jesus, or on a life after death that is exclusive to religious believers, or even on the existence of a divine being who will bring it about, the New Testament writers clearly thought otherwise. Although it may be logically conceivable that the soul could survive the death of the body, simply because we *feel* that it has an existence and identity apart from the body, this is not satisfactory to the New Testament writers. Only a supremely powerful divine being, motivated by love for his people to the extent that he sent his only son to die for them in order that they might fully realise the loving relationship he wants to share with them, can have the incentive and the ability to bring about such an existence. Without God, we are left to ask why human potential should be fulfilled beyond the grave, why good should be rewarded, and why the value of human life should be recognised post mortem. If it is only because we think it should, then it reflects nothing more than humankind's inflated sense of its own importance, and a tendency to exaggerate humankind's ability to influence and shape its own destiny. The New Testament writers would argue that postmortem existence must be firmly placed within the hands of God, and that the resurrection of Jesus, and the promise that his resurrection offers to all believers, guarantees its reality.

For some thinkers, the language of life after death alone poses a problem. To speak of life after death could be thought to be a contradiction in terms. Antony Flew considered that it is and that therefore it is not meaningful even to talk about life after death, still less to consider what form it might take. He argued that the notion of life after death is incoherent because death and life are two mutually exclusive categories. In a plane crash there may be those who survive and those who die, but there is no one who 'survives death'. Flew also argued that pronouns and proper nouns — I, me, you, father, brother, Tallulah, Anthea — refer to real, living human beings and not to souls or to dead persons or to immortal beings to whom one cannot ascribe personal identity.

Proponents of language game theory can resolve this by claiming that talk of postmortem existence is part of a religious language game and has meaning to those who participate in it. Furthermore, language becomes stretched and applied to new situations, becoming meaningful in new contexts even if it was not previously communicable. If the phrase 'surviving death' is meaningful and not misleading to those who hear it, then it is a legitimate way of speaking. It is possible to argue that the New

Testament writers, and the Fourth Evangelist in particular, did exactly this. If the concept of a future postmortem existence in which the body is replicated or resurrected by the power of God in a place inhabited by resurrected beings is potentially meaningless, then the concept of eternal life available in the present, and representing a *quality* of life which is available to those who share a set of beliefs to which it coheres, may acquire a meaning rooted in its use and application among those who share that belief. This is known as the **coherence theory of truth**, which does not demand that a statement corresponds to objects or situations within the physical world, but rather that truth or falsity is related to the other statements with which it is associated.

The Fourth Gospel's use of realised eschatology seems to apply very well to this way of understanding life after death. In the Fourth Gospel, the emphasis on salvation as a present experience overshadows the idea of future salvation and bodily resurrection. Although the evangelist does not completely remove all future concepts, they are something of an addendum to his more dominant eschatology of eternal life and all its blessings achieved and enjoyed in the present through the act of accepting and receiving Jesus. Although some future elements remain, Robert Kysar proposed a 'preserver theory', which suggests that the evangelist included some traditional elements alongside his own perspective, even though they were contradictory, and arguably no longer meaningful. For the Fourth Evangelist, therefore, the phrase 'surviving death' becomes an **anti-realist** phrase, something which is not verifiable or falsifiable in a literal or physical sense, but which has a truth value nevertheless.

However it is described, the New Testament writers have such confidence in the reality of life after death that they have accepted and incorporated it into their belief system without question. For the philosopher, however, this may not be so easy. Hick resolved this with the principle of eschatological verification. He envisaged two travellers walking down a road, one of whom believes it leads to the celestial city and one who believes that there is no final destination. Which one of them is right will not be verified until they reach the end of the road, although their particular positions will have a vital influence on the way they experience and interpret what happens to them on the road.

Life after death

Christian beliefs in life after death

Belief in an afterlife is an essential part of Christian belief. This belief is supported by the view that a loving God would not create finite human beings with enormous potential, only to drop them out of existence at the end of their earthly life, and so in most cases when a person believes in God it is natural to assume the existence also of an afterlife where humankind (or at least some people) can encounter God and live with him. Christians believe that since human beings are part of nature and yet they also transcend it, they lead a double life — a mortal life, which is over-lapped by an eternal life. Although Jesus did not specify the mode of the afterlife, Christian eschatology incorporates two main ideas:

- **The immortality of the soul:** the soul, which is indestructible, survives the death of the physical body and goes to a place where God dwells.
- **The resurrection of the dead:** at some future date all the dead will be raised again to life and those who believe in God and Jesus Christ will be given an immortal, spiritual body.

Of these ideas, the one closer to a biblical perspective is the resurrection of the body, which offers the view that the body is a psychophysical unity reconstituted by God after death, and able to inhabit a different place, but one in which there is full continuity of personal identity between this life and the next.

Christian eschatology offers two wider eschatological perspectives:

- **Individual eschatology:** each individual human being will suffer death and judgement relative to their beliefs and their actions. Death is the historical and spiritual consequence of Adam's sin, bringing to an end the period of human-kind's probation, when our eternal destiny is decided. The way in which an individual lives their earthly life brings about the conditions for the next stage of their existence, after which those judged to have been saved at the time of their death will enter heaven and enjoy the company of God, Christ and the angels. Those who die in a state of unrepented personal sin go to **hell** to suffer punishment, although Catholic eschatology allows for some to enter **purgatory**, where they undergo purification in order to qualify for heaven.

- **Universal eschatology:** the world will come to an end, all the dead will be raised to face a general, last judgement, and all things will come to their final consummation. Although Jesus did not specify a time, the early Christians lived in active expectation of the end of all things. The return of Jesus (the **parousia**) will be the signal for the resurrection of the dead, the good and the bad. The present heaven and earth will be destroyed and new ones will take their place. Jesus will reign in glory for ever, and those who have been saved will share his reign with him.

Christians are divided on the notion of hell, which appears to many to be contrary to the Christian view of a loving God. The concept of a place of eternal punishment as an incentive to believe in God may also be thought to degrade true faith. However, as J. S. Whale (1957) observed: *'It is illogical to tell men that they must do the will of God and accept his gospel of grace, if you also tell them that the obligation has no eternal significance and nothing ultimately depends on it.'* Christians who believe in a literal hell are usually from the conservative tradition, in which two main interpretations exist:

- **Annihilationism:** unsaved individuals will be punished in hell for a period of time relative to the sinfulness of their earthly lives and when the penalty is paid they will be annihilated (cease to exist in any form).
- **Traditionalism:** unsaved individuals will be punished in hell for all eternity.

Despite their differences, both positions agree that hell exists as a place of punishment for individuals who have rejected the gospel or never heard it; *and*, although unceasing torture and imprisonment of individuals for their beliefs is considered uncivilised on earth, it is the norm in hell.

Eschatology and human purpose

Christian eschatology interprets death as giving significance to the life of every individual. The ultimate meaning of creation is revealed by what happens to it at the end, and the ultimate meaning of a person's life acquires sense by making sense of their death. Death is *predictable*, but although it is natural, Christian eschatology is aware of a tension that must be resolved in the death of every individual. That tension is resolved by the notion of an afterlife, which is nothing to do with earthly immortality — living on through descendants, for example. The world is impermanent, and so life after death must be in another realm altogether. The individual soul reaches a crisis at death when no middle course is possible, and only those who have chosen belief in God win victory over the despair of death and thus discover the purpose of their whole existence.

Human history as a whole reaches its climax at the end of time. The Old Testament depicts a world in which the Day of the Lord is vividly expected. C. H. Dodd wrote: *'Not an event in history at all, for it is described in terms which remove it from the conditions of time and space…in it the whole purpose of God is revealed and fulfilled'* (cited in Whale, 1957). In the New Testament, Jesus brings the future into the present and a far-off divine event bursts into human history. Life still has to be lived in the flesh, however, and a final consummation awaits. The coming of Jesus makes possible a life that is to be judged in terms of its quality rather than quantity — humans still have to die, but the meaning of death is changed in the light of eternal life. Christian eschatology is therefore set in a tension between eternal life in the present and the final accomplishment of God's purpose in the Last Judgement.

Christian belief is that eschatology raises urgent issues: does Christian faith matter? If so, how, and how much? Dying is seen as inevitable, but arriving at the destination God offers to all humankind is not. Humans have to make a choice and we may miss the offer of eternal life.

The problem of mortality

Christian eschatology colours the reality and awareness of human mortality. Death is still an unknown quantity, but, as John Hick (1968) observed: *'it should not evoke the sickening fear with which we face what we know to be evil…. It is a fuller stage in the outworking of the Creator's loving purpose for his children.'*

Mortal life, Hick suggested, is the place in which Christians can recognise God's goodness and make a response to it.

Islamic beliefs in life after death

Islam observes that all the prophets of God called their people to worship him and to believe in an afterlife, a belief so significant that to deny it made all other beliefs meaningless. God's revelation of the afterlife has been made in the same way over thousands of years, and although the prophets were opposed by many people because of their teaching on the subject, it has endured unchanged. Islamic teaching on life after death has always appealed to the rational consciousness of human beings. When the people of Makkah denied the possibility, the Qur'an advanced logical and rational arguments in its favour: *'Who can give life to dry bones and decomposed ones at that? Is not He who created the heavens and the earth able to create the life thereof? Yea, indeed! For He is the Creator Supreme, of skill and knowledge infinite'* (36:78–81). Similarly, the Qur'an states that non-believers can offer no good argument to deny life after death: *'And they say, "What is there but our life in this world?"…. But of that they have no knowledge, they merely conjecture…. Their argument is nothing but this: they say "Bring back our forefathers, if what you say is true!"'* (45:24–25).

Islamic beliefs in the afterlife are, in many ways, very similar to Christian beliefs:

- God has a plan for the whole universe and all human beings.
- At the day of judgement the whole universe will be destroyed and the dead raised to stand before him.
- That day will be the beginning of an unending life on which every individual will be judged and rewarded by God according to their deeds.

The Qur'an offers the argument that life after death is vital in order to make sense of morality. If there is no afterlife then belief in God is irrelevant and even for those who did believe in God, he would be an unjust and indifferent God. A just God must punish the wicked and reward the good. Since this is clearly not possible in this life, however, there must be a Day of Judgement on which God will decide the fate of each individual:

The unbelievers say, 'Never to us will come the hour'…. But most surely, he may reward those who believe and work deeds of righteousness, for such is forgiveness and a sustenance most generous. But those who strive against our signs, to frustrate them, for such will be a chastisement, of painful wrath.　　　　　　　　　　　　　　　　　　　　(34:3–5)

Muslims believe that the day on which the dead will be raised will reveal God's attributes of justice and mercy, especially made manifest on those who have suffered for his sake during their earthly life in the confidence of eternal bliss. The Qur'an draws a comparison between such Muslims and those who have rejected God, and states that the worldly life is a preparation for eternal life after death. For those who have simply served their earthly desires and mocked those who have lived for God, it will be too late to be given another chance on the Day of Judgement:

Until, when death comes to one of them, he says 'O, my Lord! Send me back to life, in order that I may work righteousness in the things I neglected'. By no means…. The fire will burn their faces and they will therein grin with their lips displaced.　　　　(23:99–104)

Islamic eschatology teaches that belief in an afterlife ensures a successful outcome on the Day of Judgement because it will encourage an individual to be responsible and dutiful in earthly life. This has important ramifications for this life too, since a life lived with the next one in view is more likely to be characterised by soberness, modesty, peace and discipline. A society that rejects teaching on the afterlife will be open to corruption and evil. The Qur'an cites examples of civilisations that failed to accept eschatological truths and suffered as a consequence:

The Thamud and the Ad people disbelieved in the Day of Noisy Calamity! But the Thamud, they were destroyed by a terrible storm of thunder and lightning. And the Ad, they were destroyed by a furious wind, exceedingly violent. He made it rage against them seven nights and eight days in succession, so that thou couldst see the whole people lying overthrown in its path, as if they had been roots of hollow palm trees tumbled down. Then seest thou any of them left surviving? (69:4ff.)

For individual Muslims, everything they do, every intention they have, every thought and every word are all counted up and kept in accurate records to be brought up on the Day of Judgement. Those individuals with good records will be rewarded and welcomed into heaven, while the wicked will be cast into hell. Those who think that they will be able to negotiate their way out of punishment will be proved wrong, as absolute justice will prevail. Only God knows the exact nature of heaven and hell, however, and the descriptions offered in the Qur'an and other traditions are not intended to be taken literally.

Muslims believe that the Day of Judgement will bring the final answer to many complicated and unanswerable questions of this life. Those who appear to be successful in worldly terms despite their sins will no longer be able to escape the penalty of their deeds, so the important truth that morality and goodness are worth pursuing, even if they do not appear to be so in this life, will be revealed to be the only way to live if there is to be hope for an afterlife. Islamic teaching on the afterlife should, therefore, serve as an important warning to the wicked that the justice of God will prevail: *'The unbelievers among the People of the Book and the pagans shall burn for ever in the fire of Hell. They are the vilest of all creatures'* (98:1–8). The sin of disbelief is essentially the outcome of rejecting what is good and right and presupposes that good actions and thoughts lead to belief in God. Someone who does and thinks aright has a clear conscience: *'Any who believe in Allah and the Last Day, and work righteousness, shall have their reward with their Lord; on them shall be no fear, nor shall they grieve'* (2:62).

Islam teaches that moral laws, like physical laws, work on the principle of cause and effect, and that those who do wrong deliberately must face the consequences, even if those consequences lie some way ahead in the future.

Synoptic question and answer

Question 6 World Religions (Islam) and Christian Belief

With reference to texts or religious traditions you have studied:

(a) Outline and explain the key features of their belief in an afterlife.

(b) Examine and evaluate the view that an afterlife may be understood as a means of controlling our behaviour in this life.

(a) For those who believe in the existence of a loving, omnipotent, creator God, it is inconceivable that humankind has nothing to look forward to after the death of the physical body and the end of earthly life. For God to create human beings, only to bring their existence to an end before they can even begin to realise the full potential of a relationship with him, seems at best arbitrary, and at worst callous. For both Christians and Muslims, human beings are part of nature and yet they also transcend it. The physical body is part of the material, created order, but alone of creation God has implanted into human beings a spiritual, non-physical identity that overlaps humankind's earthly existence. This non-physical part of humankind's persona can survive the death of the physical body with its personal identity intact, and enter the afterlife with a complete continuity of identity, personality and memories, and in the afterlife reap the rewards or suffer the punishments of the earthly life. How this is accomplished is not made clear in either Christian or Islamic texts, but that it is accomplished by the action of God is without doubt, and in most cases it is understood as involving a resurrection or replication of the body.

Christian teaching incorporates two main ideas — the immortality of the soul and the resurrection of the body — and of these the one closest to a biblical world-view is resurrection. The resurrection of the body will have both individual and universal implications. For each individual, death is the historical and spiritual consequence of Adam's sin, and it brings to an end the period of probation on earth during which humanity's eternal destiny is decided. However, Christianity also teaches that when the world order is brought to an end (an event that is thought to coincide with the parousia — the return of Jesus in glory), all the dead will be raised to face a general, last judgement. Those who have not chosen to believe in God and accept the implications of Jesus's act of salvation on the Cross will face the consequences of that failure.

For the Muslim, a similar picture is offered. Islam teaches that all the prophets of God taught an eschatological doctrine against which all other beliefs are to be evaluated: *'Who can give life to dry bones and decomposed ones at that? Is not He who created the heavens and the earth able to create the life thereof? Yea, indeed! For He is the Creator Supreme, of skill and knowledge infinite'* (36:78–81). The rejection of that belief was, however, common, and would bring great calamity on all those who failed to recognise its rational truth: *'And they say, "What is there but our life in this world?".... But of that they have no knowledge, they merely conjecture.... Their argument is nothing but this: they say "Bring back our forefathers, if what you say is true!"'* (45:24–25).

In common with Christianity, Islam teaches that God has a plan for the whole universe and all human beings, and at the Day of Judgement the whole universe will be destroyed and the dead raised to stand before him. That day will be the beginning of an unending life on which every individual will be judged and rewarded by God according to their deeds. The Qur'an puts forward the argument that without life after death, belief in God and the incentive to live a moral life is pointless and irrelevant. If God is a just God he must punish and reward, otherwise he is simply indifferent: *'The unbelievers say, "Never to us will come the hour".... But most surely, he may reward those who believe and work deeds of righteousness, for such is forgiveness and a sustenance most generous. But those who strive against our signs, to frustrate them, for such will be a chastisement of painful wrath'* (34:3–5). On the day that the dead will be raised God's attributes of love and mercy will be fully revealed for those who have suffered for his sake during their earthly life, while for those who have served their earthly desires and mocked those who have lived for God, it will be too late: *'Until, when death comes to one of them, he says "O, my Lord! Send me back to life, in order that I may work righteousness in the things I neglected". By no means.... The fire will burn their faces and they will therein grin with their lips displaced'* (23:99–104).

It is not just the events of the Day of Judgement that are important to Christians and Muslims, however, but the meaning and significance that the hope of an afterlife gives to earthly existence. For a Christian, the ultimate meaning of creation is revealed by what happens to it at the end, and the ultimate meaning of a person's life acquires purpose by making sense of their death. Death is predictable but is not an evil, and it is not to be feared by those who love and serve God; those who have chosen belief in God win the victory over the despair of death which, Christians believe, will be inescapable for those who have rejected him. Human history too will reach a climax at the end of time. C. H. Dodd observed: *'Not an event in history at all, for it is described in terms which remove it from the conditions of time and space...in it the whole purpose of God is revealed and fulfilled'* (cited in Whale, 1957).

Christian teaching on the afterlife also encompasses a belief in realised eschatology — the view that while life has to be lived in the flesh, Jesus brings the future into the present and makes it possible for the believer to live a life that is qualitatively eternal

A2 Religious Studies Synoptic Guide

while they await its consummation. In a similar way, Muslims believe that living with the prospect of an afterlife in view changes the quality of the life that the individual and the community live in the present, since the society which anticipates an afterlife is more likely to be characterised by sobriety, modesty, peace and discipline.

(b) From what we have examined so far, it is clear that religious teachings on an afterlife are inextricably linked with the view that the way in which believers live their earthly lives will have a significant impact on the destiny that awaits them after the death of the body. It is assumed that belief in an afterlife gives relevance to earthly life, and that every word, deed and thought of the Christian or Muslim on earth is to be accounted for in the hereafter. For the Muslim, everything he or she does, every intention they have, is counted up and kept in accurate records to be reviewed on the Day of Judgement. Those individuals with good records will be welcomed into heaven, while the wicked will be cast into hell. There will be no last-minute negotiations possible, and absolute justice — which can never be exercised on earth — will prevail. Only God knows the exact nature of heaven and hell, and the descriptions offered in the Qur'an and other traditions are not to be taken literally. There is no doubt, however, that while heaven will be a place of unspeakable joy, hell will be a place of utter misery and despair.

Christians are divided on the notion of hell, which seems to many to be contrary to the prevailing view of a loving and forgiving God. However, as J. S. Whale (1957) observed: *'It is illogical to tell men that they must do the will of God and accept his gospel of grace, if you also tell them that the obligation has no eternal significance and nothing ultimately depends on it.'* Nonetheless, Christians who believe in a literal hell — an objectively real place where sinners and unbelievers suffer punishment — tend to be from the conservative tradition, whereas liberals, positivists and modernists tend to prefer non-literal images — the *idea* of separation from God, or a *sense* of exclusion from his blessing, rather than actual punishment and torture. Like Islam, however, Christian eschatology does not shy away from the notion that there are important implications for human beings if they choose to reject God's revelation. Christian belief is that eschatology raises urgent issues. Dying is inevitable, but arriving at the destination God offers to all humankind is not. Humanity has a choice to make and we may miss the offer of eternal life. Is this right? Should religious doctrine effectively attempt to influence the choices we make in this life with the carrot or the stick of eschatological reward or punishment? And if it attempts to do so, does it succeed?

The issue at stake is really one of freedom to express a religious view of the world and human destiny, and of whether, in expressing this view, the religious belief is attempting to control, or indeed *is* actually controlling, the behaviour and choices of others. Ultimately, we can only be controlled if we choose to be controlled. We are free human agents and the choices we make are rarely truly coerced. That we may *feel* coerced or controlled is really quite another matter. Even a child who acts in obedience to his or her parents is choosing to be obedient, since there is a genuine alternative choice that they could have made — not to obey. In adulthood our freedom to be controlled or to refuse control is even greater. We are free to break the law, free to stay in an undesirable situation or to remove ourselves from it, free to conform to the expectations of others or to choose our own path. If we argue that we are not free to break the law because the law of the land exercises control over us, we need to consider why we think this is the case. The law cannot physically restrain us — we are not (in most cases) physically incapable of committing a burglary or murder, for example — so the control it exercises must be more subtle. We are controlled by it because we choose to submit to its claims, not because it has coerced us into submitting.

If this is so, then what are these subtle claims? The law of cause and effect is well known to philosophers and scientists; we make associations between events, objects, people and situations because we have known them to be linked before and we trust that they will be so linked in the future. It may not be logically necessary that such associations are made, and the principle of induction may not work on every occasion, but it works often enough for us to establish what seems to us to be a law: if I bang my head against the wall, it will hurt. Both Christianity and Islam teach that moral laws, like physical laws, work on the same principle, and for those who deliberately do wrong (flout the moral laws) there are consequences that must be faced, even if they lie some way ahead in the future. If we choose to break the law of the land, we have demonstrated that we do not intend to be controlled by it — we make a free choice to obey or disobey — but we cannot expect to be free from its consequences. Christian and Muslim teaching on the afterlife works on the same principle. We have a genuine choice to believe or not to believe the teaching both religions have to offer on the relationship between behaviour and beliefs in this life and the next, and so we are not mindlessly controlled by it. Whether we choose to believe or not, however, the consequences are unavoidable.

But the problem still remains that those who believe in a direct and unavoidable link between this life and the next are operating on the basis of faith, not fact. Life after death is only eschatologically verifiable, so in this life Christians place their faith in the teaching of the Bible and their experience of God, and Muslims in the teaching of the Qur'an. However, we will only receive absolute and irrevocable proof that what we have believed is true, or not, after death. If I believe that everything I do is recorded by red dwarves who live underground and who, after my death, will reward or punish my doings according to their evaluation of morality, my life will be significantly influenced by that belief. But would I have any right to attempt to influence others to think and act in the same way and according to the same belief? Our instinctive answer is no, because we 'know' that this is not a reasonable basis for morality. So what makes it any more reasonable to propose a system of eschatological rewards and punishments on the basis of the Bible, the Qur'an, the teachings of Jesus or Muhammad, or religious leaders? Tradition, consensus and revelation assure us that it is more reasonable, but for those who cannot see any meaning or rationality in religious belief and all that goes with it, religious believers might as well tell them to be controlled by red dwarves as by the belief that an omnipotent and loving God will reward or punish them in the afterlife.

The graphic pictures of hell that have been painted over the centuries by religious believers may offer sufficient support for the view that religion attempts to control people's lives through teaching on the afterlife. Furthermore, the concept of a place of eternal punishment as an incentive to believe in God and obey him may be thought to degrade faith. The Qur'an states: *'The unbelievers among the People of the Book and the pagans shall burn forever in the fire of Hell. They are the vilest of all creatures'* (98:1–8) and Jesus warns his hearers: *'If your eye causes you to stumble, tear it out: it is better for you to enter the kingdom of God with one eye than to have two eyes and to be thrown into Hell, where their worm never dies and the fire is never quenched'* (Mark 9:47–48). These pictures are utterly uncompromising and believers, as well as non-believers, may maintain that they are so contrary to the picture of the God of love as to be unsupportable. If they are used to frighten people into believing in God and adopting a lifestyle compatible with that belief, then there may be questions to be asked. However, both Islam and Christianity are religions with a missionary or evangelical spirit. Any committed Christians who are convinced that humankind's eschatological destiny stands or falls on our acceptance of Jesus, or Muslims who believe that it stands on obedience to the Qur'an, must be free to warn others of the penalty of not accepting these beliefs. The onus is then on the hearer to accept or refuse their message.

Both Christian and Muslim views of the world make an important link between the moral law and the afterlife. In this life, it is clear that the good do not necessarily prosper and the evil are not necessarily punished. However, a just and loving God is not a God who considers this arbitrary or unimportant. The afterlife is the place in which rewards and punishments are finally bestowed, and the Day of Judgement will bring the final answer to many complicated and unanswerable questions of this life. The important truth that morality and goodness are worth pursuing, even if they do not appear to be so in this life, will be revealed to be the only way to live if there is to be hope of an afterlife. For both the Christian and the Muslim, teaching on the afterlife should serve as an important warning that the justice of God will prevail, and so can and must serve as a controlling medium. The freedom to submit to that control, however, remains in humankind's free hands.

Chapter 7
Philosophy of Religion and New Testament

Miracles

Miracles in the New Testament

The miracles of Jesus in the Synoptic Gospels

In the Synoptic Gospels the miracles of Jesus emphasise the authority and power of God over both the natural and the spiritual world. The miracles are shown as acts of power that not only reveal Jesus's authority but also highlight his teachings about God. The miracle stories come under three broad headings — **healings**, **exorcisms** and **nature miracles**.

The following miracles all deal with healings and exorcisms:

The casting out of an evil spirit (Mark 1:21–27)

This story illustrates the authority of Jesus over the spiritual world — he simply utters the word of command and such is his authority that the spirit must leave.

The healing of the paralytic (Mark 2:1–13)

Jesus acts in response to the faith of the man and his friends by forgiving his sins and, hence, curing the man. The Jewish leaders are outraged, believing that only God himself can forgive sins — yet Jesus's healing of the man in this way shows he has the power and authority of God himself: *'Which is easier: to say to the paralytic, "Your sins are forgiven", or to say "Get up, take your mat and walk"? But that you may know that the Son of Man has authority on earth to forgive sins'* (Mark 2:9–10).

The sick woman (Mark 5:25–34)

Here Jesus highlights the importance of faith. He requires the woman to declare her action and faith aloud rather than keep it secret, in order that she can truly understand and accept what has happened. As R. Alan Cole (1990) observed: *'This brought a realization of the means by which she had entered the experience, an assurance of God's peace and a sense of security for the future.'*

Jairus's daughter (Mark 5:21–24, 35–43)

The miracle reveals Jesus's ultimate authority over death itself. This is the same authority exercised by God, who is the creator of life and rules over death, and it serves as a prelude to Christ's own resurrection. Jesus begins by telling Jairus: *'Don't be afraid: just believe'* (5:36) — God requires his people to have faith and to acknowledge both the limits of human helplessness and the extent of God's grace.

The Centurion's servant (Matthew 8:5–13; Luke 7:1–10)

This miracle also highlights the importance of the Centurion's faith: *'I tell you, I have not found such great faith even in Israel'* (Luke 7:9). The Jews believe that when the Messiah comes there will be a great banquet, at which they will sit down to feast — the Messianic banquet. Yet Jesus controversially suggests that Gentiles will be invited too and that the Jews themselves may lose their places.

The calming of the storm (Matthew 8:23–27; Mark 4:35–41; Luke 8:22–25)

Jesus gives clear evidence to his disciples of his divine power and control over the forces of nature and questions the disciples over their lack of faith; they are simply amazed: *'Who is this? He commands even the winds and the water, and they obey him'* (Luke 8:25).

The miracles of Jesus in the Fourth Gospel

The author of the Fourth Gospel uses the word **semeia**, or 'signs', to describe the miracles of Jesus. This is different from the word **dunameis**, or 'act of power' or 'mighty work', which is the term used in the Synoptic Gospels. The sign points beyond itself to highlight a spiritual truth. Moreover, when Jesus himself speaks of the miracles he uses the word **erga**. This term is used in the Old Testament to mean God's work in creation and salvation. Thus, in the Fourth Gospel Jesus links God's work in the past with his own in the present — God's power continues in him. This is highlighted in John 5:36: *'For the very work that the Father has given me to finish, and which I am doing, testifies that the Father has sent me.'* Jesus performs signs because he has been sent by God and has a unique relationship with the Father. However, the signs have not always led people to believe. Instead, they have often brought controversy, conflict and condemnation. The signs are an aid to faith, yet Jesus often seems to imply that people should believe without the signs. Nevertheless, to believe with the signs is better than not believing at all: *'Do not believe me unless I do what my Father does. But if I do it, even though you do not believe me, believe the miracles,* *that you may know and understand that the Father is in me, and I in the Father'* (10:37–38).

The healing of the official's son (John 4:46–54)

The official *believes* Jesus and does not require any further signs or evidence; he has such great faith in Jesus that he is able to accept his word without question and goes home to his healed son. Moreover, as a result of the sign, all his family believe too. The message of the sign is clear — by the word of Jesus, life is given. The son symbolises Jesus's work: death is followed by life. The nature of true belief is to show obedience and trust in the word and power of Christ.

The feeding of the five thousand (John 6:1–15)

Jesus does not give the bread to the disciples to distribute but gives it to the people himself, just as he gives his body on the Cross. Moreover, there is a Eucharistic link here with the priest giving the bread to the people, with hints of the Messianic banquet. The believers share bread together, just as the disciples will later share it at the Last Supper, and this prefigures how all the faithful will share a table with the Messiah at the end of time (Revelation 19:17). Moreover, there are 12 baskets of fragments, which is the same number as the tribes of Israel; this therefore offers an image of the new nation of God's people.

The healing of the blind man (John 9:1–41)

Jesus restores the man's sight by spitting into some clay and anointing the man's eyes with it — the same technique God uses in Genesis 2 to create Adam. The symbolism is clear: Jesus is making the blind man into a new person. Once the man washes his eyes in the Pool of Siloam the healing is confirmed and he receives his sight. This is again symbolic as Siloam means 'sent' and the man is thus 'sent' by Jesus to be cleansed in 'living water'. He receives a new baptism, in which his physical disability is removed and he receives spiritual enlightenment and faith in Christ. The 'Light of the World' has entered into him.

The raising of Lazarus (John 11:1–44)

The sign takes place among people who believe in Jesus and love Lazarus, a friend and follower of Christ. B. Warfield (1950) observed: *'The raising of Lazarus thus becomes a decisive instance and open symbol of Jesus's conquest of death and hell.'* Lazarus has been dead and buried for 4 days before Jesus arrives. However, Martha, Lazarus's sister, seems to believe that Jesus can still do something and her faith makes her bold enough to claim: *'But I know that even now God will give you whatever you ask.'* (11:22). But she does not really understand the power of Christ. She is probably thinking that Jesus will be able to do something for Lazarus in the life to come, as she mentions the *'resurrection at the last day'* (11:24). Yet this futuristic eschatology is about to be overtaken by a realised eschatology as Jesus declares that he is *'the resurrection and the life'* (11:25).

Were the miracles of Jesus genuine historical events or are they simply symbolic? John Marsh suggested that they can be both; for the author, the actions of Christ are real and also have symbolic meaning, to enable the reader to see that Jesus is the Son of God. Historically accurate or not, the purpose of the gospel writer is to convince his readers of those aspects of the person of Christ that will lead them to belief and eternal life. The signs also highlight the most important aspects of faith — life, light, glory and the sacraments — as well as showing the perceived superiority of that faith over Judaism. The aim is also to lead the reader to a greater understanding of Christ.

Miracles: philosophical issues

What is a miracle?

Miracle: a violation of a law of nature by the direct intervention of God. A miracle occurs when the world is not left to itself, when something distinct from the natural order as a whole intrudes into it.

Miracles are a special category of religious experience, in that they are events attributed to the supernatural power of God. Miracles have always had the power to convert people and to confirm religious belief, and there are thousands of testimonies given throughout the ages of people who claim to have experienced miracles.

For Aquinas there were three kinds of miracles, all of which fulfilled the general definition he offered (cited in Hick (ed.), 1964): *'Those things most properly be called miraculous which are done by divine power apart from the order generally followed in things.'* The three kinds are:

- events done by God which nature could never do, e.g. stopping the course of the sun (Joshua 10:13)
- events done by God which nature could do, but not in that order, e.g. healings and exorcisms (Mark 1:31)
- events done by God which nature can do, but which God does without the use of natural laws, e.g. healing by forgiving sins (Mark 2:5)

This is not without its difficulties, however. What Aquinas was suggesting was a kind of interventionist God, who only acts on certain, almost random, occasions. Brian Davies argued that to talk about God 'intervening' suggests that he is otherwise little more than a spectator in human affairs, rather than a loving father who constantly interacts with his creation.

There seems to be broad agreement among scholars that a miracle must contain three basic notions:

- breaking of the laws of nature
- purpose and significance
- openness to religious interpretation

The problem of natural law

Since we may not actually know all natural laws, nor how they operate, we might not therefore be able to tell if a natural law has been broken or not. John Hick (1973) suggested that natural laws may, in fact, be no more than *generalisations formulated retrospectively to cover what has, in fact, happened'*. Similarly, if a natural law is claimed to have been broken, this may be no more than saying that something happened that we did not understand or expect. Mel Thompson (1996) argued that: *'The idea of a miraculous event introduces a sense of arbitrariness and unpredictability into an understanding of the world.'* By contrast, Richard Swinburne said that the laws of nature are reasonably predictable and if an impossible event happens, then it is fair to call it a miracle. He gave examples of such events in the Bible (1971): *'The resurrection from the dead in full health of a man whose heart has not been beating for twenty four hours and who was dead also by other currently used criteria; water turning into wine without the assistance of chemical apparatus or catalysts; a man getting better from polio in a minute.'*

The purpose of miracles

Just to say that a miracle is defined as God intervening in natural laws is not enough — there must, surely, be a reason for God's actions. Swinburne, in *The Concept of Miracle*, suggested that a miracle must also have a deeper religious significance: *'If a god intervened in the natural order to make a feather land here rather than there for no deep, ultimate purpose, or to upset a child's box of toys just for spite, these events would not naturally be described as miraculous.'*

This raises serious criticisms of miracles on moral grounds, for many testimonies of miracles seem to have no real point. Peter Vardy (1996) questioned such miracles on moral grounds: *'A God who intervenes at Lourdes to cure an old man of cancer but does not act to save starving millions in Ethiopia — such a God needs, at least, to face some hard moral questioning.'* Other modern philosophers agree. For example, Maurice Wiles (1986) observed: *'It seems strange that no miraculous intervention prevented Auschwitz or Hiroshima. The purposes apparently forwarded for some of the miracles acclaimed in the Christian tradition seem trivial by comparison.'*

This leads on to the criticism that the actual occurrence of certain miracles seems to be incompatible with the notion of the love and justice of God. For example, within Judaism, he saved the Jews in the Exodus, yet he did not save the millions of Jews who died in the Holocaust. This may not be altogether fair, however, since Jesus himself said the purpose of his miracles was to bring people to belief in him. He did not cure everyone he met — his miracles were for this specific purpose: *'Just believe it — that I am in the Father and the Father is in me. Or else believe it because of the mighty miracles you have seen me do'* (John 14:11).

Are miracles just a matter of interpretation?

R. F. Holland suggested that a miracle is nothing more than an extraordinary coincidence that is seen in a religious way. He used the example of a small boy who is stuck on a railway line. The driver of the express train, who cannot see the boy, unexpectedly faints onto the brake lever and the train stops, saving the boy. His mother says 'It's a miracle!' According to Holland, a coincidence can be taken religiously as a sign and called a miracle. This view makes a miracle dependent on personal assessment, and this may vary from person to person — one says an action is a miracle, the other says it is not. How are we to judge?

Are miracles symbolic?

Those who subscribe to the **realist** point of view have suggested that miracles are purely for the faithful and that, if there is a God, he would indeed make them happen to increase the faith of his people. **Anti-realists**, however, say that coincidences and similar events are not miracles because God plays no part in them. They suggest that miracles are events that help believers to understand the nature of God — they may be symbolic rather than real, and are only understood properly by the religious believer, such as the signs in John's Gospel.

The views of Hume and Swinburne

- David Hume (1975 edn): *'A transgression of a law of nature by a particular volition of the Deity.'*
- Richard Swinburne (1971): *'Nothing is esteemed a miracle, if it ever happens in the common course of nature.'*

In *An Enquiry Concerning Human Understanding*, David Hume argued that it will always be impossible to prove that a miracle has happened. He took the view that all questions of truth have to be answered by the evidence of experience, and that the evidence we have is unreliable: *'No testimony is sufficient to establish a miracle unless it is such that the falsehood would be more miraculous.'* He suggested that there are no grounds for believing the evidence we have for miracles, giving four reasons:

- *There is not to be found in all history, any miracle attested by a sufficient number of men, of such unquestioned good sense, education and learning, so as to secure against all delusion.*
- *The passion of surprise and wonder, arising from miracles…gives a tendency towards belief of those events…. A religionist may be an enthusiast and imagines he sees what has no reality.*
- *It forms a strong presumption against all supernatural and miraculous relations that they are observed chiefly to abound amongst ignorant and barbarous nations.*
- *In matters of religion, whatever is different is contrary…every miracle, therefore, pretended to have been wrought in any of these religions…destroys the credit of those miracles.*

Swinburne was prepared to consider the possibility that the best explanation for an event is indeed that it is a miracle. He claimed that the evidence in favour of a miracle must be considered properly, not simply dismissed because it may not be scientific. It is wrong simply to assume that miracles cannot occur. The principle of Ockham's Razor could be applied here — this principle argues that the simplest explanation for an unusual event is generally the most philosophically viable explanation. There is no reason why, when all other issues have been considered, the simplest explanation for an unexpected event should not be that it is, in fact, a miracle. Swinburne argued (1996) that as a principle of credulity we should normally accept what people tell us to be the truth: *'We ought to believe things as they seem, unless we have good evidence that we are mistaken.'*

Synoptic question and answer

Question 7 **Philosophy of Religion and New Testament**

'The accounts of miracles in the New Testament can neither prove nor disprove the existence of God.' Examine and evaluate this claim.

A miracle occurs when the world is not left to itself, when something distinct from the natural order as a whole intrudes into it. (J. L. Mackie, 1982)

Miracles are a special category of religious experience. They are events attributed to the supernatural power of God. Miracles have always had the power to convert people and to confirm religious belief, and there are thousands of testimonies given throughout the ages of people who claim to have experienced miracles. The New Testament is full of accounts of miracles, and they are a vital part of the ministry of Christ. In the Synoptic Gospels, miracles show the authority of Christ and the power of God (*dunameis*) over both the physical and the spiritual world: *'Who is this? He commands even the winds and the water, and they obey him'* (Luke 8:25). In the Fourth Gospel, the miracles are signs (*semeia*) which highlight spiritual truth — they show the link between Jesus and the Father and are intended to lead the believer into eternal life: *'…believe the miracles, that you may know and understand that the Father is in me, and I in the Father'* (John 10:37–38). *'After the people saw the miraculous sign that Jesus did, they began to say, "Surely this is the Prophet who is come into the world"'* (John 6:14). In all cases, the New Testament writers are convinced that miracles prove the existence of God. Indeed, it is not even open to debate and it is assumed that both protagonists and readers will take this for granted.

For Thomas Aquinas (Hick (ed.), 1964), miracles are: *'Those things most properly called miraculous which are done by divine power apart from the order generally followed in things.'* Aquinas suggested that there are three kinds of miracles: first, those actions done by God which nature cannot do, such as the raising of Lazarus from the dead. Second, those actions done by God which nature could have done, but not in that order. Such miracles might include exorcisms, the healing of the paralytic (Luke 5:17–26) and the healing of the crippled man at the pool (John 5). Third, Aquinas spoke of those actions done by God which nature could do, but which God has worked outside nature, for instance the healing of Peter's mother-in-law of a fever (Mark 1:29–31). She has presumably been suffering from something akin to a severe cold or flu, and would have recovered naturally in due course, but Jesus's action expedites the process. Many Christians may believe that God regularly answers their prayers in such a way, so that they may indeed not even consider such events especially miraculous (in the strongest sense of the term) but, rather, loving responses by God to the prayers of his people.

In all these kinds of miracles Aquinas was suggesting the existence of an interventionist God, who acts on random occasions. The philosopher Brian Davies, however, argued that to talk about God intervening in such a way suggests that he is otherwise little more than a spectator in human affairs. This is contrary to Christian teaching, which claims that God, as a loving father, constantly interacts with his creation. Aquinas's argument is based on the notion that God breaks natural laws. The problem here is that we may not actually know all natural laws, nor how they operate, and we might therefore not be able to tell whether or not a natural law has been broken. However, Richard Swinburne suggested that the laws of nature are reasonably predictable and that, if an apparently impossible event occurs, then it is fair to call it a miracle. He used two New Testament examples — the raising of Lazarus and the wedding in Cana — to support his view (1971): *'The resurrection from the dead in full health of a man whose heart has not been beating for twenty four hours and who was dead also by other currently used criteria: water turning into wine without the assistance of chemical apparatus or catalysts...'* Swinburne suggested that people actually do recover from illness — some are even resuscitated from death — and water can be turned into wine with the aid of chemicals, and thus, it is not the *actual event* that is miraculous, but rather the time-scale and the way in which they occur. They take place outside the normal conditions in which such cures might usually happen.

The New Testament contains many such accounts. While miracles are clearly not presented as the reason why men and women should put their faith in Jesus, they are an intrinsic part of his ministry. Miracles confirm belief: *'This, the first of his signs, Jesus did at Cana in Galilee, and manifested his glory, and his disciples believed in him'* (John 2:11); they demonstrate Jesus's authority: *'What is this? With authority he commands even the unclean spirits and they obey him'* (Mark 1:27); and they identify him as the Son of God: *'And when they got into the boat, the wind ceased, and those in the boat worshipped him, saying, "Truly you are the Son of God"'* (Matthew 14:32–33). Such events are greeted with amazement, wonder and awe; they are evidently beyond the experience of those who witness them, who demand an explanation for them or who are further convinced of what they have already believed about Jesus as a result of listening to his teaching. Through the divine power working in him, Jesus performs deeds that are at least beyond regular experience, and at most violations of a natural law: *'Transgressions of a law of nature, by the volition of the deity, or by the interposition of some invisible agent'* (David Hume's classic definition of miracle).

Just to say that a miracle can be defined as God intervening in natural laws is not enough, however — there must be a reason for God's actions. Swinburne, in *The*

Concept of Miracle, suggested that a miracle must have a deeper religious significance: *'If a god intervened in the natural order to make a feather land here rather than there for no deep, ultimate purpose, or to upset a child's box of toys just for spite, these events would not naturally be described as miraculous.'* This is supported by evidence from the New Testament itself. In the Synoptic Gospels the healing of the paralytic is achieved by Jesus's words: *'Son, your sins are forgiven'* (Mark 2:5). This miracle is used as a sign of Jesus's Messiahship: he displays the power and authority of God to forgive the man his sins. Similarly, the healing of the sick woman and of Jairus's daughter in Mark 5 are used to highlight the religious significance of faith in Christ. Moreover, in the Fourth Gospel the miracles are used specifically and significantly to lead people into faith in God, through Jesus: *'Jesus did many other miraculous signs in the presence of his disciples...these are written that you may believe that Jesus is the Christ, the Son of God and that by believing you may have life in his name'* (John 20:30–31).

However, serious criticisms against miracles can be made on moral grounds. Peter Vardy (1996) wrote: *'A God who intervenes at Lourdes to cure an old man of cancer but does not act to save starving millions in Ethiopia — such a God needs, at least, to face some hard moral questioning.'* Other modern philosophers have made similar claims. For example, Maurice Wiles (1986) argued: *'It seems strange that no miraculous intervention prevented Auschwitz or Hiroshima. The purposes apparently forwarded for some of the miracles acclaimed in the Christian tradition seem trivial by comparison.'* The occurrence of certain miracles seems, therefore, to be incompatible with the notion of the love and justice of God. God appears to help some people by way of miracles, but not others. If he is indeed all-loving and just, should he not treat everyone equally? This may not be altogether fair, however, since Jesus himself made clear that the purpose of his miracles was to bring people to believe in him. He did not cure everyone he met — his miracles were for a specific purpose: *'Just believe it — that I am in the Father and the Father is in me. Or else believe it because of the mighty miracles you have seen me do'* (John 14:11).

Furthermore, what we may read at one level as biblical accounts of violations of natural law may be explained quite easily in other ways. Rudolph Bultmann famously wrote: *'It is impossible to use electric light and the wireless and to avail ourselves of modern medical and surgical discoveries and, at the same time, to believe in the New Testament world of demons and spirits'* (cited in Green, McKnight and Marshall (eds), 1992). In other words, biblical accounts of miracles owe their origin to an age when the world-view was significantly different from that of our own scientific, rational age. The biblical writers may well have interpreted the recovery of the Gerasene Demoniac to the casting out of demons, but modern psychiatry might identify him as a victim of multiple personality disorder, calmed and soothed by the presence of Jesus. In a sense, we no longer need (although we may choose) to explain phenomena in terms of the spirit world, and this gives rise to the question of whether the biblical writers were accurate in their assessment of events. The miracles of the Old Testament might be explicable in the same way. Did the Red Sea part through a miraculous act of God, or did a freak wind blow back the waters at the precise moment that the Israelites were pondering how to circumnavigate this watery obstacle, an event so fortuitous and *'stupendous as to be ever impressed on her [Israel's] memory'* (John Bright, 1981)?

Such interpretations do not necessarily eliminate God from the equation, but they force us to reconsider our understanding of what occurred. God's hand, or that of Jesus, may still be at work in an event which goes utterly against our expectations and which blesses the recipient in ways that had seemed otherwise impossible, but this need not demand that the natural law be broken or that logical impossibilities are achieved. God may work within rather than outside the natural order, bringing to pass things that may happen naturally, but at such times and places when he can breach the epistemic distance and make himself and his nature directly evident to his people. It is not necessary for God to do the logically impossible in order to interact with his people, although if he is omnipotent, then there are strong reasons for believers to maintain that sometimes he will do so.

Perhaps the notion of whether or not an action is a miracle depends more on individual interpretation. R. F. Holland suggested that a miracle is nothing more than an extraordinary coincidence that is seen in a religious way. He used the example of a small boy who is stuck on a railway line. The driver of the express train, who cannot see the boy, unexpectedly faints onto the brake lever and the train stops, saving the boy from almost certain death. His mother claims that a miracle has occurred. According to Holland, however, coincidence can be taken religiously as a sign and called a miracle. But this interpretation may miss an important point — throughout the ages, millions have claimed to have experienced miracles and had their lives changed by them. Have they all been deceived by mere coincidences? The coincidence theory may well apply to any of the New Testament miracles. For example, Lazarus may not have been raised from the dead — he may simply have been in a coma, from which he emerged at the moment Jesus called 'Lazarus, come out'. Furthermore, even if Mary and Martha had been given such a naturalistic explanation of what had happened, they may still have continued to believe that a miracle had occurred, an explanation which fitted their interpretation of the events perfectly well.

Nevertheless, the crucial question is whether or not miracles have actually happened. In *An Enquiry Concerning Human Understanding*, David Hume argued that it is always impossible to prove that a miracle has taken place. He took the view that all questions of truth have to be answered by the evidence of experience, and that the evidence we have is unreliable: *'No testimony is sufficient to establish a miracle unless it is such that the falsehood would be more miraculous.'* Hume suggested that there has never been a miracle which has been witnessed by a sufficiently large number of reliable, objective people and that, in fact, those who see miracles tend to be religious believers anyway — people who are almost looking out for miracles. Moreover, he claimed, miracles are not seen in 'civilised' countries, but rather in 'primitive' ones. He argued that the different religions cannot *all* be true, yet they all claim that their deities perform miracles. Hume suggested that these testimonies therefore cancel each other out, making all testimony unreliable. Interestingly, the society from which the New Testament emerged, although not hugely advanced, could not be considered to be primitive. The level of learning among the Jewish scribes, for example, would have been exceptionally high. Furthermore, the New Testament miracles do not cancel out those from the Old Testament, but build upon them, showing that Jesus's ministry supersedes the revelation of the Old Testament but does not render it null and void.

Swinburne, nevertheless, considered the possibility that the best explanation for an event is indeed that it is a miracle. He claimed that the evidence in favour of a miracle must be considered properly, not simply dismissed because it may not be scientific. It is wrong simply to assume that miracles cannot occur. The principle of Ockham's Razor could be applied here. This principle argues that the simplest explanation for an unusual event is generally the most philosophically likely one. There is no reason why, when all other issues have been considered, the simplest explanation for an unexpected event should not be that it is, in fact, a miracle. After all, if there is a God, this is surely how he would act: *'If there is a God, one might expect him to make his presence known to man, not merely through the over-all pattern of the universe in which he has placed them, but by dealing more intimately and personally with them'* (Swinburne, 1996). Nevertheless, surely it is questionable whether the simplest explanation of something can ever be that it is a miracle. Surely, for example, a more *simple* explanation of the disappearance of the body of Jesus from the tomb would be that is was done by grave robbers rather than by the miracle of the Resurrection.

John Marsh argued that the miracles in the New Testament are both genuine historical events *and* symbolic religious actions. They are indications of the power of God and the saving message of Christ. They are more than merely descriptions of actions and events since they are there to lead people into a greater understanding of Christ. C. K. Barrett (1955) observed that there are *'clear indications that he by whom the signs are wrought is the Son of God and equal to God himself.'* This is supported by the words of Christ himself: *'For the very work that the Father has given me to finish, and which I am doing, testifies that the Father has sent me'* (John 5:36).

To conclude, if philosophers seek to know if the miracles of the New Testament actually occurred, then it is possible to conclude that some, if not all of them, may not literally have happened. The sick, the blind and the lame may have simply recovered naturally, the demon-possessed may just have been mentally ill. We don't know. But this is not the most important thing. Miracles seen only as physical actions neither confirm nor deny God's existence. However, if we regard the miracles not as physical actions, but as signs that point to the existence of God, then we get an altogether different picture. Perhaps the best example of this is the resurrection of Jesus himself, which is,

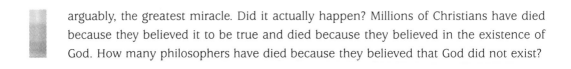

arguably, the greatest miracle. Did it actually happen? Millions of Christians have died because they believed it to be true and died because they believed in the existence of God. How many philosophers have died because they believed that God did not exist?

Chapter 8
Philosophy of Religion and World Religions (Judaism and Buddhism)

Evil and suffering

The problem of evil

Types of evil

- **Natural evil** — the malfunctioning of the natural world, which produces diseases, famine and natural disasters.
- **Moral evil** — the result of human actions, such as cruelty, murder and war.

The consequence of evil is **suffering**, which can involve **physical pain** and **mental anguish**, and which often appears to be unjust. The issue of evil poses a problem for those who uphold the notion of the all-loving, all-powerful God of Judaism and Christianity:

- God has created the universe out of nothing and is totally responsible for it. If he is all-powerful, then he can do anything that is logically possible. This means he could create a world that is free from evil and suffering.
- God is omniscient and omnipotent; he must, therefore, know how to stop evil and suffering and be able to do so.
- God is omnibenevolent and, in his love, would wish to end all evil and suffering. No all-loving God would wish his creation to suffer for no reason.
- *The name of God means that He is infinite goodness. If, therefore, God existed, there would be no evil discoverable; but there is evil in the world. Therefore God does not exist* (Aquinas, cited in Hick (ed.), 1964).
- Hence, either God is not omnipotent *or* God is not omnibenevolent *or* evil does not exist.

However…

It is conceivable that God allows evil to exist as part of his greater plan of love and in such a case there is no logical contradiction in God still being regarded as all-loving and all-powerful.

Theodicies

The Augustinian Theodicy	The Irenaean Theodicy
God saw all that he had made, and it was very good (Genesis 1:31)	Evil is the inevitable outcome of God engaging the willing cooperation of human beings
Soul-deciding	Soul-making
Man in the likeness of God	Man created imperfectly
Man with true moral autonomy	Man with true moral autonomy
Freedom leads to the Fall	Freedom gives potential for growth
Free will leads to suffering as punishment for sin	Free will leads to development
Humanity redeemed through Christ	Humanity redeemed through its own actions
God foresaw the Fall	God remains at an epistemic distance so as not to compromise human freedom
Evil is part of an aesthetic pattern	Suffering is necessary for growth
Evil is a privation	Evil can lead to good
Weaknesses	*Weaknesses*
It is a logical contradiction to say that a perfectly created world has gone wrong.	It is not fair or reasonable that everyone should gain heaven through their own efforts and that love can be expressed through suffering.
If the world was perfect and there was no knowledge of good and evil, how could there be the freedom to obey or disobey God?	The challenges of this world do not always result in genuine human development.

Process Theodicy

Process Theodicy claims that God is not omnipotent and the universe is an uncreated process of which God is himself a part. God began the evolutionary process but is bound by the laws of the universe. He does not have total control and humans are free to ignore him. God suffers when evil happens and is a fellow sufferer who understands. *'God is responsible for evil in the sense of having urged the creation forward to those states in which discordant feelings could be felt with greater intensity'* (D. Griffin, 1976). God's actions are justified on the grounds that the universe has produced sufficient good to outweigh evil — in other words, this universe is better than no universe at all.

Criticisms of Process Theodicy

Process Theodicy denies that God is all-powerful in the first place and brings into question the idea of whether a limited God is worthy of worship. If God cannot guarantee victory over evil, then what is the point of human efforts? And while it may be the case that good outweighs evil, this is little comfort to those who have suffered; it offers no certainty that the innocent will be rewarded.

Other solutions

If we argue that certain evils are simply too great, then we have to reconsider how much evil is acceptable. John Hick suggested that if we deem certain evils as being too great, we begin to work down the scale of evils until even the slightest suffering becomes too much. He suggested that we must either demand a world with no evil and suffering or accept what we have now.

A generous God will seek to give us great responsibility for ourselves, each other, and the world, and thus a share in his own creative activity of determining what sort of world it is to be. And he will seek to make our lives valuable, of great use to ourselves and to each other. The problem is that God cannot give us these goods in full measure without allowing much evil on the way.
(Richard Swinburne, 1979)

The Buddhist perspective

Karma is a central concept in Buddhism, upon which pivots the whole question of why life is as it is. Karma means 'action' and highlights the relationship between what people do and what happens to them as a result. This is not what Westerners might call 'fate' or 'luck' but is concerned with what has happened and what will happen as a consequence. For the Buddhist, it may relate retrospectively to actions done in a previous lifetime and the effect of that karma on a present lifetime. Karma is the key to the liberation of the individual from a state of ignorance and suffering. People are born, die and are reborn in a great cycle. This is a **samsaric existence** — karmic behaviour governs whether or not they will be born again. Because people cannot recognise the effect of their karmic actions, they cannot conceive of the result. Actions are like addictive habits and karmic conditioning determines a person's thoughts and actions.

The quest for true happiness and peace is at the heart of Buddhism. Earthly life is unsatisfactory and is characterised by suffering and impermanence. Humans are themselves responsible for these things, which stem from their own greed, selfishness and ignorance of the true nature of reality.

Buddhists believe that people do not possess any unchanging inner self, or soul, and, like everything else, they change from moment to moment. While people remain ignorant and selfish, this cycle of change continues from one life to the next, through the cycle of rebirth. The Buddha claimed that this state of being is one of ignorance and craving, over which we have lost control. People crave but, because of their ignorance, they do not understand why and so cannot be freed. If a person becomes enlightened, however, and realises the truth about life, they can be liberated from the cycle and will find peace; they will no longer be reborn.

Karma is rooted in the process of rebirth, or re-becoming. People live through successive rebirths, which are determined by karmic habits — when actions bring about bad effects, the consequences will be reaped in a later life. Equally, good actions will produce a better rebirth. People may be reborn in a higher or lower human station, or as an animal, and therefore suffer even greater ignorance, but Buddhism teaches the individual to recognise this state of craving and ignorance and offers an end to the continual cycle of rebirths — the imprisonment in samsara.

To explain this, the Buddha taught about the Wheel of Becoming. At its centre this cosmic wheel has the driving forces — ignorance, desire and aversion, represented by a pig, a cockerel and a snake — and the hub of the wheel is formed by each biting the others' tails. Surrounding the hub is a circle in two parts — a white part, indicating figures ascending, and a black part, showing figures moving downwards into a lower existence. The spokes of the wheel are the six samsaric realms. At the top are the **devas**, or gods, dwelling in a place of luxury. Alongside them are the **asuras**, or jealous gods, fighting to reach the top realm. Below them are the animals, which seek only for more food and dwell in ignorance. At the base is the realm of tortured beings, filled with pain and fear. Above them are the **pretas**, or hungry ghosts, whose hunger and thirst can never be satisfied. Finally, there is the realm of humans, who go about their daily lives, mostly oblivious to what goes on. The wheel is held by Yama, the Lord of Death, who has ultimate control over the fate of those who live in samsara and who, conditioned by their ignorance, see it as reality. The six realms represent the inevitability of past and future rebirths — rebirths into the same and into the other realms. This is part of the ceaseless rhythm of nature from which liberation can only be achieved by seeing through its illusion of the material world (**maya**). Through understanding the truth taught by the Buddha, ignorance can be transformed into wisdom.

The ending of suffering comes through **nirodha** — the control of the craving or attachment to the material world. This craving ends by rooting out the attachment, and when this is done the believer achieves **nirvana**. This is the end of craving, the end of desire, the end of all those things that cause suffering (**dukkha**). Many Western thinkers have equated nirvana with heaven, but this is not so. Nirvana is the ending of everything and can be realised in the midst of everyday living. In *What the Buddha Taught*, W. Rahula explained it as follows:

He who has realised the Truth, Nirvana, is the happiest being in the world. He is free from all 'complexes' and obsessions, the worries and troubles that torment others. His mental health is perfect…. He gains nothing, accumulates nothing, not even anything spiritual, because he is free from the illusion of Self, and the 'thirst' for becoming.

The way to achieve nirvana is to follow the path to the cessation of suffering (**magga**), through living out one's life in accordance with the **Middle Way**, or the **Noble Eightfold Path** — the wisdom of right understanding, intention and speech, the ethics of right action, livelihood and effort and the mental discipline of right mindfulness and concentration.

Buddhism is not just about personal spiritual development, however, but also about concern for others, since the two are closely linked — selfishness is the main obstacle to spiritual enlightenment. Compassionate concern for others is shown in many ways — through leading a morally responsible life, looking after the family, being loving and faithful, earning a living in an ethical way and giving of your best in all things. Indeed, the most important Buddhist moral guideline is to be compassionate. It emphasises dealing with the causes of problems rather than the symptoms — this involves wisdom and clarity of mind, which becomes easier as enlightenment approaches.

In *Buddhism in the Modern World*, Dumoulin and Maraldo noted the Buddha's own words concerning the mystery of life and death:

Those who have died after the complete destruction of the three bonds of lust, of covetousness, and of the egotistical cleaving to existence, need not fear the state after death. They will not be in a state of suffering; their minds will not continue as a Karma of evil deeds or sin, but are assured of final deliverance. When they die, nothing will remain of them but their good thoughts, their righteous acts and the bliss that proceeds from truth and righteousness. As rivers must at last reach the distant main, so their minds will be reborn in higher states of existence and continue to press on to their ultimate goal, which is the ocean of truth, the eternal peace of Nirvana.

The Jewish perspective (with special reference to the Holocaust)

When people suffer great evil they ask themselves 'Why?' This question is a kind of protest against something that seems to threaten the whole of life's meaning — evil and suffering, in a sense, just should not be. For Jews, the Holocaust is the great challenge. Human life is unique — and so great a loss of life demands an answer.

Traditionally, Jewish theologians have responded to the problem of evil and suffering in the manner of Job's friends in the Bible. They maintain that there is a direct link between goodness and reward on the one hand and evil and punishment on the other. Suffering is sometimes the inevitable result of God's justice. However, by far the most common view among Jewish theologians, certainly before the Holocaust, was the doctrine of the world to come — that God is ultimately good and just and he will reward the good and punish the evil in the afterlife. But how do these explanations of the problem of evil stand up in the face of the Holocaust? It raises new questions that, some have contended, cannot be answered in traditional ways. It is a unique and awful occurrence — in its scale, its dehumanisation and its cruelty. Indeed, for 20 years after the Holocaust Jewish theologians said little. Jonathan Sacks described it as *'a mystery wrapped in silence'*.

For some Jewish thinkers, however, the traditional answers still apply. Some Jews believe that Hitler and the Nazis will receive God's punishment in the afterlife, while the ultra-Orthodox community believes that the Holocaust was God's punishment of Jewish secularism. Others suggest that the Holocaust, like so much before it, is one of the mysteries of God's plan for the world. Some, including Robert Gordis, claim that the Holocaust shows the folly of the free-will argument — that the secular free-will society that was Nazi Germany highlights the fact that human beings cannot be trusted to be moral on their own — only a God-centred society can truly act morally in the face of evil.

Rabbi Albert Friedlander, in his book *Riders Towards the Dawn*, said that Jews must face up to the evils of the Holocaust and must address the questions it raises, otherwise the memories of the concentration camps will continue *'to poison the atmosphere'* and Jews will then never be able *'to move out of the shadow of the Holocaust'*. Friedlander argued that Christians too must look at the questions the Holocaust asks of them: the part played by anti-Judaic teaching within Christianity, leading to the rise of anti-Semitism, the failure of the various parts of the Christian Church to oppose Hitler and the need for present-day Christians to take a fresh approach and heal the religious divide.

The difficulty in understanding the place of the Holocaust in history is highlighted by the problems raised in remembering it. Many Jews use the term **Shoah** (whirl-wind) to refer to the Holocaust. In 1951, the Israeli government set aside a special day of commemoration and remembrance, the Yom Ha-Shoah (Day of the Shoah), which is held on 27 Nisan, the anniversary of the uprising in the Warsaw Ghetto. Many Jews are uncomfortable with this, however, and want to see the Holocaust assimilated into the remembrance fast of Tishah B'Av, which commemorates many other destructions, notably the first and second Temples in Jerusalem.

A difficult question is raised for Jewish theologians: should the Holocaust be viewed as one event, albeit awful, among many in Jewish history, or should it be singled out as unique? It is a question Jewish theologians have wrestled to answer, because it challenges the very heart of the Jewish faith — if God is good, if God is all-powerful and if God has a special purpose for the Jewish people in the history of the world, then why did he permit the Holocaust to happen? Does such an evil action question the very existence of God?

Within post-Holocaust Judaism there seem to be two different theological arguments. The first is encompassed in the writings of Richard Rubenstein in his work *After Auschwitz*. He challenged the very basis of traditional Judaism, saying that the notion that God acts in history and that the Jews have a special place within it is irreconcil-able with the Holocaust. God is a 'Holy Nothingness'. If God did not intervene in an evil programme as awful as the Holocaust, then God can never be expected to intervene in human history. Rubenstein challenged those Jews who claim that the Holocaust was, in some sense, God's punishment of his covenant people and suggested that Hitler was not God's agent of punishment. Moreover, he refused to celebrate the Passover as a celebration of God's saving providence. He wrote:

When I say we live in a time of the death of God, I mean that the thread uniting God and man, heaven and earth, has been broken. We stand in a cold, silent, unfeeling cosmos unaided by any purposeful power beyond our own resources. After Auschwitz, what else could a Jew say about God?

Rubenstein challenged the Jewish people to turn their focus away from God and towards the community of Israel — Jews have to create meaning for life and not assume that meaning comes from God. He called for a return to primal origins, the importance of nature and the sanctity of life and the land of Israel. But there are others who claim that Rubenstein was wrong to see the Holocaust as *the* decisive event in Jewish history and claim that he ignored the wider, panoramic picture. Eliezer Berkovits argued that the traditional Jewish faith can be retained despite the Holocaust. In his book *Faith after the Holocaust*, Berkovits stated that the Jewish scriptures have always spoken of God as, on occasions, 'hiding his face', so that people can develop their own responsibilities and freedom. He cited Isaiah 45:15: *'Truly, you are a God who hides himself, O God of Israel, the Saviour.'* He argued that God must give humans space to develop as moral beings for themselves, suggesting that the traditional views can combine with the free-will defence to provide an answer: *God cannot, as a rule, intervene whenever man's use of freedom displeases him.... If God did not respect man's freedom to choose his course in personal responsibility, not only would the moral good and evil be abolished from the earth, but man himself would go with them. For freedom and responsibility are the very essence of man. Without them, man is not human.*

Berkovits said that God must *'absent himself from history'* and not intervene. Yet God only appears to be absent — he is still silently present: *'Why do you hide your face? Why do you forget our affliction and oppression?'* (Psalm 44:24). In *With God in Hell*, Berkovits rejected the view that the Holocaust was a punishment from God for the sins of humanity. He questioned what these sins could have been, if they were to merit such terrible punishment. Berkovits did not see the Holocaust as unique in Jewish history and insisted that it be seen instead as part of the greater whole. He used another biblical notion, that of Israel being the 'suffering servant' depicted in Isaiah 52, who suffers not for his own wrongs but for the wrongs of others; his suffering is, in some way, part of God's purpose for the world.

There are, however, important criticisms of Berkovits's view. First, the Nazis took away the free will of the Jews and, hence, the freedom of those who chose the good was destroyed by those who chose the bad. Second, in a perverse sense it could be argued that the Nazis, by their awful actions, were actually assisting the Jews to develop love, forgiveness and other moral attributes. But the big question is surely, 'Was the Holocaust worth it?' Given the extent of the evil of the Holocaust, might it not be better to do without human beings capable of courage and faith? For the millions who died, there was no chance for moral growth. Berkovits suggested that the Holocaust could have no meaning without reference to an afterlife, where all will be made whole through God: *'There must be a dimension beyond history in which all suffering finds its redemption through God. This is essential to the faith of a Jew.'*

Emil Fackenheim, in his book *Quest for Past and Future*, called upon Jews to work on a new response. Instead of trying to excuse God, they should look to themselves and their own obligations. He said that, in addition to the 613 commandments in the Torah, a 614th should be added, which comes from Auschwitz — that the memory of the Holocaust should be used by the Jews to inspire them to fight for all the Jewish people and for the Jewish faith.

Finally, Irving Greenberg argued that the Holocaust was a real challenge, not only to Judaism but to Christianity as well. He said that the Holocaust denied the infinite and absolute values that both religions give to human life and challenged the Christian Church for its failure to act against the Holocaust. He claimed that these events undermine modern secular culture's promises of humanitarianism and universalism. In *Living in the Image of God* he wrote: *'No statement, theological or otherwise, should be made that would not be credible in the presence of the burning children.'*

Synoptic question and answer

Question 8a Philosophy of Religion and World Religions (Buddhism)

> 'The doctrines of karma and rebirth mean that evil and suffering do not present the same problems in Buddhism as they do in Western philosophy.' Examine and comment on this view.

The consequence of evil is suffering, which can involve physical pain and mental anguish. In addition to the pain it produces, suffering often appears to be unjust and the innocent are sometimes seen to suffer most. The problem of evil is very difficult for those who uphold the notion of the all-loving, all-powerful God of Christianity. For such believers there is only one God and he is the all-powerful creator of the universe. This leads to a dilemma: *'The name of God means that He is infinite goodness. If, therefore, God existed, there would be no evil discoverable; but there is evil in the world. Therefore God does not exist'* (Aquinas, cited in Hick (ed.), 1964).

In Buddhism, however, there is not the same pressing requirement to explain the existence of evil and suffering in the face of an all-powerful, all-loving God. For Buddhists, evil and suffering are due to human action and ignorance of the true state of things; God, as such, is not responsible. Karma is the central concept upon which pivots the whole question of why life is as it is. Karma means action, and highlights the relationship between what people do and what happens to them as a result. It is rooted in the process of rebirth. People live through successive rebirths, which are determined by karmic habits — evil actions bring about bad effects and the consequences will be reaped in a later life. Equally, good actions will produce a better rebirth.

This depends, of course, on what one believes. If a person goes through many rebirths, then there is sufficient time and opportunity to make amends for evil actions, and suffering becomes a transient thing. For Christians, however, who believe that there is only one life and no rebirth, then the causes and consequences of evil and suffering become more serious.

There are similar themes in Western philosophy. In his work *Confessions*, Augustine argued that there is a God who is wholly good and who has created a world that is perfectly good and free from defect. There is no evil and suffering. Like the Eastern religions, Augustine argued that evil itself is not a thing or a substance. Evil is really the going wrong of something that is good.

It is at this point, however, that the traditions depart from one another. Augustine said that the state of perfection was ruined by human sin and the delicate balance of the world was destroyed. Natural evil came through the loss of order in nature, and moral evil from the knowledge of good and evil which humanity discovered through its disobedience. Evil is a punishment and all humans deserve to suffer because they are all 'in the loins of Adam'. As a result, God is right not to intervene to put a stop to suffering, since the punishment is justice for human sin and God is a just god.

Buddhists would argue that although humans are responsible for their suffering, which stems from their own evil actions — greed, selfishness and ignorance of the true nature of reality — evil and suffering are not a punishment inflicted by God. Instead, they are consequences of karmic actions. While people remain ignorant and selfish, the cycle of rebirth will continue. However, the Buddhist depiction of this bears a striking similarity to the Christian notion of hell and God's punishment of the wicked.

The consequences of evil and suffering in Buddhism are shown in the Wheel of Becoming. This cosmic wheel, driven by ignorance, desire and aversion, is a circle in two parts — a white part, indicating figures that are ascending, and a black part, showing figures moving downwards into a lower existence. The spokes of the wheel are the six samsaric realms. At the top are the devas, or gods, dwelling in a place of luxury, having led good previous lives. Alongside them are the asuras, or jealous gods, fighting to reach the top realm. Below them are the animals, which seek only more food and dwell in ignorance. At the base is the realm of tortured beings — those who have caused evil and suffering — now filled with pain and fear. Above them are the pretas, or hungry ghosts, who have a hunger and thirst that can never be satisfied. Then there is the realm of humans, who go about their daily lives, mostly oblivious to what goes on. The wheel is held by Yama, the Lord of Death. If a person becomes enlightened, however, and realises the truth about life, they can be liberated from the cycle and will find peace and no longer be reborn. They will no longer suffer the consequences of evil and suffering.

Such a view has links with the views of Irenaeus, who suggested that evil could be traced back to human free will. He argued that God created humans imperfectly in order that they could develop into perfection. In other words, absolute goodness and perfection have to be developed by humans themselves, through willing cooperation with God. This means God has to give us free will, because that is the only way in which we can give willing cooperation. Moreover, freedom requires the possibility of choosing good instead of evil, and therefore God has to allow evil and suffering to occur.

John Hick argued that God had to create human beings at an epistemic distance from himself. This is a distance in dimension or knowledge which allows humans to choose freely. Moreover, the world has to be imperfect. If it were a paradise in which there was no evil and suffering, then humans would not be free to choose, since only good could actually occur. Without the existence of evil and suffering, humans would not be able to develop the positive qualities of love, honour, courage and so on, and would lose the opportunity to develop into God's likeness.

This view has similarities with the Buddhist doctrine of liberation. Here again, responsibility lies in the hands of humanity; liberation can only be achieved by seeing through the illusion of it all — the fact that people cannot see what lies beyond the material world (maya) is due to ignorance. Through understanding the truth taught by the Buddha, ignorance can be transformed into wisdom. The ending of suffering comes through nirodha — the control of the craving or attachment to the material world. This craving ends by rooting out the attachment. When this is done, the believer achieves nirvana. This is the end of craving, the end of desire, the end of all those things that cause suffering (dukkha).

Yet herein lies the difference. In Western philosophy, the endurance of evil and suffering can lead to perfection with God in the paradise of heaven. However, for Buddhists, nirvana is not like heaven. Nirvana is the ending of everything and can be realised within everyday life. W. Rahula (1986) explained it as follows: *'He who has realised the Truth, Nirvana, is the happiest being in the world. He is free from all 'complexes' and obsessions, the worries and troubles that torment others. His mental health is perfect.... He gains nothing, accumulates nothing, not even anything spiritual, because he is free from the illusion of Self, and the "thirst" for becoming.'*

Yet although the ends — heaven or nirvana — are radically different, similarities do remain. Modern Western philosophers, such as David Griffin, have suggested that the problem of evil and suffering is a human one and not something for which to blame God. God is not, in fact, omnipotent at all. He did not create the universe, because the universe is an uncreated process of which God is himself a part. In other words, God is part of the world and the universe and is bound by natural laws. God's role in creation was to start off the evolutionary process that, eventually, led to the development of humans. But God does not have total control and humans are free to ignore him. God cannot stop evil since he lacks the power to change the natural process. Yet he bears some responsibility for it, since he started off the evolutionary process knowing that he would not be able to control it. Griffin wrote (1976): *'God is responsible for evil in the sense of having urged the creation forward to those states in which discordant feelings could be felt with greater intensity.'*

God's actions are justified on the grounds that the universe has produced sufficient good to outweigh evil — in other words, this universe is better than no universe at all.

The existence of God apart, the approach to the problem of evil and suffering is similar in Buddhism. The way to achieve nirvana is not to rely on the actions of God, but to follow the path to the cessation of suffering (magga), through living out one's life in accordance with the Middle Way, or the Noble Eightfold Path — the wisdom of right understanding, intention and speech, the ethics of right action, livelihood and effort, and the mental discipline of right-mindfulness and concentration.

Moreover, Buddhism is not just about personal spiritual development; it is also concerned for others, since the two are closely linked: selfishness is the main obstacle to spiritual enlightenment. Compassionate concern for others is shown in many ways — through leading a morally responsible life, looking after the family, being loving and faithful, earning a living in an ethical way and giving of your best in all things. Indeed, the most important Buddhist moral guideline is to be compassionate. It emphasises dealing with the causes of problems rather than the symptoms — this involves wisdom and clarity of mind, which becomes easier as enlightenment approaches.

There are certainly differences between the ways in which Buddhists on the one hand, and Western philosophers on the other, approach the problem of evil and suffering. Both sides recognise the issues but for the former, the answer lies in human actions, karma and the opportunity to make amends through the cycle of rebirth. For the latter, however, there is only one lifetime and reliance upon the love of an all-powerful but mysterious God.

Synoptic question and answer

Question 8b Philosophy of Religion and World Religions (Judaism)

'Since the Holocaust, Jewish theologians have been unable to provide an adequate answer to the problem of evil and suffering.' Examine and comment on this statement.

No statement, theological or otherwise, should be made that would not be credible in the presence of the burning children.

(Irving Greenberg)

The consequence of evil is suffering, which usually involves physical pain and mental anguish. Suffering often appears to be unjust, and the innocent are frequently seen to suffer most. Evil and suffering simply should not be, and for Jews, the Holocaust is the ultimate and awful challenge posed by evil and suffering. The problem of evil is very difficult for those who uphold the notion of the all-loving, all-powerful God of Judaism and Christianity. For such believers there is only one God and he is the creator of the universe. This leads to a dilemma, however. As Augustine wrote in *Confessions*: *'Either God cannot abolish evil or he will not: if he cannot then he is not all-powerful; if he will not, then he is not all good.'*

Traditionally, Jewish theologians have responded to the problem of evil and suffering in one of two ways. First, they suggest that there is a direct link between goodness and reward on the one hand, and evil and punishment on the other, and that suffering is the inevitable result of God's justice. Second, they advocate the doctrine of the world to come — that God is ultimately good and just and he will reward the good and punish the evil in the afterlife. But how do these explanations of the problem stand up in the face of the Holocaust? It raises questions that some have contended cannot be answered in traditional ways. It is a unique and terrible occurrence — both in its scale and in its cruelty.

In his work *Confessions*, Augustine argued that the Old Testament/Jewish Bible shows that God is wholly good and that he has created a world that is perfectly good and free from defect. Evil itself is not a thing and therefore God did not create it. Evil is the going wrong of something that is good, and has come not from God, but rather from those entities that have free will — angels and humans. This perfect world was ruined by human sin. Natural evil came through the loss of order in nature, and moral evil from the knowledge of good and evil which humanity had discovered through its disobedience to God. Augustine said that both forms of evil are a punishment for human sin — suffering sent by a just God.

For some Jewish thinkers such traditional answers do apply to the Holocaust. Many believe that Hitler and the Nazis will receive God's punishment in the afterlife, while the ultra-Orthodox community believes that the Holocaust was God's punishment against Jewish secularism. Modern Jewish theologians have begun to oppose this view, however. Richard Rubenstein, in his work *After Auschwitz*, challenged the very basis of traditional Judaism. He suggested that the notion that God acted in history and that the Jews have a special place within that is irreconcilable with the Holocaust. For him, God is a 'Holy Nothingness'. If God did not intervene in a programme as evil as the Holocaust, then God can never be expected to intervene in human history. Rubenstein denied that the Holocaust was God's punishment against his covenant people and said that Hitler was not God's agent of punishment. He wrote: *'When I say we live in a time of the death of God, I mean that the thread uniting God and man, heaven and earth, has been broken. We stand in a cold, silent, unfeeling cosmos unaided by any purposeful power beyond our own resources. After Auschwitz, what else could a Jew say about God?'*

Rubenstein offered a challenge to the Jewish people to turn their focus away from God and towards the community of Israel — Jews have to create meaning for life and not assume that meaning comes from God. He called for a return to primal origins, the importance of nature and the sanctity of life and the land of Israel.

Rubenstein may be right, but there are other possibilities and the answer may lie in a different approach. Irenaeus argued that evil has a valuable part to play in God's plans for humanity. God created humans imperfectly in order that they could develop into perfection. Such perfection has to be developed by humans themselves, through willing cooperation with God. This means God had to give humans free will, and such freedom requires the possibility of choosing good instead of evil. Therefore God has to permit evil and suffering to occur. John Hick said that God had to create human beings at an epistemic distance from him, a distance in dimension or knowledge. This means that God must not be so close that he would overwhelm humans. If he were, they would have no choice but to believe and obey. By keeping at a distance, God allows humans to choose freely. The world is a place of 'soul-making', that is, a world where humans have to strive to meet challenges in order to gain perfection — and, of course, to do this, evil and suffering must necessarily occur.

Eliezer Berkovits supported this view and argued that the traditional Jewish faith can be retained despite the Holocaust. In his book *Faith after the Holocaust*, Berkovits observed that the Jewish scriptures have always spoken of God as, on occasions, 'hiding his face' so that humans can develop their own responsibilities and freedoms. He cited Isaiah 45:15: *'Truly, you are a God who hides himself, O God of Israel, the Saviour.'* In *With God in Hell* (1979), Berkovits rejected the view that the Holocaust was a punishment from God for the sins of humanity. He did not see the Holocaust as unique and insisted that it be seen as part of the greater whole of Jewish history. He used another biblical notion, that of Israel being the 'suffering servant' depicted in Isaiah 52, who suffers not for his own wrongs but for the wrongs of others and whose suffering is, in some way, part of God's purpose for the world. Berkovits suggested that the Holocaust could have no meaning without reference to an afterlife, where all will be made whole through God: *'There must be a dimension beyond history in which all suffering finds its redemption through God. This is essential to the faith of a Jew.'*

There are, however, important criticisms of Berkovits's view, not the least of which is the fact that the Nazis took away the free will of the Jews, so those who chose the good were destroyed by those who chose the bad. Robert Gordis claimed that the Holocaust showed the folly of the free-will argument — that the secular free-will society that was Nazi Germany highlighted the fact that human beings could not be trusted to be moral on their own — only a God-centred society could truly act morally in the face of evil.

Rabbi Albert Friedlander, in his book *Riders Towards the Dawn*, said that Jews must face up to the evils of the Holocaust and must address the questions it raises, otherwise the memories of the concentration camps will continue *'to poison the atmosphere'* and Jews will never be able *'to move out of the shadow of the Holocaust'*. Christians too must look at the questions the Holocaust asks of them: the anti-Judaic teaching within

Christianity, the failure of some within the Christian Church to oppose Hitler, and the need for present-day Christians to take a fresh approach and heal the religious divide.

There is another possibility: David Griffin, in his book *God, Power and Evil: A Process Theodicy*, suggested that God is not omnipotent. He did not create the universe because the universe is an uncreated process of which God is himself a part. In other words, God is part of the world and the universe and is bound by natural laws. God's role in creation was to start off the evolutionary process that, eventually, led to the development of humans. But God does not have total control and humans are free to ignore him. God cannot stop evil, since he lacks the power to change the natural process. Yet he bears some responsibility for it, having started off the evolutionary process knowing that he would not be able to control it: *'God is responsible for evil in the sense of having urged the creation forward to those states in which discordant feelings could be felt with greater intensity.'* In this way God's actions are justified on the grounds that the universe has produced sufficient good to outweigh evil — in other words, this universe is better than no universe at all. Griffin argued that God must give humans space to develop as moral beings for themselves. He argued that the traditional views can combine with the 'free-will defence' to provide an answer: *'God cannot as a rule intervene whenever man's use of freedom displeases him…. If God did not respect man's freedom to choose his course in personal responsibility, not only would the moral good and evil be abolished from the earth, but man himself would go with them. For freedom and responsibility are the very essence of man. Without them man is not human.'*

Emil Fackenheim supported this approach. In his work *Quest for Past and Future*, he called upon Jews to work on a new response. Instead of trying to excuse God, they should look to themselves and their own obligations. He said that, in addition to the 613 commandments in the Torah, a 614th should be added, which comes from Auschwitz — that the memory of the Holocaust should be used by the Jews to inspire them to fight for all the Jewish people and for the Jewish faith.

The big question remains: was the Holocaust worth it? Given the extent of the evil of the Holocaust, might it not be better to do without human beings capable of courage and faith? For the millions who died there was no chance for moral growth. Herein lies the difficulty: if we argue that certain evils are simply too great, then we have to talk about how much evil is acceptable. John Hick suggested that if we deem certain evils as being too great, then we begin to go down the scale of evils until even the slightest suffering becomes too much. He suggested that we should either demand a world with no evil and suffering in it at all or accept what we have now. In *Is There a God?*, Richard Swinburne wrote: *'A generous God will seek to give us great responsibility for ourselves, each other, and the world, and thus a share in his own creative activity of determining what sort of world it is to be. And he will seek to make our lives valuable, of great use to ourselves and to each other. The problem is that God cannot give us these goods in full measure without allowing much evil on the way.'*

The Holocaust raises more questions than answers and, for Jewish theologians, the issues it raises challenge the very heart of the Jewish faith: if God is good, if God is all-powerful and if God has a special purpose for the Jewish people in the history of the world, then why did he permit the Holocaust to happen? Does such an evil action question the very existence of God himself?

The nature of God

The nature of God in the Old Testament/Jewish Bible

The Old Testament is primarily a religious work — it does not set out to give an impartial view of events. It has a purpose, which is to depict, as the writers saw it, the sacred history of the Jewish people in the light of God's action in the world. **Salvation history** is the history of God's saving works performed for the benefit of his chosen people. The writers of the Old Testament saw the whole of history in the light of God working out his will and purpose for humanity and, in particular, for the people of Israel. The Old Testament view of the nature of God depicts him as the holy one, the creator of all things. He is shown as the unchanging sovereign Lord of creation — the all-powerful, all-knowing, eternal God of love, grace, providence, morality and truth.

Creation itself is not divine, God is. Humanity must affirm that the universe is, indeed, God's creation and it should be honoured and respected as such. As creator, God has authority over his creation. Humans are themselves a part, albeit a special part, of that creation and have special functions within it. The Bible talks of humans having stewardship over creation (Genesis 1:28). Humans do not own the world but are stewards who hold the world in trust for God. This stewardship is a matter of deepest responsibility — humans are required to look after the world, and each other, in a serious and responsible manner.

The writers of the Old Testament make it clear that God is encountered through the history of Israel's national life and he is in control of history — all that happens is part of his plan for his people. John Drane (2000) observed:

Life is not just a meaningless cycle of empty existence. It has a beginning and end, and events happen not in a haphazard sequence, but as part of a great design that in turn is based on the character of God himself. And this God is encountered by his people in the ordinary events of everyday life.

The Bible speaks of God in personal terms. He is said to be loving and trustworthy and to have a personal relationship with his people, rather like a parent and child. He chooses certain individuals, such as Abraham and Moses, to play a special part in his plan, but he also interacts with the people as a whole through his saving actions. God is seen to be deeply concerned both for the world and for his people. He acts out of love and concern, expressing his love in a personal way: *'The Lord is my shepherd, I shall not be in want'* (Psalm 23:1).

The law given to the people by God (the **Torah**) is a crucial part of the Old Testament. God is depicted as the law-giver, and obedience to God's law does not mean blindly following religious rules — it is about experiencing God's love and, in obedience to God, learning how to love one another.

The concepts of justice and righteousness are very significant. They mean more than just treating people fairly. The leaders of the people of Israel had to live their lives in accordance with the requirements of justice and righteousness, which meant righting wrongs and acting with mercy, love and trust when enforcing God's laws. Obedience to the Law would lead to righteousness in life; righteousness was an act of love from an obedient and holy people: *'But let justice roll on like a river, righteousness like a never-failing stream!'* (Amos 6:24).

God is depicted as a suffering God, who feels the anguish of his people and identifies with their needs. God also has a personality that is recognisably human, in order to highlight the sense of personal relationship. He is therefore depicted as a loving parent, guide and protector of his people: *'When Israel was a child, I loved him'* (Hosea 11:1); *'As a mother comforts her child, so will I comfort you'* (Isaiah 66:13). One of the most potent images is that of God as the bridegroom, with Israel as his bride: *'I will betroth you to me forever: I will betroth you in righteousness and justice'* (Hosea 2:19).

God identifies with the poor and the oppressed, and believers are urged to do the same. This does present theological difficulties, however. In *Proslogion*, Anselm argued that God is compassionate in terms of our human understanding of him, but in divine terms he is not; we experience God as compassionate, but this does not mean that God *is* actually compassionate: *'you are compassionate, in that you save the miserable and spare those who sin against you; you are not compassionate, in that you are not affected by any sympathy for misery.'*

Aquinas, too, believed that since love implies being vulnerable, God can therefore never be truly affected by human sorrow. Similarly, Spinoza observed that if God is truly perfect, then he can never change, and to experience suffering inevitably involves change. The Old Testament, however, clearly depicts God sharing in the suffering of the people of Israel. Nevertheless, after the First World War many theologians argued that God was apparently not affected by the evil and suffering in the world. This even prompted J. Moltmann to describe this argument, against a seemingly invulnerable God, as *'the only serious atheism'*. Moltmann (2001 edn) maintained that a truly perfect God must be able to experience suffering, and that while God cannot be forced to suffer, he can choose to experience suffering because that is, or should be, the nature of his love: *'A God who cannot suffer is poorer than any human. For a God who is incapable of suffering is a being who cannot be involved...the one who cannot suffer cannot love either. So he is also a loveless being.'*

Worship is humanity's response to God. It may be through silence, stillness, wonder, praise or dedication. In the Old Testament the most common Hebrew word used for worship was *ebed*, meaning 'servant', and worship itself was akin to acts of service and dedication towards God. According to the Bible, God alone is to be worshipped. He is to be worshipped and served with the believer's whole being — emotions, physique and feelings should all come together to praise God. In the Old Testament, rituals are widely used in order to please God and allow for the forgiveness of sins. The principles behind them — holiness, sincerity and purity — are requirements, as is the offering of one's best to God.

The nature of God in liberation theology

Humans make religion; religion does not make humans. Religion is the self consciousness and self esteem of people who either have not found themselves or who have already lost themselves again.
(Karl Marx)

The Christian Church is constantly faced with the task of adapting to the changing demands and circumstances of the modern world. This has not proved to be easy and the church has faced a major dilemma in recent years concerning the growth in personal awareness among those whom the Bible calls 'the poor'. These are people, particularly in the developing world, who are engaged in evaluating the teaching of the Bible in the light of their own lives and circumstances.

The 'poor' in the Bible are not just those who are financially lacking. The 'poor' also means the 'poor in spirit' — those who know the weakness of the human condition and understand their complete dependence on the love of God. In the modern world there are many differing groups who lay claim to this — in particular, those who feel they have suffered racism, sexism and exploitation. In *The Church in Response to Human Need*, Sugden wrote: *'Rather, the wealthy need the poor to learn from them the nature and meaning of the deliverance God brings to them both.'* The issue is not primarily one of economics, although charity is important. It is about what it means to be poor. Society may give the poor little value or status but the grace of God turns the poor into God's people.

Liberation theology

The starting point of Liberation Theology is commitment to the poor, the 'non-person'. Its ideas come from the victim.   (Gustavo Gutierrez, 2001)

God is clearly and unequivocally on the side of the poor.   (José Miguez Bonino, 1985)

Liberation theology is the name given to a wide-ranging movement that first began in Latin America in the 1960s. It is Roman Catholic in orientation and seeks to interpret the Bible from the point of view of the poor and oppressed, searching for hope in a world of poverty and injustice. The origins of the movement come from the experience of extreme poverty found in Latin America — an area that had been deeply Christian for centuries. The liberation theologians declared that such suffering was against the will of God and contrary to the teaching of Christ: *'We are on the side of the poor, not because they are good, but because they are poor'* (Gutierrez, 2001). Many of the ideas of liberation theology come from European political theology and the work of scholars such as Moltmann and Bonhoeffer, who had called for Christianity to enter the political and social arenas of life. But more than this, liberation theology was rooted in Roman Catholicism. When Vatican II (1962–65) examined the social and economic conditions of the world it opened up the chance for a re-examination of the situation of the church in Latin America. This was undertaken in the Medellin Conference of Latin American Bishops in 1968. The outcome of this meeting was the shocking acknowledgement that the Roman Catholic Church had often sided with oppressive governments in the region. In future, it was declared, the church would be on the side of the poor: *'Theology has to stop explaining the world, and start transforming it'* (Bonino, 1975).

The papacy of John Paul II was suspicious of the movement, however, and its alleged Marxist connections. In the Puebla Conference of Bishops in 1979 the Pope declared that: *'those who sup with Marxism should use a long spoon.'* In 1984, the church interrogated liberation theologian Leonardo Boff and later issued a criticism of the 'excesses' of liberation theology in the *Instructions of the Sacred Congregation for the Doctrine of the Faith*. The position softened a little in 1986, when the Vatican issued the *Instruction on Christian Freedom and Liberation*, which recognised some forms of liberation theology and gave a higher priority to the relief of the poor in Latin America. However, the supposed links between liberation theology and Marxism remained a thorny issue, particularly with the use of notions of class struggle and the economic system as factors of oppression.

Certainly, liberation theology is changing. At the beginning, it was found in the universities and among the educated middle classes, but it has since moved into the lives of the common people and there has been a growth in **Base Ecclesial Communities** — small groups of people who meet to pray and address the social and political issues that affect their lives. Writers such as Gutierrez have become less academically orientated and now use non-specialist language, while in the churches priests have striven to restore the faith of the people into mainstream Catholicism.

Liberation theology declares that the poor and oppressed should not be pitied, but are to be seen as the shapers of the new path for humanity: *'The poor are the authentic theological source for understanding Christian truth and practice'* (Sobrino, 1978). The mission of the church is seen in terms of the historical struggle for liberation, and theology is something to be done, not learned. This is the concept of **praxis**, or 'action', whereby believers are urged to seek actively to change society on behalf of the poor.

In *Liberation Theology: From Confrontation to Dialogue*, Leonardo Boff argued that the kingdom of God is concerned with the liberation of the poor. Liberation theology emphasises the notion of **structural sin** — it is society, rather than individuals, that is corrupted and requires redemption. To its critics, however, liberation theology is too simplistic and avoids some of the deeper theologies concerned with sin, salvation and atonement. It has reduced salvation to a purely worldly affair and neglected the spiritual dimension. But it has brought new challenges and raised important questions that cannot be ignored. Conn (1989) posed the question: *'Is there a "hidden agenda" in our theological formulations that has helped to make the worldwide church more comfortable with the middle and upper classes than with the poor?'*

Synoptic question and answer

Question 9 Old Testament/Jewish Bible and Christian Belief

'The teaching on the nature of God in the Old Testament/Jewish Bible is incompatible with the teaching of liberation theology.' Examine and comment critically on this statement.

Life is not just a meaningless cycle of empty existence. It has a beginning and end, and events happen not in a haphazard sequence, but as part of a great design that in turn is based on the character of God himself. And this God is encountered by his people in the ordinary events of everyday life.

(John Drane, 2000)

The Old Testament view of the nature of God depicts him as the holy one, the creator of all things. He is the unchanging sovereign Lord of creation — the all-powerful, all-knowing, eternal God of love, grace, providence, morality and truth. God's nature is divine. He has authority over all creation, of which humanity is a part. God has given to humanity a special role within the created order and he requires humanity to respect his creation. The Old Testament talks of humans having stewardship over creation. Humans do not own the world but are stewards who hold the world in trust for God. This stewardship is a matter of the deepest responsibility — humans are required to look after the world, and each other, in a serious and responsible manner: *'God blessed them and said to them, "Be fruitful and increase in number; fill the earth and subdue it"'* (Genesis 1:28).

God himself is personal in nature. He is said to be loving and trustworthy and to have a personal relationship with his people, rather like a parent and child. God is seen to be deeply concerned both for the world and for his people: *'The Lord is my shepherd, I shall not be in want'* (Psalm 23:1).

The law (Torah) given to the people by God is a crucial part of the Old Testament. God is depicted as the law-giver, although obedience to God's law does not mean blindly following religious rules — it is about experiencing God's love and, in obedience to God, learning how to love one another. The concepts of justice and righteousness are very important. They mean more than just treating people fairly. The leaders of the people of Israel had to live their lives in accordance with the requirements of justice and righteousness, which meant righting wrongs and acting with mercy, love and trust when enforcing God's laws. Obedience to the Law would lead to righteousness in life; righteousness was an act of love from an obedient and holy people: *'But let justice roll on like a river, righteousness like a never-failing stream!'* (Amos 6:24). God's nature, therefore, according to the Old Testament, is to respond not only with love and concern for his people, but also with a sense of justice and righteousness. Is this compatible with the teachings of liberation theology?

Liberation theology is the name given to a movement that began in the experience of extreme poverty found in Latin America in the 1960s. It seeks to interpret the Bible from the point of view of the poor and oppressed, searching for hope in a world of poverty and injustice: *'God is clearly and unequivocally on the side of the poor'* (José Miguez Bonino, 1985). Liberation theologians declared that such suffering was against the will of God: *'We are on the side of the poor, not because they are good, but because they are poor'* (Gustavo Gutierrez, 2001).

The Christian church has been challenged throughout the centuries on its response to the treatment of the 'poor' of the world. The 'poor' in the Bible are not just those who are financially lacking. The 'poor' also means the 'poor in spirit' — those who know the weakness of the human condition and understand their complete dependence on the love of God. Responding to this challenge has not proved to be easy and the church has faced a major dilemma, particularly in recent years, concerning the growth in personal awareness amongst those whom the Bible calls 'the poor'. These are people, particularly in the developing world, who are evaluating the teaching of the Bible in the light of their own lives and circumstances. As Sugden observed in *The Church in Response to Human Need*: *'the wealthy need the poor to learn from them the nature and meaning of the deliverance God brings to them both.'* The issue is not primarily one of economics, although charity is important. It is about what it means to be poor. Society may give the poor little value or status, but the grace of God turns the poor into God's people: *'The starting point of Liberation Theology is commitment to the poor, the "non-person". Its ideas come from the victim'* (Gustavo Gutierrez, 2001).

It could be argued that God's nature requires the churches to make a positive response. The Old Testament depicts God as a 'suffering God', who feels the anguish of his people and identifies with their needs. God also has a personality that is recognisably human, in order to highlight the sense of personal relationship. He is therefore depicted as a loving parent, guide and protector of his people: *'When Israel was a child, I loved him'* (Hosea 11:1); *'As a mother comforts her child, so will I comfort you'* (Isaiah 66:13). Indeed, one of the most potent images is that of God as the bridegroom with Israel as his bride: *'I will betroth you to me forever: I will betroth you in righteousness and justice'* (Hosea 2:19).

God, therefore, identifies with the poor and the oppressed, and believers are urged to do the same. As a result, modern scholars, such as Moltmann and Bonhoeffer, have long called for the Christian church to enter the political and social arenas of life and to begin to identify with the suffering of God's people. In response, Vatican II (1962–65) examined the social and economic conditions of the world. Soon after, the Medellin Conference of Latin American Bishops in 1968 made the shocking acknowledgement that the Roman Catholic Church had often sided with oppressive governments in the region. In future, it was declared, the church would be on the side of the poor: *'Theology has to stop explaining the world, and start transforming it'* (Bonino, 1985).

On the face of it, it seems that the Old Testament teachings on the nature of God — with the emphasis on stewardship, caring for the poor and identifying with the suffering of others — has a very strong parallel in the teachings of liberation theology. It is not that simple, however, and there are teachings on both sides that suggest that there may be serious differences. The Catholic Church condemned the alleged connections that liberation theology was said to have with Marxism, particularly with the use of notions of class struggle and the economic system as a factor of oppression. In the Puebla Conference of Bishops in 1979, the Pope declared that: *'those who sup with Marxism should use a long spoon'* and in 1984 the church criticised the so-called excesses of liberation theology in the *Instructions of the Sacred Congregation for the Doctrine of the Faith*. The position softened a little in 1986, when the Vatican issued the *Instruction on Christian Freedom and Liberation*, which recognised some forms of liberation theology and gave a higher priority to the relief of the poor in Latin America.

The heart of this conflict lies with the notion of the kingship of God and obedience to him. The Old Testament refers to the people of Israel as God's servants, who should live in reverence of him as the ultimate ruler and source of authority: *'Praise the Lord, Praise, O servants of the Lord'* (Psalm 113:1). If Marxism is a major feature of liberation theology, then this could present problems, since Marxism fails to recognise the kingship of God and places human beings, and not God, at the centre of the universe.

In the same way, liberation theology is based firmly on the notion of identifying with the suffering of oppressed people. We have seen how the Old Testament talks of a suffering God. However, there are difficulties with such a concept that could make this incompatible with liberation theology. In *Proslogion*, Anselm argued that God is compassionate in terms of our human understanding of him, but in divine terms he is not; we experience God as compassionate, but this does not mean that God is actually compassionate: *'you are compassionate, in that you save the miserable and spare those who sin against you; you are not compassionate, in that you are not affected by any sympathy for misery.'*

The Old Testament shows God sharing in the suffering of the people of Israel. After the First World War, however, many theologians argued that God appeared not to be affected by the evil and suffering in the world. Moltmann (2001) said that while a truly perfect God cannot be forced to suffer, he can choose to experience suffering because that is the nature of his love: *'A God who cannot suffer is poorer than any human. For a*

God who is incapable of suffering is a being who cannot be involved...the one who cannot suffer cannot love either. So he is also a loveless being.' This is a serious challenge, for liberation theology revolves around the need to identify with the sufferer in a real and practical way. Liberation theology argues that theology must start with the view from below — with the sufferings of the oppressed. It is a commitment to the poor, who are seen as the future builders of a new humanity: *'How can we believe in God in a society that crushes the poor and marginalizes their humanity?'* (Conn, 1989).

Marxism rejected the practices of the established church — the false hopes that worship and liturgy brings; yet, for believers, worship is humanity's response to God. It may be through silence, stillness, wonder, praise or dedication. In the Old Testament the most common Hebrew word for worship was *ebed*, meaning 'servant', and worship itself was akin to acts of service and dedication towards God. In the Old Testament, rituals are widely used in order to please God and allow for the forgiveness of sins. The principles behind them — holiness, sincerity and purity — were requirements, as was the offering of one's best to God. Marxists, however, would argue that doing away with the wretched conditions in which much of humanity lives is what really matters. Do away with these conditions and religion will wither away because it will no longer be needed. As Karl Marx wrote: *'Religious reflections of the real world will not disappear until the relations between human beings in their everyday lives have assumed the aspect of reasonable relations.'*

In *Liberation Theology: From Confrontation to Dialogue*, Leonardo Boff argued that the kingdom of God is concerned with the liberation of the poor. Liberation theology emphasises the notion of structural sin — it is society, rather than individuals, that is corrupted and requires redemption. However, Conn (1989) posed the question: *'Is there a "hidden agenda" in our theological formulations that has helped to make the world-wide church more comfortable with the middle and upper classes than with the poor?'*

The Old Testament's teachings on God's nature concerning justice and righteousness do stand uneasily against some of the excesses of capitalistic greed. Yet, at the same time, the church in the West seems to support the broad tenets of capitalism. Herein lies the fundamental difference between the two belief systems. Marxism, looking to humanity rather than God, challenges the church to 'praxis' (action), whereby believers are urged to seek actively to change society on behalf of the poor. The church, for its part, rejects liberation theology because it is too simplistic and avoids some of the deeper theologies concerned with sin, salvation and atonement. Liberation theology has reduced salvation to a purely worldly affair and neglected the spiritual dimension.

At grassroots level, there are certainly areas of conflict between the church and the followers of liberation theology. At the beginning, liberation theology was found in the universities and among the educated middle classes, but it has since moved into the lives of the common people and there has been a growth in Base Ecclesial Communities — small groups of people who meet to pray and address the social and political issues that affect their lives. Writers such as Gutierrez have become less academically orientated and now use non-scholarly language. Meanwhile, in the churches, the priests have striven to restore the faith of the people into mainstream Catholicism, often with little success.

Ultimately, it is not the teachings concerning the nature of God in the Old Testament that are incompatible with liberation theology — caring for the poor, respect for one another and stewardship of the world are common to both. The incompatibility lies in the way the church interprets the word of God and how liberation theology perceives it. The church needs to be more open to the needs of the poor, particularly in the developing world, and to practise what it preaches concerning love, justice and righteousness. In turn, liberation theology needs to recognise that simplistic answers to the problems of the world are not sufficient. Perhaps for both sides, greater attention to the teachings of the Bible may, in the end, produce the right answer.

Significant people

Old Testament/Jewish Bible (Significant person: Moses)

Background

Moses (*c.* 1350–1230BCE) was the great leader and law-giver of the people of Israel, who led them out of slavery in Egypt and made them into a holy nation of God's people. An Israelite by birth, he was brought up in the Pharaoh's court (Seti I) before fleeing for his life after killing an Egyptian officer. He went to the land of Midea, where he lived as a shepherd with the family of Jethro and married Jethro's daughter, Zipporah. In the wilderness God spoke to Moses from a burning bush (Exodus 3), telling him that he had chosen him to lead the Israelites out of slavery and into freedom. Pharaoh's (Rameses II) refusal to set them free led to a series of ten plagues, culminating in the death of the Egyptian first-born. The angel of death who passed over their houses spared the Israelites, and the waters of the Red Sea, which had parted to allow the Israelites across, destroyed the pursuing Egyptian army. Forty years of wilderness wanderings ensued before God's people entered Canaan, the Promised Land.

The character of Moses

The many sidedness of this man and the multiplicity of functions which he has performed have long suggested that the tradition has exaggerated the contribution of one man.

(John Bright, 1981)

Moses is, arguably, the greatest figure in the Old Testament and is the supreme leader of his people, constantly interceding with God on their behalf: *'It is a tribute to the leadership and resourcefulness of Moses that he was able to lead them successfully through the desert'* (John Hyatt, 1980).

Through Moses, God renews the covenant with his people that has been made earlier with Noah and Abraham (Deuteronomy 29:1). Moses becomes the model for all the later prophets and the forerunner of the Messiah (Deuteronomy 18:18). He gives the people God's law, of which he himself is judge and arbitrator (Exodus 18). It is through the Law and the covenant that the people develop a sense of national identity. Moses' role in the history of the Israelites is therefore of paramount importance; it is through him that the people escape from slavery to freedom and, in his role as mediator, he is able to bring the Law of God to the people and enable them to understand the nature and significance of their relationship with God.

It is with Moses that Israel's distinctive faith begins. The events of the Exodus and Sinai require a great personality behind them and a faith as unique as Israel's demands a founder.

(John Bright, 1981)

The wilderness experiences

At the Burning Bush Moses receives his divine call. God speaks to him in a direct and personal way and tells Moses his name, which defines the very character of this God: *'God said to Moses, "I AM WHO I AM. This is what you are to say to the Israelites: I AM has sent me to you"'* (Exodus 3:14). In Hebrew, 'I am' translates as 'YHWH' (Yahweh), which may stem from the Hebrew verb 'to be' or from 'to cause to be' — thus, 'He who will cause to be', which encompasses all of God's divinity and power.

According to Exodus 29:36, a great many Israelites leave Egypt with Moses — 600,000 men and an unknown number of women and children, together with their herds and flocks. It is clear that this is one of the most crucial events in the history of the people of Israel, affirming not only that God is with his people, but also that he has freed them from bondage and is leading them to a Promised Land. Martin Noth (1996) observed that it was understood as an event *'so unique and extraordinary that it came to constitute the essence of the primary Israelite confession and was regarded as the real beginning of Israel's history and the act of God fundamental for Israel'*, while John Bright (1981) commented that it was so *'stupendous as to be ever impressed on her memory'*. During this time they develop a consciousness of identity, a common way of life and a shared history — they become the people of God, although it is a testing time and the people complain to Moses of their harsh existence. At Sinai, Moses again meets God, who gives him a new message to bring to the people: *'Now if you obey me fully and keep my covenant, then out of all nations you will be my treasured possession. Although the whole earth is mine, you will be for me a kingdom of priests and a holy nation'* (Exodus 19:5–6). Moses presides over a covenant-making ceremony and reads from the Book of the Covenant, including the Ten

Commandments (Decalogue) as well as the ordinances, or minor laws, found in Exodus 20–23. The people gladly accept the terms of the covenant: *'When Moses went and told the people all the Lord's words and laws, they responded with one voice, "Everything the Lord has said we will do"'* (Exodus 24:3).

It is precisely the emphasis upon the worship of God that we associate with Moses, and he is depicted as the kind of leader who would have been capable of issuing a general set of commandments.
(John Hyatt, 1980)

Later, impatient while Moses delays returning from Sinai, the people break the covenant agreement, worshipping a golden calf they have fashioned themselves. When Moses returns he is outraged, smashing the tablets of stone on which God has written the Law, destroying the calf and ordering the execution of those who have been worshipping it. However, Moses then returns to God and pleads with him to give his people a second chance.

Eventually, although the people reach the Promised Land of Canaan, Moses himself does not enter; he dies on Mount Nebo in the land of Moab, according to God's will: *'This is the land I promised to Abraham, Isaac and Jacob…I have let you see it with your own eyes, but you will not cross over into it. And Moses, the servant of the Lord, died there in Moab'* (Deuteronomy 34:4–5).

World religions (Judaism) (Significant person: Rashi)

Historical and family background

Rashi (Rabbi Shlome Yitzchaki, 1040–1105CE) was the most outstanding biblical commentator of the Middle Ages. His commentary on the Bible aimed to elaborate and explain every word, while using as few of his own words as possible. He made extensive use of Midrash, applying it specifically to biblical texts to clarify their meaning, and his characteristic method was to dictate his thoughts to his students. He transliterated many obscure Hebrew words into Old French, and consequently had an important impact on the development of the French language. Rashi's commentary was so significant that it was contained in Bomberg's 1517 Bible and in subsequent years 200 commentaries on Rashi's commentary were written. Rashi's commentary on the Talmud was even more significant, explaining all the Gemara discussions and making it accessible to the non-scholar. After Rashi's death, Talmud scholars (known as Tosafists), including members of his own family, developed his work further. Their additions to the Talmud — critical glosses in the margins of Rashi's work — are called Tosafot.

Rashi came from a distinguished scholarly family — his uncle was Rabbi Simon ben Isaac the Elder — and inherited his intellectual gifts from a long chain of scholars going back to Rabbi Johanan haSandler. Although he had no sons, two of his daughters married Rabbinic scholars who became important Tosafists. His grandsons became important figures in the Rabbinic world and after Rashi's death, Samuel ben Meir (Rashbam), the eldest, assumed the spiritual leadership of his grandfather's community. Rashi's descendants were the disseminators of Rabbinic scholarship throughout western Europe, shifting the centre of Jewish learning from North Africa to Europe.

Rashi was born in France, spending his student life in Germany. Jews had come to Europe as captives of the Romans, but over the centuries liberated Jews had chosen to settle in the Rhenish areas, although they suffered persecution and threats of expulsion. By Rashi's time they enjoyed comparative tranquillity and prosperity, however, and the community in Mayence appears to have been particularly prominent, producing a number of famous scholars, including Rabbenu Gershom, who founded the Talmudic academy there. It was here that Rashi gained access to a definitive and accurate text of the Talmud; he relied heavily on this, although he did not hesitate to deviate from it when he felt that other versions were more accurate or logical. Relations between Christians and Jews were commercially significant and influenced much of Rashi's teaching. It is also evident that Rashi engaged in discussions with Christian clergy and that he had some knowledge, at least, of Latin biblical commentaries. On occasion he responded to the interpretations of Christian commentators, most notably Jerome.

The significance of Rashi

The achievements of great men are reflections of their personalities. The reactions of men to the environment in which they live, and the manner in which they express these reactions, mirror their own innermost beings and convey their character and temperament to posterity.

(Esra Shereshevsky, 1996)

Rashi drew his interpretations of the biblical text from centuries of Midrashic and Talmudic material. He selected that with which he felt he could best identify and the way in which he introduced this material into his own commentary reveals his personality and interests.

Rashi was known to be a man of great personal modesty and humility, despite his intellectual achievements. In a letter, he stated that he was not qualified to set aside an excommunication imposed by another Rabbinic authority, with the words: '*Far be it from me to assume the title and appoint myself an accepted Bet Din…who am I to make myself part of another place, I being rather poor in wisdom and young in years?'* His quest for the truth and his readiness to admit to error or failure of understanding are quite remarkable. He relied completely on the teaching of his own masters, to whom he frequently made reference. However, he was prepared to disagree with them when their views challenged his own integrity. Esra Shereshevsky (1996) observed: *'With this sincere, almost agonizing quest for the truth, Rashi demonstrates his own integrity and his courage to confront even his most revered teachers on the battlefield of Torah.'*

Rashi prized peace and harmony above all else. In his commentary on Leviticus 26:6 he noted: *'If there is no peace, there is nothing; peace outweighs everything.'* This extended to a considerable leniency before condemning a fellow Jew, encouraging others to consider that an apparently ill-intentioned act may have been well-intentioned. He was deeply compassionate, even when faced with hostility on the part of those who thought it inappropriate — for example, when he conducted a Kaddish during a festival holiday. He dismissed those who handed down prohibitions for their own sake and who did not consider the financial suffering that this may cause a fellow Jew. He was pragmatic concerning money-lending, dealing in wine and trading with Gentiles, and although he remained concerned not to encourage assimilation, he declared that it was forbidden to humiliate Jews who had assimilated (blended in with the local or national community) out of fear. Whenever he sought to impart moral values, he did so by suggesting or illustrating the desirability of certain behaviour, rather than categorically demanding or forbidding an action. His work demonstrates a great sensitivity to human behaviour and he covers all the essentials of everyday life — dress, health, commerce and industry, food, the household and utensils.

Rashi valued time-honoured customs over the explicit law, encouraging unity within a community who shared the customs and with their ancestors who had established them. He insisted on the unalienable right of his people to the Land of Israel, declaring that no Jew could consider himself homeless, having been given the land by God: *'There is not one person among the Jewish people who has no soil in the Land of Israel. The Gentiles may have seized it and captured it but they have no permanent right to it…even if we do not have political sovereignty over it'* (Teshuvot Rashi).

Rashi's teachings are dominated by his personal piety and fear of God, which he believed must supersede the study of the Torah. In his commentary on Proverbs 1:7 he wrote: *'Before you set out to acquire knowledge, learn first to fear your Creator, and that should motivate you to acquire knowledge.'* Fear of God, he claimed, is the only reason for man to be moral, since morality is not an automatic outgrowth of society. Rashi described those who study the Torah inspired by the love of God in the most lyrical and romantic language — as tender and pleasant as roses, and like the verdant forests.

Ultimately, Rashi's aim was to produce a commentary that would explain the biblical text in the clearest manner possible, and in so doing he often rejected earlier interpretations from the sages on the grounds that they did not correspond with the intention of the text. He sought primarily for a literal interpretation of the text, though he was ready to concede to an allegorical one if the text did not readily lend itself to a literal reading.

Rashi accompanied the Jew in his studies throughout the lights and shadows of his tragic history. Like a mentor's guiding hand, Rashi's commentaries molded the character of the Jew from early childhood on through his formative years and until the last conscious stirrings of his intellectual life.
(Esra Shereshevsky, 1996)

Moses and Rashi compared

Moses	Rashi
An innovator, who delivered God's revelation to the people	Explained, developed and elucidated God's word
His work has been significant for thousands of years	His work was so significant it kept scholars active for centuries after his death
Laid emphasis on the truth of God's revelation	Concerned that all people should understand God's word
His character developed throughout his experiences. He was in an ideal position to help God's people and his own authority increased	From a scholarly family, he used his intellectual prowess to make the text meaningful to generations of Jews
Disciples: Aaron was appointed as his right-hand helper; Joshua was to take over from Moses when Israel entered Canaan	Disciples: Tosafists. His grandson, Rabbenu Tam, was among most significant. Rashi's impressive descendants were responsible for continuing his work
Emerged at a time of crisis — Israel's oppression in Egypt	Survivor of the First Crusade (1095–99) when many Jews were massacred
Was he a historical figure? His significance may be exaggerated, but there is no serious case for being fictional	No doubts about his historical existence

Received God's revelation through direct, personal experience	Interpreted God's revelation through reason and scholarship
Revealed the big picture; interpretation of the minutiae of the Law left to others later in a different historical setting	Concerned with the detail of the text and clarifying fine points
Demanding and authoritarian, quick to anger, but ultimately concerned with the well-being of the people	Pragmatic, compassionate and realistic
Initially resistant to his call, Moses emerged as a confrontational and challenging leader	Dealt with his teachers and other rabbinic authorities with dignity and humility

Synoptic question and answer

Question 10 Old Testament/Jewish Bible and World Religions (Judaism)

Explain and consider critically the importance of one person in the Old Testament [Moses] with the status of a figure in the world religion you have studied [Rashi].

The achievements of great men are reflections of their personalities. The reactions of men to the environment in which they live, and the manner in which they express these reactions, mirror their own innermost beings and convey their character and temperament to posterity.

(Esra Shereshevsky, 1996)

The place of Moses in the history of God's people is among the best-known aspects of the Old Testament. He is the great leader and law-giver of the people of Israel, who leads them out of slavery in Egypt and makes them into a holy nation of God's people. An Israelite by birth, Moses is brought up in the court of Pharaoh (Seti I) before fleeing for his life after killing an Egyptian officer. He goes to the land of Midea, where he lives for a time as a shepherd with the family of Jethro and marries Jethro's daughter, Zipporah. In the wilderness, God speaks to him from a burning bush (Exodus 3), telling Moses that he has chosen him to lead the Israelites out of slavery and into freedom. Pharaoh's (Rameses II) refusal to set them free leads to a series of ten plagues, culminating in the death of the Egyptian first-born, which enables the Israelites, under Moses' leadership, to leave Egypt by way of the Red Sea. Once in the wilderness, the people wander for 40 years, facing many physical and spiritual challenges. Eventually, although they reach the Promised Land of Canaan, Moses himself does not enter, but dies on Mount Nebo in the land of Moab, according to God's will: *'This is the land I promised to Abraham, Isaac and Jacob.... I have let you see it with your own eyes, but you will not cross over into it. And Moses, the servant of the Lord died there in Moab'* (Deuteronomy 34:4–5).

During this time Moses emerges as a larger-than-life character and although initially resistant to God's call, he develops into a confrontational and challenging leader, set apart from those whom he leads by his intimate and personal relationship with God. John Bright (1981) observed tellingly: *'The many sidedness of this man and the multiplicity of functions which he has performed have long suggested that the tradition has exaggerated the contribution of one man.'* However, although there have been attempts (as with the Patriarchs) to dismiss the historical existence of Moses, they have not been particularly compelling. Nevertheless, the character of Moses is no everyday figure and his greatness is seen against a background of miraculous divine activity and pivotal events in salvation history.

The figure of Rashi (Rabbi Shlome Yitzchaki), the most outstanding Jewish biblical commentator of the Middle Ages, is, at first glance, remarkably different from Moses. Born in France nearly 2,000 years later than Moses (*c.* 1040CE), he spent his student years in Germany at a time when Jews enjoyed comparative tranquillity and prosperity. This had not always been the case, however. Like Moses' compatriots, Jews had first come to Europe as captives, and although liberated Jews settled in the Rhenish areas, they had suffered persecution and threats of expulsion. The attitude of cooperation between Jews and Gentiles which prevailed in Rashi's time was not something to be taken for granted, and it had a significant influence on his work. Unlike Moses, Rashi was not engaged in confronting Gentile authorities and although he was concerned not to encourage assimilation, he declared that it was forbidden to humiliate Jews who had assimilated out of fear. He was pragmatic about the implications of trading with Gentiles, without which many Jews would have suffered economic hardship. Essentially, Rashi's work was intimately concerned with and connected to the daily life of the Jew, not with great events in salvation history, but the impact of this work is not to be underestimated.

Rashi was born into a distinguished scholarly family — his uncle was Rabbi Simon ben Isaac the Elder — and he inherited his intellectual gifts from a long chain of scholars going back to Rabbi Johanan haSandler. Although he had no sons, two of Rashi's daughters married Rabbinic scholars who became important Tosafists (commentators on Rashi's commentary). His grandsons too became important figures in the Rabbinic world and after Rashi's death the eldest, Samuel ben Meir (Rashbam), assumed the spiritual leadership of his grandfather's community. Rashi's descendants were the disseminators of Rabbinic scholarship throughout western Europe, shifting the centre of Jewish learning from North Africa to Europe. Rashi's pedigree made it almost inevitable that he would become pivotal in the development of Jewish learning, but Moses' pedigree, although radically different, also serves to prepare him for his task.

Saved soon after birth, by divine accident, from the Egyptian massacre of Israelite boys, Moses grows up in the royal court but with the benefit of close association with his mother and sister, who evidently ensure that he does not forget his Israelite heritage. His sense of religious and national identity is roused when he sees an Egyptian task-master beating a fellow Israelite, and he kills the Egyptian. He is then forced to become a desert-dweller, after the luxuries of court life. Nevertheless, despite his change of circumstances, Moses is then given another opportunity to prepare for the task ahead of him. His courtly upbringing enables him to face Pharaoh with God's demand for freedom for his people, while his desert experience equips him for the challenges faced in the wilderness. John Hyatt (1980) observed: *'It is a tribute to the leadership and resourcefulness of Moses that he was able to lead them successfully through the desert.'*

Furthermore, Moses' task is preceded by a vivid encounter with God when at an apparently burning bush Moses receives his divine call. God speaks to Moses in a direct and personal way. He tells Moses his name, which defines the very character of that God: *'God said to Moses, "I AM WHO I AM. This is what you are to say to the Israelites: I AM has sent me to you"'* (Exodus 3:14). In Hebrew, 'I am' translates as 'YHWH' (Yahweh), which may stem from the Hebrew verb 'to be', or from 'to cause to be' — thus, 'He who will cause to be', which encompasses all of God's divinity and power. Moses receives the assurance that God will be with him in power and presence, although his reaction is initially uncertain. Unsure of his ability to communicate effectively or to convince the people of the reality of his experience, Moses needs to be persuaded that God will provide everything he needs to fulfil his calling — the assistance of the otherwise rather two-dimensional Aaron, the ability to perform miracles in Pharaoh's court, and the presence of God himself in cloud and fire as they travel through the wilderness. Interestingly, however, once Moses gets into his stride he develops into an indomitable and confrontational figure. He takes the people to task for their criticism of God when they complain that they have no good food to eat, he acts as judge over the people in the wilderness, challenges them to accept the uncompromising conditions of the covenant agreement, and explodes with righteous anger when they build the golden calf.

Rashi's character emerges quite differently, and this should not, perhaps, be a surprise. A man who is called to take on the might of Pharaoh and to lead a restless and angry people through 40 years of desert-dwelling needs to develop a resilience not required in the study of the Torah. However, although Rashi was characterised by his humility, modesty and compassion, he was not a weak man. On the one hand he stated in a letter that he was not qualified to set aside an excommunication imposed by another Rabbinic authority, with the words: *'Far be it from me to assume the title and appoint myself an accepted Bet Din…who am I to make myself part of another place, I being rather poor in wisdom and young in years?'* His quest for the truth and his readiness to admit to error or failure of understanding were quite remarkable and he relied heavily on the teaching of his own masters, to whom he frequently made reference. However, he was prepared to disagree with them when their views challenged his own integrity. Esra Shereshevsky (1996) observed: *'With this sincere, almost agonizing quest for the truth, Rashi demonstrates his own integrity and his courage to confront even his most revered teachers on the battlefield of Torah.'*

Rashi prized peace and harmony above all else. In his commentary on Leviticus 26:6 he noted: *'If there is no peace, there is nothing; peace outweighs everything.'* This extended to a considerable leniency before condemning a fellow Jew, encouraging others to consider that an apparently ill-intentioned act may have been well-intentioned. He was deeply compassionate, even when faced with hostility by those who thought it inappropriate, for example, when he conducted a Kaddish during a festival holiday. Whenever he sought to impart moral values he did so by suggesting or illustrating the desirability of certain behaviour, rather than categorically demanding or forbidding an action.

Rashi's work shows a great sensitivity to human behaviour and he covers all the essentials of everyday life — dress, health, commerce and industry, food, the household and utensils — the very substance of the Law handed down to Moses on Mount Sinai. However, while Moses is not described as interpreting the Law or considering the many ways in which it may have had to be applied once the people of Israel were in the Promised Land, Rashi's life was spent on that very task. Although, as John Bright (1981) observed, *'it is with Moses that Israel's distinctive faith begins'*, Rashi *'accompanied the Jew in his studies throughout the lights and shadows of his tragic history. Like a mentor's guiding hand, Rashi's commentaries molded the character of the Jew from early childhood on through his formative years and until the last conscious stirrings of his intellectual life'* (Esra Shereshevsky, 1996). Rashi's ultimate aim was to produce a commentary that would explain the biblical text in the clearest possible manner, and in so doing he often rejected interpretations from the sages on the grounds that they did not correspond with the intention of the text. He sought primarily to interpret it literally, though he was ready to concede to an allegorical interpretation if the text did not lend itself readily to a literal reading.

Like those of Moses, Rashi's teachings were dominated by his personal piety and his fear of God, which he believed to be above all else. At the foot of Sinai, Moses presides over a covenant-making ceremony and reads from the Book of the Covenant, including the Ten Commandments (Decalogue) as well as the ordinances, or minor laws, found in Exodus 20–23. The people gladly accept the terms of the covenant: *'When Moses went and told the people all the Lord's words and laws, they responded with one voice, "Everything the Lord has said we will do"'* (Exodus 24:3). John Hyatt (1980) again observed: *'It is precisely the emphasis upon the worship of God that we associate with Moses, and he is depicted as the kind of leader who would have been capable of issuing a general set of commandments.'* In his commentary on Proverbs 1:7 Rashi wrote: *'Before you set out to acquire knowledge, learn first to fear your Creator, and that should motivate you to acquire knowledge.'* Fear of God, he claimed, was the only reason for man to be moral, since morality was not an automatic outgrowth of society. Those who study the Torah inspired by love of God, Rashi describes in the most lyrical and romantic language — as tender and pleasant as roses, and like the verdant forests. Separated by so many centuries, Rashi and Moses are not that far apart in their understanding of the essential connectedness of obedience, piety and true love of God.

Under the leadership of Moses, the people of Israel experience an event that gives meaning to the rest of their history — the Exodus. Martin Noth (1956) observed that it was understood as an event: *'so unique and extraordinary that it came to constitute the essence of the primary Israelite confession and was regarded as the real beginning of Israel's history and the act of God fundamental for Israel'*, while John Bright (1981) commented that it was so *'stupendous as to be ever impressed on her memory'*. During this time the people of Israel develop a consciousness of identity, a common way of life and a shared history — they become the people of God, although it is time of many challenges and the people complain to Moses of their harsh existence. Rashi was aware of this inheritance and valued time-honoured customs over the explicit law, encouraging unity within a community who shared the customs and with their ancestors, who had established them. He insisted on the unalienable right of his people to the Land of Israel, declaring that no Jew could consider himself homeless, having been given the land by God: *'There is not one person among the Jewish people who has no soil in the Land of Israel. The Gentiles may have seized it and captured it but they have no permanent right to it...even if we do not have political sovereignty over it'* (Teshuvot Rashi).

How then to evaluate the relative significance of Moses and Rashi? Living in radically different times and circumstances and with contrasting roles, they have both had an enormous significance for Jewish history and learning. Without Moses, the Jews may not have had the Law and made the covenant with God in the wilderness, and by implication he stands out as a great man; on the other hand, the work of Rashi must clearly not be underestimated. His aim was to make every word of the Torah clear and meaningful to the non-scholar, and in so doing he also influenced the development of the French language. His commentary was so significant that it was contained in Bomberg's 1517 Bible. Both men valued true and pure obedience to God, and both produced a life's work so influential that it has kept scholars busy for centuries after their deaths.

Significant people

New Testament (Significant person: Paul)

And Paul and Barnabas spoke out boldly saying, 'It was necessary that the word of God should be spoken first to you. Since you thrust it from you, and judge yourselves unworthy of eternal life, behold we turn to the Gentiles.' (Acts 13:46)

Paul, or Saul, as he was originally known, was probably born around 6BCE in Tarsus. He was a Jew, a Roman citizen and a Pharisee of the tribe of Benjamin. He was educated in Jerusalem under Rabbi Gamaliel the Elder. As a learned Pharisee, he probably shared the view that God would intervene in history to rescue the Jewish people from their enemies. In particular, he would have believed that the Messiah would arrive from God in dramatic fashion, drive out the Romans and establish God's kingdom on earth. He would, therefore, have felt contempt for the followers of Jesus, the crucified Messiah, who were claiming that after his crucifixion Jesus had risen from the dead and was the true Messiah.

Paul believed that Christians were moving into all parts of the Roman empire and needed to be stopped from spreading their message. He gained permission from the high priest to go to the nearby city of Damascus and bring the Christians who lived and worshipped there back to Jerusalem for punishment. On the road to Damascus a bright light from heaven shone down and the risen Christ challenged Paul, saying: *'Saul, Saul, why do you persecute me?'* (Acts 9:4). Paul was blinded and his life was changed for ever. He was taken to Damascus, unable to see, and overwhelmed by his experiences. His sight was restored 3 days later and Paul was converted to Christianity, developing a burning inspiration to carry the Christian message to the furthest corners of the known world. I. Howard Marshall (1980) observed: *'Paul was no sooner converted and called to be a witness to Jesus Christ than he began to fulfil his commission.'* Furthermore: *'The death of Jesus at the hands of the Roman authorities…was a political event which Paul transformed in his imagination into a moment of cosmic religious significance'* (A. N. Wilson, 1998).

In 43CE, during the height of the persecution of the early church, Paul met the leaders of the Jerusalem church and agreed to undertake a crucial mission — to bring the word of God to the Gentiles throughout the known world. Paul and his companion Barnabas embarked upon a missionary journey — the first of three to the Gentile world. They went first to Cyprus, then on to Asia Minor, across the mountains to Pisidia and Antioch (Pisidian Antioch). From there they travelled east to Lycaonia and through several towns in Galatia, before returning to Antioch. In every town they followed the same pattern, which became the model for all the missionary journeys. First, they would preach in the local synagogue, where they might meet sympathetic Jews as well as Gentiles who would accept their message and become the centre of the new community. Later, on the return journey, they would revisit the new congregations of Christians that had been formed, and encourage them in their new faith and help their leaders.

For his second missionary journey Paul took a new companion, Silas, with him. They revisited the churches that had been founded earlier, where Paul received a vision from God of a 'man of Macedonia', beckoning him to come to Macedonia (Acts 16:9–10). So Paul travelled to Greece; he visited Athens, where he had to adopt a different approach because the city was a place of learning and there were many young Romans and Greeks who were studying philosophy and the mystery religions. They had no Jewish or scriptural background and to talk of Jesus as the Messiah would have meant nothing to them. Paul began first by observing what was going on and listening to the debates. When at last he did speak, he began from the Greek view of God as creator and invisible presence in the universe and then spoke of humanity's search for God. He referred to the many shrines and altars in the city, including the altar 'to the unknown god', which he identified with Jesus. His message received a mixed reception and Paul was not able to establish a Christian community.

The third missionary journey centred on Ephesus and Corinth. In Ephesus Paul baptised many believers and was able to perform many miracles there, including healing the sick and casting out demons. He did encounter problems, however. Ephesus was a centre of spiritual traditions, at the middle of which was the temple of the city's patron goddess, Artemis (Diana). It was also home to many magicians and astrologers and one rich idol-maker called Demetrius incited the people to riot against the Christians in the city: *'Paul has convinced and led astray large numbers of people here in Ephesus.... He says that man-made gods are no gods at all'* (Acts 19:26). Paul left Ephesus and before returning to Jerusalem made final visits to the communities he had helped to establish in the area. In Troas, Paul was able to restore Eutychus to life after he fell from an upstairs window (Acts 20:12).

Paul met the leaders of the Jerusalem church and reported on the success of God's work among the Gentiles. At first there was great rejoicing, but soon Jews from Asia saw Paul at the temple and were convinced that he had defiled the sacred site by taking Gentiles into the inner court (Acts 21:27–37). A riot followed. Paul was taken captive by the Romans because the crowd wanted to kill him and, on hearing of a Jewish plot against Paul's life, the Romans took Paul under armed guard to Caesarea.

According to John Drane (1999): *'Paul...still believed that, as the "apostle to the Gentiles", he had something to contribute to the church in the most strategic position of all: Rome, the capital of the empire.'* Paul chose to exercise his right as a Roman citizen to appeal to the supreme court of the empire — the emperor himself. Paul set sail for Rome on a prison ship and remained there for 2 years under house arrest in a property he rented for himself. Protected by Roman guards, whom he also had to pay, he spent the 2 years preaching. E. M. Blaiklock (1959) observed: *'when he came to Rome, the purpose for which he had toiled and striven was virtually achieved.'* We do not know exactly what happened, but the traditions of the early church say that Paul met a martyr's death, probably by beheading, during the persecution of Rome's Christians by the Emperor Nero in 64CE.

The religion of Paul...contains all the makings of a religion with universal appeal even though he himself, like Jesus, would perhaps have been astonished by the turns and developments which the Christian religion was to take after his death...The essential things — the certainty of human unworthiness before the perfection of God, the atoning sacrifice of Christ on the Cross, the glorious promise of the Resurrection and everlasting life — these are the core of Paul's religion. And above all, the knowledge that Christ, the drama of his passion, death and resurrection, but also the continuing presence in the world are in us. That is the winning formula.

(A. N. Wilson, 1998)

For Paul, the whole world — indeed, the whole universe — was the stage on which the drama of redemption was to be played out. Personal and individual salvation was important, but could never be separated from social and cosmic salvation. The life, death and resurrection of Jesus was the hinge on which the whole of world history turned; it was the beginning of God's 'new creation'.

(John Drane, 1999)

Paul believed that what he taught came from Jesus Christ, the Son of God, through whom God was revealed to humanity: *'The gospel I preach is not of human origin. I did not receive it from a human source, nor was I taught it, but I received it through a revelation of Jesus Christ'* (Galatians 1:11–12). *'If you confess with your mouth, "Jesus is Lord", and believe in your heart that God raised him from the dead, you will be saved'* (Romans 10:9). Paul made clear in the epistles that salvation is through God's love — an act of God's grace to his undeserving people. In turn, the believer needs to make a response to God's love — to believe in God's love and have faith in him. Drane (1999) observed: *'These then were the key features of Paul's gospel: God's undeserved love ("grace") shown to humankind through Jesus, to which the appropriate response was "faith", which included a commitment to God that was based not on wishful thinking, but on the absolute facts of Jesus' life, death and resurrection, and the arrival of God's kingdom.'*

For Paul, belief was based on personal experience and had to have some connection with real-life social and cultural realities. For example, it meant that Christians could not remain in an enclosed group — if God accepted them without conditions, so they should accept other people without conditions. This openness in relationships to others was a key part of Paul's teaching: *'there is no longer Jew nor Greek, slave nor free, male or female; for you are all one in Christ Jesus'* (Galatians 3:28).

Paul believed that Christians were intended to become children of God — Jesus had fulfilled God's will perfectly and believers could now do the same, thanks to the presence of the risen Christ living within them, through the work of the Holy Spirit: *'The Spirit himself testifies with our spirit that we are God's children. Now if we are children, then we are heirs — heirs of God and co-heirs with Christ, if indeed we share in his sufferings in order that we may also share in his glory'* (Romans 8:16–17). Nevertheless, Paul taught that there was only one way to escape the judgement of God. It was not through obedience to the Law, nor through doing good works, but rather through faith in Jesus Christ: *'This righteousness from God comes through faith in Jesus Christ to all who believe. There is no difference, for all have sinned and fall short of the glory of God and are justified freely by his grace through the redemption that came by Christ Jesus. God presented him as a sacrifice of atonement, through faith in his blood'* (Romans 3:22–25). F. F. Bruce (1995) observed: *'The gospel of justification by faith sets human beings by themselves before God. If it humbles them to the dust before God, it is that God may raise them up and set them on their feet.'*

Paul made it clear that although Christians were set free from the need to observe formal rules, this did not mean that they had no responsibility for their actions. They had entered into a new kind of life where, instead of being slaves to sin, they were *'slaves to God'* (Romans 6:22). Christ had set them free, not in order to do as they pleased, but so that they might become like Christ himself. In this they were aided by the work of the Holy Spirit: *'Therefore, there is now no condemnation for those who are in Christ Jesus, because through Christ Jesus the Law of the Spirit of life set me free from the law of sin and death'* (Romans 8:1–2). Paul saw the resurrection of Jesus as the core of Christian belief. Jesus was resurrected and this guaranteed that

Christians would be raised to life on the last day, just as Jesus was: *'For as in Adam all die, so in Christ all will be made alive'* (1 Corinthians 15:22).

Paul regarded God as the source of all authority, and those who exercise authority on earth do so by delegation from God. Hence, those who disobey the authorities are disobeying God: *'he who rebels against the authority is rebelling against what God has instituted'* (Romans 3:2). Christians, therefore, should obey the laws of the state, pay their taxes and respect the authorities — not because of the fear of punishment but because it is a way of serving God: *'This is also why you pay taxes, for the authorities are God's servants'* (Romans 13:6).

The ministry of Paul was not bounded by the limits of a life. It influenced decisively all European history, and through European history the history of the whole modern world. Paul's was the most significant human life ever lived. (E. M. Blaiklock, 1959)

World religions (Islam) (Significant person: Muhammad)

'La ilaha ilallah wa Muhammadur rasul al-Lah.' (There is no God but Allah, and Muhammad is the Prophet of God.) Thus declares the creed of Islam. It highlights the two essential truths of the faith: that there is 'One God, Supreme and Unique'; and that the revelation given through the prophet Muhammad is the final and complete revelation of God, which supersedes all that came before it.

The prophet Muhammad was born in Makkah, Saudi Arabia, around 570CE. Andrew Rippin observed: *'The religious importance of Muhammad is such that it is not really feasible (nor necessarily desirable) to distinguish later religiously inspired fiction from what might be called historical "fact"'* (2000). It seems that Muhammad's parents died when he was very young and his grandfather, Abd al-Muttalib, and his uncle, Abu Talib, raised him. Despite the fact that Arabia at that time was a predominantly pagan country, Muhammad (strongly influenced by his grandfather) grew up to be a devout and deeply religious believer in One God. At that time Makkah contained the most important of Arab shrines, the Ka'aba temple, said to have been built by Adam himself and dedicated to the One True God, though later taken over by the worshippers of Baal.

When he was 25, Muhammad married a wealthy widow, Khadijah; they lived happily together and had six children. The wealth they enjoyed meant that Muhammad could devote a good deal of time to prayer and meditation and he often went away for days on end into the mountains around Makkah to be close to God. One day, in 610CE, at the age of 40, he had a powerful religious experience in the Cave of Hira. The angel Gabriel came to him and ordered him to recite the words that appeared before him. Muhammad protested that he could not understand the words, but the angel opened his eyes and he understood their meaning. The angel ordered him to learn them and to repeat them to others. This was the first revelation of verses of the book that was to become known as the Qur'an (the Recitation). From this moment of his calling, Muhammad's life was no longer his own; he devoted himself to God (Allah) and spent the rest of his life doing God's will as his prophet, by preaching the message of God to the people.

After this initial vision, Muhammad had to go through a period of waiting, when he was unsure of what he was to do. Two years later the revelations began again and continued for the rest of his life — a period of about 20 years. At first Muhammad did not preach in public, but instead spoke privately to those who wanted to hear him. When he did finally begin preaching in public he often faced ridicule by those who thought he was mad and by those, like the Quraish tribesmen, who had a vested interest in idol worship and saw him as a threat to their position in the temple.

Muhammad taught a way of life that became known as Islam, which means 'submission to the will of Allah', and his followers were known as Muslims ('those who submit'). But many people caused trouble for Muhammad and his followers. Some were forced to flee to Abyssinia, anticipating a sympathetic response among Christians and Jews ('People of the Book'), while others were refused food and water and many lived in great poverty. Muhammad himself attempted to find a new place to live in Arabia and finally settled in Yathrib, later to be called Medina — 'the town of the prophet'. As ruler, Muhammad offered justice and freedom to both the Arabs and the Jews who lived there and taught equality and justice for all. The move to Yathrib is known as the **Hijrah** and the year of its occurrence (622CE) is the focal point of the Muslim calendar as the year in which the Muslim community (the **Ummah**) came into being and defined the Islamic sense of identity.

Some years earlier, in 619CE, Muhammad's wife had died and he was grief-stricken. For a while he left Makkah and, soon after, he experienced the *Lailat ul-Miraj* ('Night of Ascent'). He felt God take him to the site of the Jewish temple in Jerusalem and from there up to heaven. There he spoke to Jesus and the other prophets and was given the rules of Muslim prayer, which have become a central part of the Islamic faith. The experience gave Muhammad great comfort and the strength to carry on his mission, but despite his position Muhammad lived very simply. His teachings, sayings and anecdotes about his life, which ran to many thousands, became known as **Hadiths**. Muhammad taught humility and kindness to one another and advocated the freeing of slaves and the giving of charity:

'Charity is for the poor, the needy, those working at collecting it, those whose hearts are being reconciled to yours, for freeing of captives and debtors and in striving along God's way, and for the wayfarer, as a duty imposed by God' (Qur'an 9:60).

Yet Muhammad's was not to be a life of peace. The Quraish tribes still opposed him and he was forced to go to war. In 627CE Muhammad defeated an army of 10,000, led by Abu Sufyan, which had threatened Medina, and the following year Muhammad decided to return to Makkah. Leading 1,400 unarmed followers dressed in white, he made a pilgrimage to the city. They were refused entry but met with the Quraish chief, Suhayl, who made peace with them. The following year they returned and were allowed to enter the city unhindered.

Muhammad wanted Makkah to surrender to him and become converted to Islam. In November 629CE, however, the Makkans attacked one of the tribes who were friendly with the Muslims. In response, Muhammad took an army of 10,000 to the gates of Makkah. The Makkans did not fight him and Muhammad entered the city. He went to the Ka'aba and destroyed all the idols. Soon the Quraish swore their loyalty to Muhammad.

Muhammad returned to Medina and in 632CE he made a pilgrimage to the Ka'aba shrine; this became known as the 'Final Pilgrimage', or *Hajjat ul-Wida*. During this time he received revelations concerning the rules of pilgrimage (**hajj**), which Muslims follow to this day. Muhammad delivered his final sermon at Mount Arafat, in which he said: *'Regard the life and property of every Muslim as a sacred trust.... Hurt no one, so that no one may hurt you. Remember that you will indeed meet your Lord, and that he will reckon your deeds.... You will neither inflict nor suffer injustice.... Worship Allah, say your five daily prayers.'*

Muhammad contracted a heavy fever and died on 8 June 632CE at the age of around 62. His tomb is now part of the sacred mosque complex in Medina.

Synoptic question and answer

Question 11 New Testament and World Religions (Islam)

> Compare and contrast the life and teaching of a leading figure in the New Testament [Paul] with that of a leading figure in a religion you have studied [Muhammad]. To what extent did they preach a similar message?

Paul and Muhammad held unique and distinctive positions within their respective faiths. Paul was the Apostle to the Gentiles, the one who brought the message of Christ to the known world, and whose epistles and letters make up a great deal of the New Testament. It is claimed that Muhammad was the last prophet (the 'Seal of the Prophets'), the one to whom was given the Qur'an, the final and complete revelation of God, which superseded all that came before it. The two men came from vastly different religious traditions and were separated by five centuries; yet both lives have common threads running through them, and their influence within their respective traditions is unsurpassed.

Paul, or Saul, as he was originally known, was born around 6BCE in Tarsus. He was a strict Jew and a Pharisee of the tribe of Benjamin. As a learned Pharisee, he believed that God would intervene in history to rescue the Jewish people from their enemies. He expected that the Messiah would arrive from God in dramatic fashion, drive out the Romans and establish God's kingdom on earth. He felt contempt for the followers of Jesus, who were claiming that he had risen from the dead and was the true Messiah. He wanted to stop the early Christians from spreading their message and obtained permission from the high priest to go to the nearby city of Damascus and bring the Damascene Christians back to Jerusalem for punishment. On his way there a bright light from heaven shone down and the risen Christ challenged Paul, saying: *'Saul, Saul, why do you persecute me?'* (Acts 9:4). Paul was blinded and his life was changed for ever. He was taken to Damascus, unable to see and overwhelmed by his experience. His sight restored, Paul was converted to Christianity, developing a burning inspiration to carry the Christian message to the furthest corners of the known world: *'Paul was no sooner converted and called to be a witness to Jesus Christ than he began to fulfil his commission'* (I. Howard Marshall, 1980).

The prophet Muhammad was born in Makkah, Saudi Arabia, around 570CE. Like Paul, he was brought up in a strict religious setting. His parents died when he was very young and his grandfather, Abd al-Muttalib, and his uncle, Abu Talib, cared for him. Despite the fact that Arabia at that time was a mainly pagan country, Muhammad, strongly influenced by his grandfather, grew up to be a devout religious believer in One God. At that time Makkah contained the most important of Arab shrines, the Ka'aba temple, said to have been built by Adam himself, and dedicated to the One True God, though taken over by the worshippers of Baal.

Unlike Paul, who remained unmarried, Muhammad married Khadijah; they lived happily together and had six children. The wealth they enjoyed meant that Muhammad could devote a good deal of time to prayer and meditation and he often went away for days on end into the mountains around Makkah to be close to God. Just as Paul had received a dramatic revelation from God, so too did Muhammad — in 610CE he had a religious experience in the cave of Hira. The angel Gabriel appeared and ordered him to recite the words that appeared before him. Muhammad protested that he could not understand the words, but the angel opened his eyes and he understood their meaning. The angel ordered him to learn them and to repeat them to others. This was the first revelation of verses of the book that was to be known as the Qur'an (the Recitation). Like Paul, from the moment of his calling Muhammad's life was no longer his own; he devoted himself to God (Allah) and spent the rest of his life doing God's work as his prophet.

After this initial vision, Muhammad went through a period of waiting, unsure of what he was to do. Then, 2 years later, the revelations began again and continued for the rest of his life — a period of about 20 years. Paul's experience was similar. The leaders of the early church in Jerusalem were wary of him; after all, he had been their sworn enemy. After a brief period of preaching he was sent back to Tarsus, where he waited for nearly 10 years before he finally received the call to begin his work. In about 43CE, during the height of the persecution of the early church, Paul met the leaders of the Jerusalem church and agreed to undertake a crucial mission — to bring the word of God to the Gentiles.

There were also similarities in the circumstances that governed the early missions of Paul and Muhammad. Both faced opposition from the religious authorities and had to leave their native city and travel elsewhere to continue their work. Paul was persecuted by the Jews in Damascus and when he fled to Jerusalem he was attacked by Hellenistic Jews, who sought to kill him. Throughout his mission he faced persecution from his opponents.

Muhammad and his followers were ill-treated by the Quraish tribe, who had a vested interest in the Ka'aba shrine since they provided many pilgrims with food and shelter. They were fearful that Muhammad's teaching would undermine the prestige and credibility of temple worship, especially if the people were converted to Muhammad's teaching and away from idol worship. As a result, many of Muhammad's followers were persecuted and could not find food and shelter.

A2 Religious Studies Synoptic Guide

However, the people outside Makkah began to hear his message. He was invited to stay in the town of Yathrib, where he was made leader and judge. Muhammad and his followers were made very welcome and soon the town even changed its name to Medina, the 'town of the Prophet'. Although he was the leader, Muhammad lived very simply and humbly. In a similar vein, Paul also lived a humble life, living in the homes of believers who welcomed him. When he was not preaching he worked as a tent-maker.

Paul and Muhammad taught extensively — in Paul's case many of his sayings were recorded as letters or epistles, while the anecdotes surrounding Muhammad are known as Hadiths. Both taught humility, kindness, the freeing of slaves and the giving of charity. As ruler, Muhammad offered freedom to both the Arabs and the Jews who lived in Yathrib and taught equality for all: *'Charity is for the poor, the needy, those working at collecting it, those whose hearts are being reconciled to yours, for freeing of captives and debtors and in striving along God's way, and for the wayfarer, as a duty imposed by God'* (Qur'an 9:60).

Paul embarked upon a series of missionary journeys to the Gentile world. Everywhere he went he would preach in the local synagogue, where he met sympathetic Jews and Gentiles who would accept his message and become the centre of the new community. Later, on the return journey, he visited the new congregations of Christians that had been formed and encouraged them in their new faith. Paul, although not a ruler of his people, spoke with the authority that he believed was given to him by God: *'Share with God's people who are in need. Practise hospitality. Bless those who persecute you; bless and do not curse...be careful to do what is right in the eyes of everybody'* (Romans 12:13–14, 17).

When he preached, Muhammad often faced ridicule from those who thought he was mad. He taught a way of life that became known as Islam, which means 'submission to the will of Allah', and his followers were known as Muslims ('those who submit'). But many, like the Quraish, caused constant trouble for Muhammad and his followers because they threatened the established order. Paul faced similar opposition. In Ephesus, a city with many spiritual traditions and the home of a large number of magicians, astrologers and idol-worshippers, Paul was accused of false teaching and a riot ensued: *'Paul has convinced and led astray large numbers of people here in Ephesus.... He says that man-made gods are no gods at all'* (Acts 19:26).

In the lives of Paul and Muhammad there was seldom peace, and not everything was successful. In Athens, Paul spoke to young Romans and Greeks who were studying philosophy and the mystery religions. He began from the Greek view of God as creator and invisible presence in the universe and then spoke of humanity's search for God. He referred to the many shrines and altars that there were in the city, including the altar 'to the unknown god', which he identified with Jesus. His message received a mixed reception and Paul was not able to establish a Christian community.

Later, in Jerusalem, Jews from Asia saw Paul at the temple and convinced themselves that he had defiled the sacred site by taking Gentiles into the inner court. A riot followed. Paul was taken captive by the Romans because the crowd wanted to kill him. He was taken under armed guard to Caesarea and then on to Rome for trial before the emperor. This suited Paul's vision, since he *still believed that, as the "apostle to the Gentiles", he had something to contribute to the church in the most strategic position of all: Rome, the capital of the empire'* (John Drane, 1999).

Muhammad's was also not to be a life of peace. The Quraish tribes still opposed him and he was forced to go to war. In 627CE Muhammad defeated the army of 10,000, led by Abu Sufyan, which had threatened Medina and, the following year, Muhammad decided to return to Makkah. Leading 1,400 unarmed followers dressed in white, he made a pilgrimage to the city. They were refused entry but met with the Quraish chief, Suhayl, who made peace with them. The following year they returned and were allowed to enter the city.

In November 629CE the Makkans attacked one of the tribes who were friendly with the Muslims. In response, Muhammad took an army of 10,000 to the gates of Makkah. The Makkans did not fight him and Muhammad entered the city. He went to the Ka'aba and destroyed all the idols. Soon the Quraish swore their loyalty to Muhammad.

Both Paul and Muhammad received a profound religious experience at a similar age and their work lasted about the same length of time. In addition, both died at about the same age, although in different circumstances — Paul as a prisoner and Muhammad as a revered leader. The traditions of the early church say that Paul met a martyr's death, probably by beheading, during the persecution of Rome's Christians by the Emperor Nero in 64CE. His burial spot is unknown. Muhammad contracted a heavy fever and died on 8 June 632CE at the age of 62. His tomb is now part of the sacred mosque complex in Medina.

Yet although the lives of Paul and Muhammad contain interesting similarities, it is in their teachings that the major differences occur. Paul believed that what he taught came from Jesus Christ, the Son of God, through whom God is revealed to humanity: *'the gospel I preach is not of human origin. I did not receive it from a human source, nor was I taught it, but I received it through a revelation of Jesus Christ'* (Galatians 1:11–12). Muhammad also believed that his teaching came from God, but directly and not through Jesus Christ. He received the Qur'an gradually, over a period of 23 years. The heart of Paul's teaching was that salvation was an act of God's gracious love to his undeserving people, shown by Jesus Christ. In turn, the believer needed to make a response to God's love — to believe in God's love and have faith in him. *'These then were the key features of Paul's gospel: God's undeserved love ("grace") shown to humankind through Jesus, to which the appropriate response was "faith", which included a commitment to God that was based not on wishful thinking, but on the absolute facts of Jesus' life, death and resurrection, and the arrival of God's kingdom'* (John Drane, 1999).

For Muhammad, Jesus Christ — or Isa, as he is known to Muslims — was a great prophet but he was not the Son of God. His function was not to die and rise from the dead as a sacrifice for people's sins. Jesus was a messenger of God, not a saviour. Jesus could not be the Son of God because God is One: *'La ilaha ilallah wa Muhammadur rasul al-Lah'* (There is no God but Allah, and Muhammad is the Prophet of God). Paul, however, believed that Christians were intended to become children of God — Jesus had fulfilled God's will perfectly and believers could now do the same, thanks to the presence of the risen Christ living within them, through the work of the Holy Spirit: *'The Spirit himself testifies with our spirit that we are God's children. Now if we are children, then we are heirs — heirs of God and co-heirs with Christ, if indeed we share in his sufferings in order that we may also share in his glory'* (Romans 8:16–17).

Paul taught that there was only one way to escape the judgement of God. It was not through obedience to the Law, nor through doing good works — it was through faith in Jesus Christ: *'The certainty of human unworthiness before the perfection of God, the atoning sacrifice of Christ on the Cross, the glorious promise of the Resurrection and everlasting life — these are the core of Paul's religion. And above all, the knowledge that Christ, the drama of his passion, death and resurrection, but also the continuing presence in the world are in us. That is the winning formula'* (A. N. Wilson, 1998). This is in direct contrast to Muhammad's teaching on judgement. Muhammad said that God would judge all people on Judgement Day and that no one could bear the sins of another. The believer must depend upon the mercy of God: *'O my servants who have transgressed against their own souls! Do not despair of the mercy of God, for Allah forgives all sins. He is the Compassionate, the Merciful'* (Sura 39–53).

A further major difference is in the actions of Paul and Muhammad. Although both were men of peace, Muhammad was often called upon to wage war whereas Paul never was. Of course, this needs to be considered in context — Paul was not a ruler but Muhammad was, and leadership brings special responsibilities. In that sense it ought to be noted that both men preached peace and equality among all humanity: *'There is no longer Jew nor Greek, slave nor free, male or female; for you are all one in Christ Jesus'* (Galatians 3:28); *'An Arab has no superiority over a non-Arab; a white has no superiority over a black.... Every Muslim is a brother to every other Muslim.'*

In 632CE Muhammad made a pilgrimage to the Ka'aba shrine; this became known as the Final Pilgrimage, or *Hajjat ul-Wida*. During this time he received revelations concerning the rules of pilgrimage (hajj), which Muslims follow to this day. Muhammad delivered his Final Sermon at Mount Arafat, in which he said: *'Regard the life and property of every Muslim as a sacred trust.... Hurt no one, so that no one may hurt you. Remember that you will indeed meet your Lord, and that he will reckon your deeds.... You will neither inflict nor suffer injustice.... Worship Allah, say your five daily prayers.'* We do not know Paul's final words, but the core of his message — peace, love and respect for others — is the same as that of Muhammad. The form of the faith and the source of the revelation were very different for the two men, but the heart was the same.

Ethical theory and applied ethics

New Testament teaching on divorce

A man will leave his father and mother and be united to his wife, and they will become one flesh.

(Genesis 2:24)

Marriage is the legal union of a man and woman, and divorce is the legal termination of that union. The biblical view of marriage is that it is ordained by God and that the husband and wife make a commitment to an exclusive and binding relationship that will last until the death of one of the partners. The New Testament writers did not approve of divorce and taught that, ideally, the relationship should be maintained as a holy one: *'Therefore what God has joined together, let man not separate'* (Matthew 19:6).

Paul suggests that the marriage relationship is hierarchical, modelled on the hierarchy of God and humans. In a marriage relationship the man is the head of the wife, as Christ is the head of the church. As such, the wife is called to love and respect her husband and his task is to love her in the way Christ loves the church: *'For the husband is the head of the wife as Christ is the head of the church…love your wives, just as Christ loved the church'* (Ephesians 5:23, 25). This concept of headship is a theological one because the model is Christ's headship over the church, which is rooted in love and sacrifice, not domination and power. Such love involves the husband ensuring the needs of his wife are met even if it seems to be to his personal detriment, because in loving his wife he loves himself. In turn, the wife is reminded to show respect for her husband — not because she is inferior to him but because, arguably, it is usual for a man to need to receive respect: *'Wives, in the same way be submissive to your husbands…. Husbands, in the same way be considerate as you live with your wives and treat them with respect'* (1 Peter 3:1, 7).

J. A. T. Robinson (1963), however, challenged the view that laws concerning marriage were based on the absolute command of God. Instead, he argued that the moral teachings of Jesus were not intended to '...*be understood legalistically, as prescribing what all Christians must do, whatever the circumstances...they are illustrations of what love may at any moment require of anyone...it is saying that utterly unconditional love admits of no accommodation; you cannot define in advance situations in which it can be satisfied with less than complete and unreserved self-giving.*'

The major Christian denominations all accept the New Testament's pronouncements on marriage, but while agreeing that the relationship should ideally be lifelong, denominations are divided as to how strictly they interpret the biblical teaching on divorce. Decisions about whether to allow divorced Christians to marry again in church, or even whether to accept the marriage of a Christian to a non-Christian, will often be matters of conscience. An individual minister may not be troubled by the prospect of conducting the marriage service of a divorced person but, aware that others in the church would be challenged or offended by it, may refuse to allow the service to take place.

The subject of divorce was important to the Pharisees during the time of Jesus. It is therefore not surprising that Jesus was asked — possibly in a spirit of academic interest rather than hostility — to adjudicate between the school of Hillel, who permitted divorce for trivialities, and the school of Shammai, who allowed it only for 'indecency'. Jesus appears to have said that by virtue of God's creative ordinances a partner is bound not to separate from his or her spouse (Mark 10:11–12) and that the Jewish law provides for divorce only as a concession to humanity's hardness of heart: '*Anyone who divorces his wife and marries another woman commits adultery against her. And if she divorces her husband and marries another man, she commits adultery*' (Mark 10:11–12). However, Matthew's gospel includes what is known as the **exceptive clause**: '*I tell you that anyone who divorces his wife, **except for marital unfaithfulness**, and marries another woman, commits adultery*' (Matthew 19:9). The verb *porneia*, variously translated 'marital unfaithfulness', 'premarital unchastity' or 'indecency', allows for a wide range of sexual misconduct. Matthew may have included it only to satisfy his Jewish-Christian readers, who would have been horrified at the prospect of staying married to an unfaithful partner (in fact Jewish law required that the husband should divorce his wife if she committed adultery). Some modern-day Christians continue to accept this as biblically permissible grounds for divorce. It is also unlikely that Jesus would have permitted remarriage, even for the so-called 'innocent partner' in this case, and this might explain the disciples' astonishment at his harsh teaching: '*If this is the case...it is better not to marry*' (Matthew 19:10).

Similarly, Paul condones the separation of a Christian and a non-Christian spouse if one refuses to stay with the other. This was an important provision at a time when conversion to Christianity often meant total abandonment of a traditional way of life. *'But if the unbeliever leaves, let him do so. A believing man or woman is not bound in such circumstances'* (1 Corinthians 7:15).

According to Mark, Luke and Paul, Jesus went further than the Old Testament laws on divorce in forbidding remarriage after divorce. In 1 Corinthians 7:10–11 Paul writes: *'A wife must not separate from her husband, but if she does, she must remain unmarried or else be reconciled to her husband. And a husband must not divorce his wife.'* It seems, then, that Paul has understood Jesus's teaching to imply that a couple may separate, but not divorce. This still underlies traditional Catholic teaching, which forbids divorce *a vinculo* (from the bond of marriage).

Although it is likely that both Christians and non-Christians would still argue that adultery violates the bond of exclusive commitment beyond repair, it is also possible to maintain that the Christian principle of forgiveness should be allowed to take precedence. It provides permissible grounds for divorce if a divorce is sought, but it does not command it. Selwyn Hughes, in *Marriage as God Intended*, argued that divorce need not be the inevitable end to marriage, but rather that the Christian is under a much stronger obligation than the non-Christian to seek reconciliation. Where divorce has occurred, however, the attitude of the church should surely be one of encouragement, support and forgiveness for those who are deeply in need of it. The tendency to project the view that divorce is the unforgivable sin does not support the wider biblical principles of love, grace and compassion.

Situation ethics

Joseph Fletcher coined the phrase 'situation ethics' in his 1966 book of the same title. He was responding to what he felt were the failures of **legalism** (rigid adherence to law) inherent in ethical systems that propose rules to govern human behaviour, while at the same time rejecting **antinomianism** — a total abandonment of rules and principles. His is a subjective approach to ethics, which maintains that we can only know truth through our own personal experience. Situationists take the example of Jesus in Mark 10 as a model of situation ethics in practice. When asked about divorce law by the legalistic Pharisees, Jesus refers them back to Creation, rather than the Law of Moses, which was designed to accommodate humanity's sinful nature: *'It was because your hearts were hard that Moses wrote you the law'* (Mark 10:5). The story of the woman caught in adultery (John 8:1–11) shows Jesus himself adopting a situationist approach, demonstrating love, compassion and integrity in a case where the letter of the law would usually be applied, and showing the weakness of using absolute laws as a means of judging individual moral cases: *'If any one of you is without sin, let him be the first to throw a stone at her'* (John 8:7).

Fletcher maintained that there was a middle way between legalism and antinomianism and this lay in the application of **agape**, the love which Jesus commanded: *'Love the Lord your God with all your heart and with all your soul, and with all your strength and with all your mind; and love your neighbour as yourself'* (Luke 10:27).

Fletcher proposed four presumptions of situation ethics. First, **pragmatism** demands that a proposed course of action should work and that its success or failure should be judged according to the principle. **Relativism** rejects such absolutes as 'never' or 'always', while **positivism** recognises that love is the most important criterion of all. Finally, **personalism** demands that people should be put first. Fletcher defined love as being always good, and the only norm. It should be just, and only the end or goal of love justifies the means. Crucially, it makes a decision there and then in each individual situation.

Situation ethics has many strengths. It allows for individual cases to be judged on their own merits, irrespective of what has been done in similar situations in the past. People are not subject to rules that bind them. Nothing is intrinsically wrong or right, except the principle of love. Such love seeks the well-being of others even if the course of action is not one of preference. Most importantly, it is based on the teaching of Jesus and so could be considered a truly Christian ethic.

Inevitably, however, there are weaknesses. Despite Fletcher's attempt to be anti-legalistic, the application of a single principle does make it a legalistic approach. To say no rules apply, and yet to say also that the only rule is love, is a contradiction. Also, the theory is dependent on the calculation of consequences. It is impossible to be accurate in making such a calculation. Crucially, it reduces ethics to a single principle and one way of evaluating moral action. The theory could, therefore, justify adultery, murder and even genocide in the interests of love. The approach is teleological, which demands that we are able to make reliable judgements about the long-term outcomes of actions, although such prediction is virtually impossible. At the same time, the theory is very optimistic about human ability to make judgements in favour of others without being influenced by our personal preferences, and in discrete, yet unfailingly fair ways. Fletcher said that law and love are seen as mutually exclusive yet they may, in fact, be linked. As Paul wrote: *'Love does no harm to its neighbour. Therefore love is the fulfilment of the law'* (Romans 13:10). But the principles of situation ethics do not allow for this. Glyn Simon observed: *'A false spirituality of this kind has always haunted the thinking of clever men'* (cited in Howatch, 1990).

Synoptic question and answer

Question 12 Religious Ethics and New Testament

> Examine and discuss the extent to which the ethical teaching of the New Testament in an area of your choice [divorce] is compatible with an ethical theory you have studied [situation ethics].

Marriage is a total troth communion which can be broken by any kind of prolonged infidelity, whether through the squandering of monies, unwillingness to share of self, breaking of confidences or other betrayals of trust.

(*New Dictionary of Christian Ethics and Pastoral Theology*, 1995)

Marriage is the legal union of a man and a woman, and divorce is the legal termination of that union. The Bible states that God ordained marriage as the means by which the husband and wife make a commitment to an exclusive and binding relationship that will last until the death of one of the partners: *'A man will leave his father and mother and be united to his wife, and they will become one flesh'* (Genesis 2:24). The biblical writers did not approve of divorce and taught that ideally the relationship should be maintained as a permanent, holy one: *'Therefore what God has joined together, let man not separate'* (Matthew 19:6).

The ethics of marriage and divorce have long been an issue of concern for religious believers. That concern is still relevant in the twenty-first century and has resulted in widely differing attitudes to the issues of marriage and divorce, not just among religious believers but also in the media, Parliament, law, and for moral philosophy. The law controls marriage relationships, but combines legal and moral issues in a distinctive way. For instance, adultery may be considered immoral, and it may be legitimate grounds for a legal divorce, but it is not a crime. Indeed, some thinkers argue that sexual activities that take place between consenting adults, married or unmarried, heterosexual or homosexual, are not a matter of morality at all.

Is it, therefore, possible to reconcile biblical and ethical teaching over the dilemma of divorce? One possible answer may lie in the application of situation ethics. In his book *Situation Ethics*, Joseph Fletcher argued against what he felt were the failures of legalism inherent in ethical systems that propose rules to govern human behaviour. He did not suggest a total abandonment of rules and principles, but believed that we can only know the right thing to do through our own personal experience. For example, Jesus in Mark 10, when asked about divorce law by the legalistic Pharisees, refers them back to Creation rather than the Law of Moses, which was designed to accommodate man's sinful nature: *'It was because your hearts were hard that Moses wrote you the law'* (Mark 10:5). Similarly, the story of the woman caught in adultery shows Jesus adopting a situationist approach, demonstrating love, compassion and integrity and showing the weakness of using absolute laws as a means of judging individual moral cases: *'If any one of you is without sin, let him be the first to throw a stone at her'* (John 8:7).

Cases such as these were the substance of much academic debate amongst the Pharisees during the time of Jesus, and it is not surprising that he was drawn into their discussions. As a teacher, his opinion on matters that divided the different rabbinic schools would inevitably have been sought, and his responses — which blend obedience to the will of God and compassion for the individual — can be seen to provide a model for modern Christian approaches to ethical dilemmas. Fletcher argued that the answer to ethical and moral dilemmas lies in the application of *agape*, the love that Jesus commands: *'Love the Lord your God with all your heart and with all your soul, and with all your strength and with all your mind; and love your neighbour as yourself'* (Luke 10:27). Fletcher proposed four presumptions of situation ethics. The first is pragmatism, which demands that a proposed course of action should work, and that its success or failure should be judged according to the principle. Relativism rejects such absolutes as 'never' or 'always', while positivism recognises that love is the most important criterion of all. Finally, personalism demands that people should be put first. Fletcher defined love as being always good, and the only norm. It should be just, and only the end of love justifies the means. Crucially, it makes a decision there and then in each individual situation, independent of previous cases and without making reference to a set of absolutes. The theory is thus subjective and teleological — drawing on personal experience to make judgements and considering the outcome of the action, rather than the application of absolute rules, as the important factor.

The application of situation ethics to the problem of divorce is complex, due to the conflict within Christianity itself concerning New Testament teaching. While major Christian denominations all accept the New Testament pronouncements on marriage and agree that the relationship should ideally be lifelong, denominations are divided as to how strictly they interpret the biblical teaching on divorce. Decisions about whether to allow divorced Christians to marry again in church, or even whether to accept the marriage of a Christian to a non-Christian, will often be matters of conscience. For instance, a priest may not, himself, be troubled by the prospect of conducting the marriage service of a divorced person but, aware that others in the church would be challenged by it, may refuse to allow the service to take place. The issues are so intensely personal that it is impossible to reach a consensus. As in all matters of this nature, however, people's individual beliefs are so deeply rooted that although they are inevitably subjective, through church teaching, and often the hardness of the human heart towards that which threatens their own security, they emerge as objective laws.

Even the teachings of Jesus contain apparent contradictions, a fact which should make it even harder for churches or individuals to claim that they know the 'truth'. In Mark's gospel Jesus says that a partner is bound not to separate from his or her spouse: *'Anyone who divorces his wife and marries another woman commits adultery against her. And if she divorces her husband and marries another man, she commits adultery'* (Mark 10:11–12). In Matthew's gospel, however, there appears to be an 'exceptive clause': *'I tell you that anyone who divorces his wife, **except for marital unfaithfulness,** and marries another woman, commits adultery'* (Matthew 19:9). Matthew may have included it only to satisfy his Jewish-Christian readers, who would have been horrified at the prospect of staying married to an unfaithful partner — and indeed, who would have been forbidden not to seek divorce under such circumstances. Some modern-day Christians, however, continue to accept this as biblically permissible grounds for divorce, although Selwyn Hughes argued that there is a special incentive for Christians to seek reconciliation rather than divorce in such cases.

Similarly, Paul condones the separation of a Christian and a non-Christian spouse if one refuses to stay with the other. This was an important provision at a time when conversion to Christianity often meant total abandonment of a traditional way of life, and again it is often cited as legitimate grounds for a Christian partner to be divorced from his or her non-Christian spouse without 'guilt': *'But if the unbeliever leaves, let him do so. A believing man or woman is not bound in such circumstances'* (1 Corinthians 7:15). Some Christians feel so strongly about the likely failure of the marriage of a Christian to a non-Christian that many churches actively seek to discourage, or even forbid it, and married people within the church who worship without their spouse (usually women) are frequently subjected to continual pressure to seek the conversion of their partner. Many are left feeling in some way inadequate when their partner fails to convert, and are not encouraged by the feeling that if only they had been a 'better Christian' their spouse would be worshipping alongside them.

A useful analysis of the ethics of marriage and divorce was given by John A. T. Robinson in his controversial book *Honest to God*, in which, influenced by the situation ethics of Joseph Fletcher, he offered an approach to the modern moral problems of marriage and divorce. Robinson maintained that there has been a 'wind of change' in morality which Christian thinkers have to recognise, or else we will face the downfall of Christian morality altogether. Robinson claimed that morality has traditionally assumed that morals are based on laws handed down by God and which are eternally valid for human behaviour. These laws have had the effect of making certain things always wrong (sins) or always right, and provide the basis for whether society judges them to be crimes. Robinson identified traditional thinking on marriage and divorce to be a particular arena in which this kind of thinking prevails: *'There is, for instance, a deep* *division on the interpretation of the "indissolubility" of marriage. There are those who say that "indissoluble" means "ought not to be dissolved" — ought **never** to be dissolved. There are others who take it to mean "cannot be dissolved".*

See how these varying emphases draw out different dimensions of the problem. If marriage 'ought not' to be dissolved, then it becomes a grave issue of morality if it is; if it 'cannot' be dissolved, then no legal fiction drawn up by a court of law can affect what goes on in heaven, where earthly divorce counts for nothing and a couple are as united in marriage as they were on the day they took their wedding vows. Robinson claimed that these views are grounded in the opinion that marriage is a metaphysical reality which survives independently of the actual physical relationship and which cannot be affected by any objective facts or legal manoeuvres: *'It is not a question of "Those whom God has joined together let no man put asunder": no man could if he tried.'*

Robinson challenged the view that marriage is based on the absolute command of God. Instead, he argued that the moral teachings of Jesus were not intended to *'...be understood legalistically, as prescribing what all Christians must do, whatever the circumstances...they are illustrations of what love may at any moment require of anyone...it is saying that utterly unconditional love admits of no accommodation; you cannot define in advance situations in which it can be satisfied with less than complete and unreserved self-giving.'*

Robinson argued that it is impossible to begin from a position of saying sexual relations before marriage or divorce are inherently wrong or sinful, because the only intrinsically wrong thing is a lack of love. He supported the views of Fletcher: *'If the emotional and spiritual welfare of both parents and children in a **particular** family can be served best by divorce, wrong and cheapjack as divorce commonly is, then love requires it.... And this is the criterion for every form of behaviour, inside marriage or out of it, in sexual ethics or in any other field. For **nothing else** makes a thing right or wrong.'*

In some respects Robinson's situationist view allows for the teaching of Jesus. Jesus's attitude to those on the fringes of the society in which he lived was one of true *agape*, and one for which he risked rejection by his own people. He allowed the greater purpose of love to be served when he healed lepers, spoke seriously and intimately with women, when he allowed a 'sinful' woman to anoint his head, and when he invited the hated tax collectors to share table fellowship with him. For a modern Christian to argue on the one hand that Jesus was right to do this, and would still do it today, and on the other to imply that neither Jesus nor God his Father could find room in their hearts to forgive a divorcee — whether the 'guilty' or the 'innocent' party — serves only to crystallise much of the hypocritical and narrow thinking that many people feel has come to represent Christianity over the years.

Situation ethics itself has many strengths. It allows for individual cases to be judged on their own merits, irrespective of what has been done in similar situations in the past. People are not subject to rules that bind them. Nothing is intrinsically wrong or right, except the principle of love. Such love seeks the well-being of others, even if the course of action is not one of preference. Most importantly, it is based on the teaching of Jesus and so could be considered a truly Christian ethic.

Inevitably, however, there are weaknesses. Despite Fletcher's attempt to be anti-legalistic, the application of only one principle does make it a legalistic approach. To say no rules apply, and yet also to say the only rule is love, is a contradiction. Also, the theory is dependent on the calculation of consequences. It is impossible to be accurate in making such a calculation. Crucially, it reduces ethics to a single principle and one way of evaluating moral action. The theory could, therefore, justify adultery, murder and even genocide in the interests of love.

Applying the theory to divorce, therefore, presents problems in itself. If it is the sexual tie that is crucial in marriage and if its breach is the only permissible grounds for divorce according to the New Testament, then a Christian who seeks a divorce for any other reason, including cruelty, could be said to be acting immorally and contrary to the will of God. A situationist, however, would argue that there are many ways in which the mutual bond of trust and commitment can be broken, and that it is an unreasonable imposition on the emotional and physical well-being of the individual to refuse to allow other grounds for divorce. This does not help religious believers, however, who see it as their duty to adhere to the teachings of Christ.

Yet there may be a middle ground. It is possible that both Christians and non-Christians would accept that, although adultery violates the bond of exclusive commitment beyond repair, it is also possible to maintain that the principles of love and forgiveness should be allowed to take precedence. Divorce need not be the inevitable end to marriage, and both the New Testament and situation ethics support the notion of loving reconciliation. Furthermore, when a marriage ends there must be the chance for another relationship to take its place, potentially one that is more in the spirit of Christ's love; to deny individuals any opportunity to find such a blessing is dangerously unloving. So too must be the insistence that a man or woman remain at the mercy of a violent, abusive or cruel partner, simply to justify the teachings of a church or the beliefs of a third party. The evangelists never recorded Jesus telling anyone to remain in a situation which brought them misery or put them in peril, and given the hard teachings that the New Testament does include, it seems likely that they would have included such teaching had he done so.

Christians should therefore seek a blend of law and love. Not law in its legalistic, inhibiting guise, but in the freedom it gives for humans to know that they are not acting alone, but have the revealed will of God to help them. So, despite the fact that Fletcher saw law and love as mutually exclusive, they may in fact be linked. As Paul observed: *'Love does no harm to its neighbour. Therefore love is the fulfilment of the law'* (Romans 13:10).

Ethical theory and applied ethics

Natural moral law

True law is right reason in agreement with nature. It is applied universally and is unchanging and everlasting…one eternal and unchanging law will be valid for all nations and all times, and there will be one master and rule, that is God.   (Cicero)

Thomas Aquinas was the great Christian proponent of **natural moral law**, in particular the view that all things have a purpose towards which they work. This purpose can be understood through an examination of the natural world and through the Bible, which reveals the purpose for which God has created humanity. Natural law is available to all, since everyone with some reasoning capacity would be able to see that the universe works according to certain patterns and rules that do not change. In the *Summa Theologica*, Aquinas maintained that there is a moral code towards which human beings naturally incline, which he called natural moral law. Natural law has several aspects — it is universal, unchanging, eternal and given by God. It is relevant in all circumstances and all humans can perceive it through the natural order of things. Natural law draws its inspiration from the Bible as well as from the common reasoning of humankind. *'For since the creation of the world God's invisible qualities — his eternal power and divine nature — have been clearly seen, being understood from what has been made, so that men are without excuse'* (Romans 1:20).

The principle of natural law depends on establishing the purpose of human life. Aquinas maintained that it is to live, reproduce, learn, worship God and order society. All things must operate in accordance with these principles, to which humanity is naturally inclined. God gives humans reason to accomplish these purposes and everything is created to a particular design and for a particular purpose, and fulfilling that purpose is the 'good' towards which everything aims.

However, although the natural law, instituted by God, gives humanity the opportunity to work towards the good in all things, in the New Testament Paul acknowledges that this is not always possible; humanity will fall short of God's best because this is a fallen world: *'for all have sinned and fall short of the glory of God'* (Romans 3:23). Nevertheless, the rational person will desire communication with God and will act to accomplish it, despite the limitations of humanity. Any action that takes someone closer to this goal is good, and any action that takes them further away is wrong.

Aquinas identified four kinds of law: the **eternal law**, which is God's will and wisdom and is revealed in the **divine law**, given in scripture and through the church. This is experienced by humanity as **natural law**, from which **human law** is derived. Human law, then, as exercised through the state and government, is an extension of natural and divine law: *'Everyone must submit himself to the governing authorities, for there is no authority except that which God has established'* (Romans 13:1). Natural moral law is a universal guide for judging the moral value of human actions. It makes God's commandments accessible to believers because, through Creation, humans and God share the same rationality. It means that morality is more than just a matter of what people's personal preferences and inclinations may be. Even though different cultures and individuals may reach different conclusions on the rightness or wrongness of a moral action, there is a prevailing sense that some things are eternal truths.

There are problems, however. Aquinas assumed that all people seek to worship God and that God created the universe and the moral law within it. These assumptions are not natural ones for the atheist to make. Moreover, by giving pride of place to reproduction as one of the universal aims of humankind, Aquinas opened up thorny issues for homosexuals (what if homosexuality can be explained genetically and can therefore be deemed 'natural'?) and for those who are biologically incapable of having children, let alone those who for personal reasons choose not to do so. Moreover, he suggested that human nature has remained the same since creation. This does not allow room for evolution, cultural development or even the divine redemption of humanity through Christ.

Homosexuality

Human sexuality is concerned not just with what people do, but with who people actually are. In the biblical account of Creation, the making of man and woman as sexual beings is linked to their creation in God's own image. Sexuality is an integral part of what makes a person human. The Bible makes it clear that sexual relationships are for the marriage relationship and that other forms of sexual relationship are forbidden. Any behaviour that breaks the links between sex, personhood and relationship is seen as a symptom of sin and disorder and should be avoided: *'Flee from sexual immorality…. Do you not know that your body is a temple of the Holy Spirit, who is in you, whom you have received from God?'* (1 Corinthians 6:19).

Christians are divided over the issue of homosexuality. While for some it is the ultimate taboo and homosexuals should not be welcomed into Christian fellowship, still less into the ministry, for others to be homosexual is a natural way to have been created by God. Nevertheless, the Bible teaches that all homosexual acts are prohibited: *'Neither the sexually immoral nor idolaters nor adulterers nor male prostitutes nor homosexual offenders…will inherit the kingdom of God'* (1 Corinthians 6:9–10). The biblical writers consistently condemn homosexual practices. In Leviticus 20:13 the Israelites are warned that homosexuality carries with it the death penalty: *'If a man lies with a man as one lies with a woman, both of them have done what is detestable. They must be put to death, their blood will be on their own heads.'* The most specific teaching against homosexuality is found in Romans, in which Paul suggests that it was a result of the Fall, after which: *'Men…were inflamed with lust for one another, men committed indecent acts with other men and received in themselves the due penalty for their perversions'* (Romans 1:27).

D. S. Bailey offered a re-evaluation of these traditional arguments against homosexuality, drawing attention to the use of language and the culture from which biblical teachings emerged. Condemnation of homosexual acts in the Bible often appears to relate to pagan practices, and many of the Old Testament passages seem to be condemning idolatry at the same time. In the New Testament Paul says of his own teaching on sexual morality: *'I have no command from the Lord, but I give a judgement as one who by the Lord's mercy is trustworthy'* (1 Corinthians 7:25). Paul may, therefore, be speaking entirely from his own perspective. Since it is clear that some of his teaching no longer has cultural relevance — the instruction to women to cover their heads in church, for example — it is possible that his teaching on homosexuality may also be culturally relative. Several modern thinkers have argued that stable, affectionate relationships should be defended on the grounds that the only way to judge sexual behaviour truly is through love: *'There are circumstances in which individuals may justifiably choose to enter into a homosexual relationship with the hope of enjoying companionship and a physical expression of love similar to that found in marriage'* (Church of England Working Party Paper).

Much scientific research has gone into attempts to understand the origin of homosexuality and to establish whether or not there is a fundamental medical or genetic cause. This may consist of a hormonal imbalance or a genetic predisposition and attempts have been made to identify a 'homosexual gene' which would establish in some way that homosexuality is a natural predisposition for some people. Nina Rosenstand argued that should this be established, then biblical objections to homosexuality would no longer be valid and there would be no reason to discriminate against homosexuals on the grounds of immorality. In *Sexual Deviation*, psychiatrist Anthony Storr observed that: *'[Homosexuals] have a vested interest in affirming that their condition is an inborn abnormality rather than the result of circumstances; for any other explanation is bound to imply a criticism of themselves or their families and usually of both.'*

Whatever the origins of a homosexual orientation, religious believers are deeply divided over how to deal with it in the world and in the religious community. The Lesbian and Gay Christian Movement maintain that: *'Human sexuality in all its richness is a gift from God gladly to be accepted, enjoyed and honoured.'* However, the Roman Catholic Church states in the *Declaration on Sexual Ethics* that: *'In sacred scripture homosexual acts are condemned as a serious depravity and presented as a sad consequence of rejected God.'* Recently the Methodist Church declared: *'For homosexual men and women permanent relationships characterised by love can be an appropriate and Christian way of expressing their sexuality.'* The 1998 Lambeth Conference of the Church of England Bishops established that four perspectives on homosexuality were possible:

- Homosexuality is a disorder from which the Christian can seek deliverance.
- Homosexual relationships should be celibate.
- While exclusive homosexual relationships fall short of God's best for man, they are to be preferred over promiscuous ones.
- The church should accept homosexual partnerships fully and welcome homosexuals into the priesthood.

Even if homosexuality is an important issue for religious believers, is it an issue of moral concern? In *The Value of Life*, John Harris claimed that sexual activities of any kind should not be seen in a moral context but rather as an issue of manners and etiquette. His view is not unlike J. S. Mill's **Harm Principle**, which claims that the only right that society has to interfere with the lives of individuals is in preventing them from causing harm to others. Harris maintained that as homosexuality does not cause harm to society, as a whole, the individual's sexual relationships should be private and free from moral judgements.

Nevertheless, the principle of natural law is strongly opposed to homosexuality on the grounds that the purpose and goal of a sexual relationship should be procreation. Interestingly, however, Paul himself seems not to support this view and suggests that sex could serve purposes of love and intimacy: *'Do not deprive each other except by mutual consent and for a time'* (1 Corinthians 7:5).

For many religious believers the issue is not so much being homosexual but rather the carrying out of homosexual practices. The former may not be a matter of choice but the latter is. Mark Bonnington and Bob Fyall, in *Homosexuality and the Bible*, proposed that the solution lies in loving, but non-genital, same-sex relationships: *'Warm companionship without any sexual element is not something that should be regarded as odd by the Christian community. Rather, it is to be welcomed as a valuable way of developing affectionate bonds within the church and providing the human support and comfort that most of us find we need.'*

In a similar vein, the Church of England has, while discouraging homosexual practices, acknowledged that Christians must respect those who: *'are conscientiously convinced that they have more hope of growing in love for God and neighbour with the help of a loving and faithful homophile partnership, in intention lifelong, where mutual self-giving includes the expression of their attachment.'*

Synoptic question and answer

Question 13 **Religious Ethics and Christian Belief**

> Analyse and consider critically the application of at least one ethical theory [natural moral law] to an ethical issue [homosexuality] relevant to Christianity.

Neither the sexually immoral nor idolaters nor adulterers nor male prostitutes nor homosexual offenders…will inherit the kingdom of God. (1 Corinthians 6:9–10)

Human sexuality is concerned not just with what people do, but also with who people actually are. In Christian belief, sexuality is regarded as an integral part of what makes a person human. However, the Bible makes it clear that sexual relationships are for within marriage and that other forms of sexual relationship are forbidden. Any behaviour that breaks the links between sex, personhood and relationship is seen as a symptom of sin and disorder and should be avoided: *'Flee from sexual immorality…. Do you not know that your body is a temple of the Holy Spirit, who is in you, whom you have received from God?'* (1 Corinthians 6:19).

Christians are divided over the issue of homosexuality. For some believers it is the ultimate taboo, and homosexuals should not be welcomed into the Christian Church. For others, homosexuality is the natural way in which God has created some people.

The issue of homosexuality sits in an uneasy tension with Christianity and the apparent harshness of biblical teaching has led many thinkers, Christian and non-Christian alike, to look for alternative approaches.

One ethical theory which has strong connections with Christianity and the Bible is natural moral law; its application to the problem of homosexuality offers a useful insight into the Christian approach to such a complex dilemma.

Thomas Aquinas was the great Christian proponent of natural moral law. He argued that all things have a purpose towards which they work. This purpose can be understood through an examination of the natural world and through the Bible, which reveals the purpose for which God has created humanity. Natural law is available to all, since everyone with some reasoning capacity would be able to see that the universe works according to certain patterns and rules that do not change. In the *Summa Theologica*, Aquinas maintained that there is a moral code towards which human beings naturally incline, and this he called natural moral law. Natural law has several aspects — it is universal, unchanging, eternal and given by God. It is relevant in all circumstances and all humans can perceive it through the natural order of things. Natural law draws its inspiration from the Bible as well as from the common reason of mankind. *'For since the creation of the world God's invisible qualities — his eternal power and divine nature — have been clearly seen, being understood from what has been made, so that men are without excuse'* (Romans 1:20).

The principle of natural law depends on establishing the purpose of human life. Aquinas maintained that it is to live, reproduce, learn, worship God and order society. All things must operate in accordance with these principles, to which humanity is naturally inclined. God gives humans reason to accomplish these purposes and everything is created to a particular design and for a particular purpose, and fulfilling this purpose is the 'good' towards which everything aims.

Aquinas identified four kinds of law: the eternal law is God's will and wisdom; it is revealed in the divine law, given in scripture and through the church. This is experienced by humanity as natural law — from which human law is derived. Human law, then, as exercised through the state and government, is an extension of natural and divine law: *'Everyone must submit himself to the governing authorities, for there is no authority except that which God has established'* (Romans 13:1). Natural moral law is a universal guide for judging the moral value of human actions. It makes God's commandments accessible to believers because humans and God share the same rationality. It means that morality is more than just a matter of what people's personal preferences and inclinations may be. Even though different cultures and individuals may reach different conclusions on the rightness or wrongness of a moral action, there is a prevailing sense that some things are eternal truths.

Applying natural moral law to the problem of homosexuality seems to offer little comfort, however. If the Bible is to be accepted as the word of God and as containing eternal truths, then the teaching is clear — the Bible condemns homosexual practices, both in the Old and New Testaments. Thus, in Leviticus 20:13 the Israelites are warned that homosexuality carries with it the death penalty: *'If a man lies with a man as one lies with a woman, both of them have done what is detestable. They must be put to death; their blood will be on their own heads.'*

Moreover, the most specific teaching against homosexuality is found in Romans, in which Paul suggests that it was a result of the Fall, after which: *'Men…were inflamed with lust for one another, men committed indecent acts with other men and received in themselves the due penalty for their perversions'* (Romans 1:27). The Roman Catholic Church broadly supports this view and in the *Declaration on Sexual Ethics* it states that: *'In sacred scripture homosexual acts are condemned as a serious depravity and presented as a sad consequence of rejected God.'*

Yet there may be an alternative application of the principles of natural moral law to this issue. Aquinas assumed that God created the universe and the moral law within it. This may not necessarily be the case, and is certainly not accepted by every interpretation of the universe and humanity's place in it. Moreover, Aquinas suggested that human nature has remained the same since creation. This does not allow room for evolution, cultural development or — most crucially for Christianity — the divine redemption of humanity through Christ.

The notion of redemption through Christ is at the heart of Christian teaching. It acknowledges humanity's weakness and captivity in sin and offers salvation through forgiveness. Thus, although the natural law, instituted by God, gives humanity the opportunity to work towards the good in all things, in the New Testament Paul acknowledges that this is not always possible; humanity will fall short of God's best because this is a fallen world: *'for all have sinned and fall short of the glory of God'* (Romans 3:23).

Therefore, although the principle of natural law is strongly opposed to homosexuality on the grounds that the purpose and goal of a sexual relationship should be procreation, this view is not completely supported by biblical teaching. Paul himself seems not to support this view and suggests that sex could serve other purposes — those of love and intimacy: *'Do not deprive each other except by mutual consent and for a time'* (1 Corinthians 7:5). Moreover, today many within the Church have argued that stable, affectionate relationships should be defended on the grounds that the only way truly to judge sexual behaviour is through love: *'There are circumstances in which individuals may justifiably choose to enter into a homosexual relationship with the hope of enjoying companionship and a physical expression of love similar to that found in marriage'* (Church of England Working Party Paper).

D. S. Bailey offered a re-evaluation of the biblical and natural moral law arguments against homosexuality, drawing attention to the use of language and the culture from which these teachings emerged. Condemnation of homosexual acts in the Bible often appears to relate to pagan practices, and many of the Old Testament passages seem to be condemning idolatry at the same time. In the New Testament Paul says of his own teaching on sexual morality: *'I have no command from the Lord, but I give a judgement as one who by the Lord's mercy is trustworthy'* (1 Corinthians 7:25). Paul may, therefore, be speaking entirely from his own perspective. Since it is clear that some of his teaching no longer has cultural relevance — the instruction to women to cover their heads in church, for example — it is possible that his teaching on homosexuality may also be culturally relative.

Much scientific research has gone into attempts to understand the origin and causes of homosexuality and to establish whether or not there is a fundamental medical cause. The findings pose serious challenges to the presumptions of natural moral law. Homosexuality may be the result of a hormonal imbalance or a genetic predisposition and attempts have been made to identify a 'homosexual gene' which would establish that homosexuality is a natural predisposition for some people. Nina Rosenstand argued that should this be established, then biblical and natural moral law objections to homosexuality would no longer be valid, and there would thus be no reason to regard homosexuality as an immoral choice.

Whatever the origins of a homosexual orientation, religious believers are deeply divided over how to deal with it in the world and in the religious community. The Lesbian and Gay Christian Movement maintain that: *'human sexuality in all its richness is a gift from God gladly to be accepted, enjoyed and honoured.'* In a similar vein, the Methodist Church recently declared: *'For homosexual men and women permanent relationships characterised by love can be an appropriate and Christian way of expressing their sexuality.'*

Compromises between the principles of natural moral law and broader feelings of love and compassion led to the 1998 Lambeth Conference of the Church of England Bishops establishing four perspectives on homosexuality. First, that homosexuality is a disorder from which the Christian can seek deliverance. Second, that homosexual relationships should be celibate. Third, that while exclusive homosexual relationships fall short of God's best for man, they are to be preferred over promiscuous ones. And fourth, that the church should fully accept homosexual partnerships and welcome homosexuals into the priesthood.

Even if homosexuality is an important issue for religious believers, is it an issue of moral concern? In *The Value of Life*, John Harris claimed that sexual activities of any kind should not been seen in a moral context but rather as an issue of manners and etiquette. His view is not unlike the Harm Principle of J. S. Mill, who claimed that the only right that society has to interfere with the lives of individuals is to prevent them causing harm. Harris maintained that as homosexuality does not cause harm to society as a whole, the individual's sexual relationships should be private and free from moral judgements.

Yet such compromises usually end up upsetting everyone and pleasing nobody; for many religious believers the issue is not so much one of being homosexual as of carrying out homosexual practices. The former may not be a matter of choice, but the latter is. Mark Bonnington and Bob Fyall, in *Homosexuality and the Bible*, proposed that the solution lies in loving, but non-genital, same-sex relationships: *'Warm companionship without any sexual element is not something that should be regarded as odd by the Christian community. Rather, it is to be welcomed as a valuable way of developing affectionate bonds within the church and providing the human support and comfort that most of us find we need.'* In recent times, too, the Church of England, while discouraging homosexual practices, has acknowledged that Christians must respect those who *'...are conscientiously convinced that they have more hope of growing in love for God and neighbour with the help of a loving and faithful homophile partnership, in intention lifelong, where mutual self-giving includes the expression of their attachment.'*

To apply the principles of natural moral law to the teachings of the Bible and the Christian church on the issue of homosexuality is, ultimately, unsatisfying in this modern era. The ethical teachings of both on this issue are one and the same and, it appears, most uncompromising. If the Bible is the unchanging word of God and natural moral law can be derived from it, then homosexuality is to be condemned. Yet there remains the matter of God's love and forgiveness and redemption for the sinner through Christ. Room must be found for this principle too, as Christianity looks to define its ethical and moral position in today's world: *'For all have sinned and fall short of the glory of God and are justified freely by his grace through the redemption that came by Christ Jesus'* (Romans 3:23).

Feminist theology

Biblical interpretation: the concept of divine inspiration

Inspiration as a model for biblical interpretation

The concept of divine inspiration is a model used to describe the significance of scripture and the belief that the whole Bible has its origin in God himself; in order for it to be a source of truth about God it must be of divine origin. The best-known text used to support the inspiration of scripture is 2 Timothy 3:16–17: *'All scripture is inspired by God and profitable for teaching, for reproof, for correction and for training in righteousness.'* The verb used — *theopneustos* — literally means 'God breathed' and the verse describes the inspiration being in the text itself, rather than the author. However, 2 Peter 1:20–21 suggests that men are inspired: *'men moved by the Holy Spirit spoke from God'* and in Mark 12:36 Jesus speaks of David having *'declared in the Holy Spirit'*. The Spirit's involvement gives the text a meaning and significance for a later audience and behind the human author is a divine initiative beyond that which is normally known to him. For Calvin, inspiration was the basis for asserting the unique status of scripture over and above any other post-scriptural teaching and the teaching of the church.

Inspiration is distinct from revelation. Revelation is the making known of something otherwise unknown and can take place through various media. Inspiration refers to the way in which concepts are conveyed by the Holy Spirit and the words which are used to convey those concepts. The concepts inspired may be quite commonplace but the process is unique, operating through a supernatural agency.

Inspiration was uncontroversial in patristic and medieval theology but is generally considered inconsistent with a historical and critical approach to exegesis, especially when verbal inspiration, even oral dictation, is considered an important part of the position. Scholars such as Origen, who claimed that the Holy Spirit accommodated human authors, addressed the problem of inconsistency and inexactitude in the texts. This view also accounts for the diversity of styles within the books of the Bible and usefully allows for differences which grow out of their different circumstances and situation. Sarah Heaner Lancaster (2002) observed:

If God's dictation does not violate the human author's style, neither does it violate their situation…. Though the impulse for the will to write comes from God, this impulse seems to coincide with what is also compelling about the author's particular situation.

During the renaissance and enlightenment, the drift towards studying the Bible as one would study any other work of literature led to questions about its inspiration. The word acquired an increasingly secular meaning, as non-religious writers and artists used the term to describe the feeling that something beyond themselves was given to them in the execution of their work. Most significantly, critical approaches to biblical interpretation revealed the humanness of the writings and various responses to the problem attempted to restate the doctrine of inspiration.

Problems for the inspiration model

Several issues lead to considerable problems for the model of the inspiration of scripture, especially if it is associated with the belief that it is inerrant, which characterises the conservative approach to inspiration:

The doctrine of inspiration guaranteed that scripture could be trusted but also forced Protestant scholastics to deny error of any sort. This position bore serious consequences later as [they] struggled to account both for internal and external challenges to the truth of scripture.

(Sarah Heaner Lancaster, 2002)

Millar Burrows identified several of these challenges:

- The Bible itself testifies to being the product of divine inspiration, but *'a witness cannot by his own testimony establish his competence to testify'* (Burrows, 1946).
- Direct evidence of divine origin would seem to be impossible to establish.
- The inspiration model suits some books, e.g. prophetic literature, more than others, i.e. those which are narrative-based and involve human speakers, as well as the divine. Different levels of inspiration are evident in different books of the Bible.
- What constitutes the Bible? The decision as to which books were to make up the canon of scripture was not taken at the same time and accepted unanimously by the whole church, and disputes followed for several centuries. In the light of this: *'We cannot ascribe equal authority to everything in it or exclude entirely from the category of inspired scripture such books as Ecclesiasticus or the Wisdom of Solomon'* (Burrows, 1946).

- Most Christians read the Bible in translation and no translation can be infallible, even if it were possible to argue that the original Hebrew and Greek texts were.
- Before the books of the Bible were written at all, the materials which they contain had gone through many formulations, including oral transmission. The words of the prophets were preserved in the memories of their disciples, and the books of both Old and New Testaments are products of compilation, selection, arrangement and revision.

Different ways of understanding inspiration

Verbal inspiration — this maintains that the exact wording of the biblical text is divinely inspired, a view that is characteristic of twentieth-century conservative evangelical Christianity. B. B. Warfield maintained that it is the only sufficient safeguard of the full inspiration of scripture and that any other theory concedes too much to the human element.

Oral dictation — in this process God infused concepts into the authors' intellects and instigated them to write. God's word is spoken through human words, but the word is nevertheless spoken by God. It is hard to maintain verbal inspiration without oral dictation, although alternative approaches now put more emphasis on the inspiration of the community behind the books rather than the individual.

Divine influence — W. J. Abraham argued that the process of divine inspiration is like the way in which one human being may inspire another. God influences human beings by who he is and what he has done, although the work that follows is entirely the person's own.

Biblical theology — this perspective maintains that the inspiration is inherent in the salvation history recorded in the Bible. The events are inspired, rather than the narrative accounts of them, and the whole process which leads to the existence of the Bible is itself inspired.

Inspiration without inerrancy — Alfred Loisy observed that inspiration is an issue concerning the sufficiency of the Bible in matters of morals and faith, not its perfection. Each book, being a work of its own time, is necessarily affected by errors of fact and opinion. A perfect book, valid in every respect for every period of history, is an impossibility — even for God.

Providence — scripture teaches everything we need to know for the purpose of salvation. It is by God's providence that there is a Bible at all — the inspiration is that it is complete and sufficient.

Feminist theology

Feminist biblical interpretation has its origins in the work of Elizabeth Cady Stanton, who published *The Woman's Bible* in 1895–98. She believed that the key to legislative reform lay in a new approach to biblical interpretation, and that the development of higher criticism, which was already debating the status of the Bible as the infallible word of God, supported her approach. The subsequent development of feminist interpretation has provided an alternative assessment of biblical evidence as seen through the eyes of women readers and theologians.

Feminist theologians have sought to prove that the attitude of hostility towards women and the low estimation of them derived not from the biblical text but from the *history of biblical interpretation*. The roots of an oppressive interpretation may have derived from 1 Timothy, where the author interprets the Creation narrative in a way that is clearly detrimental to the subsequent view of women in the church and the world and to the way their stories are interpreted: *'For Adam was formed first, then Eve, and Adam was not deceived, but the woman was deceived, and became a transgressor'* (1 Timothy 2:13–14).

Three routes to feminist interpretation

1 **The radical route** — this rejects the Bible in favour of an alternative, feminine religious experience. Mary Daly characterises the most aggressive end of radical feminism, observing, for example, that what may appear to be a positive feminist aspect of Catholicism — the place of Mary — has been manipulated by male theologians to become a means of female subjugation. She claimed that the Judaeo-Christian tradition is a structure in which 'god is male and the male is god' and urged that it is not enough simply to change language to make it less exclusivist. Calling God 'she' rather than 'he' is not enough, but rather God should be understood as 'Being'. She maintained that only lesbian radical feminists could rise above male patriarchy and she subsequently broke completely from Christianity and Christian feminism.

2 **The reformist route** — this reconstructs a positive theology for women. The work of Rosemary Radford Ruether, Phyllis Trible and Elisabeth Schussler Fiorenza is central to the reformist interpretation, which attempts to go directly to the text rather than through the history of interpretation. They read the text with feminist eyes and criticised the accepted interpretation of it, and as such their approach is compatible with most recent developments in biblical literary criticism.

For example, Trible took the narrative of Genesis 2. Rather than interpreting it as a story that sanctions the subjugation of women, she read it as one of equality and complementarity in which both man and woman share in sin and punishment. Ruether responded to Daly's radical approach, arguing that Daly was excluding men from the liberation which Christianity, interpreted especially through the Synoptic Gospels, offers to male and female. She used the Lucan birth narrative as an example. In it, Mary serves as a model for discipleship for all humankind, and displays a courageous faith comparable with that of Abraham. In accepting God's plan for her she does not accept in submission, but asserts her autonomy. In the Magnificat she anticipates the message of social justice which characterises Jesus's teaching, and she fuses feminist theology with liberation theology. Importantly, Fiorenza claimed that female subjugation is not part of the original gospel, but the result of the church's compromise with the Graeco-Roman world.

3 **The conservative evangelical route** — this rejects nothing in the Bible, but explains it in a positive light for contemporary women. Interestingly, while the USA has fostered the development of the radical and reformist routes, the conservative evangelical approach is unique to the UK and is characterised by the work of Elaine Storkey. The Bible continues to occupy a high position of authority and the approach is closer to apologetics, but it is nevertheless radical compared with other conservative evangelical positions. For example, Storkey interpreted Paul's use of the concept of 'headship' (Ephesians 5:22ff.) to mean 'source of life' rather than authority, and she observed that when Eve is described as Adam's 'helper' the same noun is used to describe God in relation to Israel.

Fundamental feminist concepts

Women's experience — Ruether argued that human experience is the starting and ending point of all interpretation, and since scripture must have arisen out of human experience, all interpretation of it must continue to be illuminated by it. Symbols, laws and traditions within it must be re-authenticated by a new generation or be discarded, and this is exactly what feminist theologians are doing — testing their experience against received tradition. Ruether (1983) defined 'women's experience' as: *'created by the social and cultural appropriations of biological differences in a male-dominated society'*, which make women more dependent than their male counterparts.

Feminist critical consciousness — with this in mind, feminists bring a critical bearing to biblical interpretation and assert their right to make critical evaluations based on recognising that oppression is wrong and liberation is good. This involves a fight with the authorities who have had the power to promote oppression.

Revelation — in making judgements about the relevance and truth of certain passages, feminists observe that they are not doing anything other than what has been done by other critics. In objection to this, some claim that feminist criticism places an external norm (women's experience) above the Bible itself. It is important to consider whether the authority of women as interpreters necessarily challenges the authority of the Bible. Reformists argue that they are *using* the Bible as the basis for their insights. Sarah Heaner Lancaster (2002) asked: *'[Is] there any way to bring the fundamental commitments of feminist theology into dialogue with an equally fundamental commitment to the Bible as the word of God?'*

Synoptic question and answer

Question 14 Philosophy of Religion and Christian Belief

Does feminist theology pose a significant threat to the concept of divinely inspired scripture?

The concept of divine inspiration is a model which is used to express the significance of scripture and the belief that the whole Bible has its origin in God himself. As such, it is a source of truth about God and, as described in 2 Timothy 3:16–17: *'profitable for teaching, for reproof, for correction and for training in righteousness'*. In addition, 2 Peter 1:20–21 observes that *'men moved by the Holy Spirit spoke from God'* and Jesus himself describes David as having *'declared in the Holy Spirit'* (Mark 12:26). The concept has been important throughout the development of biblical interpretation and has served to assert the unique status of scripture over and above any other post-scriptural or extra-canonical writings and the teaching of the church. While revelation is the making known of something otherwise unknown and can take place through various media, inspiration refers to the way in which concepts are conveyed by the Holy Spirit and the words used to convey them. Words are powerful tools and the wrong word, or the wrong interpretation of a word, can lead to a quite unintended interpretation of the concept. The concept of inspiration ensured the authority of the text — the divine initiative behind the human author — and the Spirit's involvement gave it a meaning and significance for a later audience.

The concept of inspiration has become a controversial one, since it carries with it many possible assumptions which are now considered anachronistic — the inerrancy of scripture in all matters, for example. Although inspiration was uncontroversial in patristic and medieval theology, it is generally considered inconsistent with a historical and critical approach to exegesis — especially when verbal inspiration, even oral dictation, is considered an important part of the position. Scholars such as Origen, however, who claimed that the Holy Spirit accommodated human authors, addressed the problem of inconsistency and inexactitude in the texts. This view also accounts for the diversity of styles within the books of the Bible and usefully allows for differences that grow out of their different circumstances and situation. The feminist critic Sarah Heaner Lancaster (2002) observed: *'If God's dictation does not violate the human author's style, neither does it violate their situation.... Though the impulse for the will to write comes from God, this impulse seems to coincide with what is also compelling about the author's particular situation.'*

The concept of inspiration is directly relevant to any discussion of biblical interpretation. As the critical movement developed in the eighteenth and nineteenth centuries, the notion that the Bible was an inerrant, inspired, homogenous work became less tenable, and the drift towards studying the Bible in the same way as any other book led to serious questions about its inspired status. The word 'inspiration' acquired an increasingly secular meaning, as non-religious writers and artists used the term to describe the feeling that something beyond themselves had been given to them in the execution of their work. Most significantly, critical approaches to biblical interpretation revealed the humanness of the writings and various responses to the problem attempted to restate the doctrine of inspiration. Feminist criticism, as a branch of biblical interpretation which, like any other, attempts to infiltrate the text irrespective (although not necessarily careless) of historical or perceived opinions about its authoritative status, will face the question of inspiration head on. This is specifically because it faces the challenge of placing an external norm — women's experience — above the Bible itself. Sarah Heaner Lancaster (2002) asked: *'[Is] there any way to bring the fundamental commitments of feminist theology into dialogue with an equally fundamental commitment to the Bible as the word of God?'*

Feminist biblical interpretation has its origins in the work of Elizabeth Cady Stanton, who published *The Woman's Bible* in 1895–98. She believed that the key to legislative reform lay in a new approach to biblical interpretation, and that the development of higher criticism, which was already debating the status of the Bible as the infallible word of God, supported her approach. The subsequent development of feminist interpretation has provided an alternative assessment of biblical evidence as seen through the eyes of women readers and theologians. Since then feminist theologians have sought to prove that the attitude of hostility towards women and the low estimation of them derives not from the biblical text but from the history of biblical interpretation. The roots of an oppressive interpretation may have derived from 1 Timothy, where the author interprets the Creation narrative in a way that clearly encourages a negative view of woman's role in man's fall and separation from God: *'For Adam was formed first, then Eve, and Adam was not deceived, but the woman was deceived, and became a transgressor'* (1 Timothy 2:13–14). Feminist theologians argue that human experience is the starting point of all interpretation of scripture and must continue to illuminate it. Scripture, however, like all literature which contains symbolism and tradition, must be re-authenticated by each new generation that encounters it, or else be discarded. Feminist theology provides a tool by which the traditions of the Bible can be re-evaluated in the light of contemporary culture and the roles of the sexes in the modern era.

This is immediately significant: feminist theologians are not essentially challenging the biblical material but rather the interpretation of it. While scripture may or may not derive directly from God, interpretation of it derives from human beings. If this needs to be reappraised and corrected, then, arguably, any tool which we may use to do this serves to get us closer to the original, inspired word, not further away from it. Three routes to feminist interpretation have emerged, however, some of which may be seen to support the inspiration model more than others.

The radical route rejects the Bible in favour of an alternative, feminine religious experience. The work of Mary Daly characterises the most aggressive end of radical feminism. For example, she observed that what may appear to be a positive feminist aspect of Catholicism — the place of Mary — has been manipulated by male theologians to become a means of female subjugation. She claimed that the Judaeo-Christian tradition is a structure in which 'god is male and the male is god' and urged that it was not enough simply to change language to make it less exclusivist. Calling God 'she' rather than 'he' is not enough, but rather God should be understood as 'Being'. She maintained that only lesbian radical feminists could rise above male patriarchy and she subsequently broke completely from Christianity and Christian feminism. This approach evidently cannot ever be compatible with the concept of inspiration, since it rejects the Bible out of hand as a source book which has done nothing more than promote female subjugation. The alternative, feminine religious experience of the radical feminists leaves no room for the Bible, inspired or not, and proponents are compelled to seek a non-biblical faith.

If the radical route to feminist interpretation rejects the inspiration model, it is not the only critical path to have done so. There are already many problems with the concept of inspiration even without the contribution of the radical feminists. Millar Burrows identified several problems with the inspiration model. The Bible itself testifies to being the product of divine inspiration, but *'a witness cannot by his own testimony establish his competence to testify'* (Burrows, 1946) and direct evidence of its divine origin would seem to be impossible to establish.

The inspiration model suits some books, e.g. prophetic literature, more than others, i.e. those which are narrative based and which involve human speakers as well as the divine — and different levels of inspiration clearly seem to be evident in different books of the Bible. In any case, what constitutes the Bible? The decision as to which books were to make up the canon of scripture was not taken at the same time and unanimously accepted by the whole church, and disputes followed for several centuries. In the light of this, as Burrows (1946) wrote: *'We cannot ascribe equal authority to everything in it or exclude entirely from the category of inspired scripture such books as Ecclesiasticus or the Wisdom of Solomon.'* Furthermore, most Christians read the Bible in translation and no translation can be infallible, even if it were possible to argue that the original Hebrew and Greek texts were. In any case, before the books of the Bible were written at all, the materials that they contain had gone through many formulations, including oral transmission. The words of the prophets were preserved in the memories of their disciples, and the books of both Old and New Testaments are products of compilation, selection, arrangement and revision. In the light of all this, it would seem virtually impossible for any interpreter to maintain the notion that the inspiration of scripture guarantees it to be free from error, as Sarah Heaner Lancaster (2002) observed: *'The doctrine of inspiration guaranteed that scripture could be trusted but also forced Protestant scholastics to deny error of any sort. This position bore serious consequences later as [they] struggled to account for both internal and external challenges to the truth of scripture.'*

Perhaps the other routes to feminist interpretation are more supportive of the inspiration model. The reformist route reconstructs a positive theology for women. The work of Rosemary Radford Ruether, Phyllis Trible and Elisabeth Schussler Fiorenza is central to the reformist interpretation that attempts to go directly to the text rather than through the history of interpretation. They read the text with feminist eyes and criticised the accepted interpretation of it, and as such their work is compatible with most recent developments in biblical literary criticism. For example, Trible took the narrative of Genesis 2 and rather than interpreting it as a story which sanctions the subjugation of women, she read it as one of equality and complementarity, in which both man and woman share in sin and punishment. Ruether made a similar analysis of the Lucan birth narrative, observing that in it, Mary serves as a model for discipleship for all humankind and displays a courageous faith comparable with that of Abraham. In accepting God's plan for her, Mary does not accept in submission but asserts her autonomy. In the Magnificat, which fuses feminist and liberation theology, she anticipates the message of social justice that characterises Jesus's teaching. Importantly for our discussion, Fiorenza claimed that female subjugation is not part of the original gospel but the result of the church's compromise with the Graeco-Roman world. If this is so, then it is possible to preserve the inspiration model virtually wholesale, since the misunderstandings which have derived from subsequent biased interpretations of it can be put down to human error rather than any failure on the part of the original authors.

The third route — evangelical conservative — accommodates the inspiration model to an even greater extent. This approach rejects nothing in the Bible but explains it in a positive light for contemporary women. Interestingly, while the USA has fostered the development of the radical and reformist routes, the evangelical conservative approach is unique to the UK and is characterised by the work of Elaine Storkey. The Bible continues to occupy a high position of authority and the approach is closer to apologetics, although it is considered radical compared with other evangelical conservative positions which traditionally hold an inerrant, inspiration model as a key doctrine. For example, Storkey interpreted Paul's use of the concept of 'headship' (Ephesians 5:22ff.) to mean 'source of life' rather than authority, and she observed that when Eve is described as Adam's 'helper' the same noun is used to describe God in relation to Israel. This positive reading does allow for inspiration, keeping the Bible in a position of authoritative centrality, while exposing the potentially chauvinistic interpretations that have arisen from earlier readings of the text.

Of the many ways of understanding the inspiration model, the concept of 'inspiration without inerrancy' may fit feminist interpretative methods best. Alfred Loisy observed that inspiration is an issue concerning the sufficiency of the Bible in matters of morals and faith, not its perfection. Each book, being a work of its own time, is necessarily affected by errors of fact and opinion and is not a 'perfect' book. In any case, a 'perfect' book, valid in every respect for every period of history, is a logical impossibility, even for God, since it would have to be constantly changing and could not therefore be, *a priori*, perfect. Feminist interpretation offers an interesting, relevant and illuminating tool to unlock truths in the biblical text which appear to have been obscured by many years of patriarchal interpretation. In this way it may be said to uncover concealed and forgotten inspirations in the text, rather than force us to abandon the inspiration model.

Concepts of authority

Authority of scripture

Two models of authority

Causative authority — scripture is inspired and the Holy Spirit produces the faith to believe what scripture has to say. It is self-authenticating and needs no further authority to confirm its truth. It leads to faith in the true sense of confidence, which leads to salvation — an internal conviction that it is based on true knowledge of God.

Canonical authority — scripture becomes the norm for knowledge of God and is both **directive** (a guide) and **corrective** (a judge). It is certain, fixed, invariable and suited to every situation — including matters of science and history — and although it needs interpretation, the only infallible interpreter is the Holy Spirit. Controversies over its meaning are not the fault of scripture, but weaknesses of interpretation. It was not accommodated to the writers' situations or to prevailing, if incorrect, notions about science, geography and chronology. It is inerrant and inspired in these, and all other matters, even in matters that are apparently contradictory. However, an *a priori* acceptance of scripture's truth in all things became increasingly difficult to maintain as science gained greater force and Protestant scholasticism, which supported the model of inerrant inspiration, itself paved the way for source criticism.

Biblical criticism

Below are three possible ways of analysing the function of biblical criticism:

1 **The rationalist and sceptical movement** — this has had the effect of 'dethroning' the Bible. Its origins lie in the assumption that the Bible can and should be read like any other book. As such it is regarded as a human creation in which inaccuracies and

inconsistencies can be detected and whose authors have been affected by their own time-bound assumptions. This position discounts the possibility of a miracle and claims that no events or persons are unique, since they are analogous to others. This viewpoint offers four alternatives: abandon biblical authority altogether and rely on personal interpretation or the interpretation of the church; abandon criticism and fall back on fundamentalism; allow criticism its place but leave room for positive, constructive theology; allow that biblical literature is valid because it is culturally relative and the texts should be read as finished wholes with regard for the authors' circumstances.

2 **German theology** — this has emphasised biblical criticism as a reflection of increased respect for scripture. Rudolph Bultmann maintained that because Christianity is justified by faith in Christ and not by the accuracy of the scriptural text, it belongs to Christian freedom to ask radical questions about the text.

3 **Intellectual curiosity and awareness of literary styles** — for example, Julius Wellhausen was concerned to reveal the Bible's fundamental status as a source of historical evidence. Academic objectivity is neither a support for, nor an attack upon, the authority of scripture.

The nature of biblical authority

While all branches of Christianity have regarded scripture in some sense to be authoritative for faith and life, they do not all agree on what the Bible teaches. What claims does the Bible make for itself? If authority lay entirely in the exact contents of the original revelation, then there would be no authoritative scripture at all, since we cannot know what those contents were. Even the original manuscripts would contain changes that had been made to the original revelation. So was it the final compiler who was divinely guided? If the Bible is to have authority it must be judged on the basis of the Bible we have now, including its imperfections. Millar Burrows (1946) observed that: *'Much ink has been wasted…in the effort to prove the detailed historical accuracy of the biblical narratives. Actually, they abound in errors, including many contradictory statements.'* Burrows maintained, however, that historical information is not the essential content of revelation, since even fictions may be true to life and convey religious truths. What is important is a valid spiritual interpretation and the religious significance given to accounts. If a miracle can be given a naturalistic explanation, this does not automatically prove that it did not happen; and the Bible treats both miraculous and non-miraculous events as having supernatural significance and origin. The Bible also expresses ideas that are clearly wrong — e.g. slavery, wars of extermination — as well as much which could be said to be permanently valid — respect for life and the rights of the disadvantaged — so it should be evident that it can only be a reliable guide when interpreted in a legitimate way. These difficulties may be viewed positively and with the intention of finding an appropriate way of interpreting the text so that it is true to itself and relevant to the reader (as Millar Burrows attempted to do). On the other hand, the difficulties may be regarded negatively: *'Truth may be hard to define but the truth of any book can be tested by its agreement with sources of its time and consistency with itself. The Bible fares badly on both counts'* (Derek Chatterton, 2000).

The relationship between God and morality

God's authority in matters of conduct

For religious believers, God's authority in matters of conduct is considered supreme, based on the twofold principles of creation and covenant. God has authority to enforce and demand, to reward obedience and punish disobedience. The sense of his sovereignty, which permeates the whole Bible, promotes this way of thinking. God's commands are not arbitrary but are true and righteous, since what God wishes man to do is that which is right in itself, even if human beings cannot perceive the reason for it. Millar Burrows (1946) wrote:

What is right is not so because God commands it; he commands it because it is right, and it is right because it is good for man. This may be true even of what we may call strictly religious rather than moral requirements such as the observance of the Sabbath.

God commands what is right for human beings because he has superior knowledge and knows all the implications of our actions, so humans should seek his advice as they would the advice of earthly experts. God is not subject to a higher source of authority and knowledge — he knows what is good because he made the world and all that is in it.

James Sire observed that the key question is how humans can tell the difference between right and wrong. Sire argued that the only satisfactory explanation lies in the existence of a personal, interactive deity. Humans are able to make moral judgements, to distinguish between right and wrong and, to a remarkable extent, to agree about the content of morality. But this does not explain *why* these moral norms are the case or whether they are only authoritative to those who claim them to be so. Sire identified a range of atheistic factors that may attempt to explain this:

- **Emotivism** — all moral statements are expressions of emotion without any scientific or rational basis.
- **Marxism** — morality is a 'phantom' formed in the human brain.
- **Nietzsche** — morality is the herd instinct of the individual.

- **Existentialism** — humans must make moral choices without having any compass to guide them.
- **Anthropology** — the diversity of human life yields no universal codes of right conduct.
- **Scientific methodology** — factual statements cannot lead to moral statements (the 'is–ought gap').

All these assume a naturalistic world — God is dead or never existed. Sire asked whether, in such a world, we can ever be good. Is there a reason to be good? The reason must derive from getting an 'ought' from an 'is'. 'Is' is simply fact, e.g. 'Child abuse is' — that is, there are instances of it. To determine why it is wrong — 'You ought not to abuse children' — there needs to be an existent moral being who is the repository of goodness, or else right and wrong are merely labels we attach for emotional, pragmatic or egotistical reasons, and moral facts are just descriptions and have no reason behind them.

Morality needs a foundation because disagreements are too vast and too important just to leave to chance, and simply thinking something is right does not make it right. However, we can only say that something actually is right or wrong if we accept that there are absolutes — otherwise everything is simply opinion. Evolution does not satisfactorily explain morality as having survival value, as this itself is simply describing a factual situation and does not offer a complete explanation which must go beyond the observable facts. Sire argued that nihilistic and relative interpretations of ethics are fundamentally damaging to society's moral character.

What is the relationship between God and morality?

Sire observed that because God created the universe and made himself known to man, he must be the source of all morality since good for the world and for humans is being what God intended it to be. He does not leave it to humans to work it out, but has communicated it directly to them. Christianity therefore does not identify a problem of good — it is easily explained. Moral responsibility is only possible if there is someone to be responsible to and this cannot be simply an absolute being, but must be a person. Jesus was the supreme revelation of God's moral character and exemplifies good, and seeking to please and glorify God provides a motivation for living a good life.

'Since God is the all-knowing knower of everything, as beings made in his image, we can be the sometimes knowing knowers of some things' (James Sire, 1994). Human knowledge is thus best explained by the notion of being made in the image of God and moral knowledge must be part of this.

In recent years there has been a noticeable increase in the number of intellectuals who embrace historic Christianity as a rational worldview.... These trends do point to the fact that a number of thinkers believe that secularism is an inadequate view of the world and that a rational apologetic can be given for historic Christianity.   (J. P. Moreland, cited in Sire, 1994)

New Testament ethics

Interpretation of the ethical teaching of the New Testament has run parallel with other branches of New Testament criticism. Some basic elements of New Testament ethics were drawn from Graeco-Roman wisdom current at the time, but its distinctive features are coloured by the prevailing eschatological perspective or the person of Jesus. Jesus established moral norms such as humility, which were not previously highly regarded. The emphasis on love is most notable. It is not without parallel in Judaism, but it does not feature so much, to the extent that it becomes programmatic for all moral judgements and teaching. It characterises the attempt made in the first decades of the early church to interpret rather than reject Jewish law, a process that ranged from conservative (e.g. Matthew's gospel) to radical (e.g. some of Paul's teaching). Distinctively Christian law emerged with the increase of predominantly Gentile congregations and the decline in a belief in the imminent parousia (Second Coming). The Old and New Testaments together became a reservoir of rules and guidance on every moral situation. The Ten Commandments became prominent at a popular level in the instruction of the laity, and it is notable that it was an Old Testament teaching, rather than Jesus's twofold formula to love God and love one's neighbour, that took central place. The latter did not do so until the 1928 prayer book reform.

In the pre-critical period, ethical material was the basis of teaching on moral growth and spiritual development. It was not until the eighteenth century that Christian ethics was identified as a distinct subject alongside other academic disciplines of Christianity. For New Testament writers it was not an independent subject, but part of their total outlook, although it clearly raises particular concerns. For example:

- How far did Paul depend on Jewish and Hellenistic aspects of his upbringing or on Christology and eschatology? Did he have God-given authority himself or was he influenced by pastoral concerns?
- What was the attitude of Jesus to the Jewish law? Did he intend to demote it from a central position in the light of new Kingdom teaching? In what sense was the prominence he gave to the teaching on love programmatic?
- How did the evangelists choose to arrange the material? Paul's teaching was

direct but we can only arrive at Jesus's teaching via the evangelists' portrayal of him, which was influenced by the concerns of the time and community.

■ As Houlden wrote:

It may be that doctrinally determined convictions about their continuing direct authority, above all if they come from Jesus himself, affect the strong investment of attention in a primary treatment of Jesus's ethics, almost regardless of the difficulties. Students should recognise that in making judgments about present-day applications of New Testament ethics, writers are inevitably conditioned by their more general doctrinal standpoint about the role of scripture in Christian judgment.... These may themselves be affected by non-theological factors, such as the degree to which a writer...has come to feel the force of the relativism of moral judgments in relation to their specific contexts.

(Coggins and Houlden, 1990)

Synoptic question and answer

Question 15 Philosophy of Religion and Religious Ethics

(a) Consider some of the traditional key philosophical and ethical issues which have faced a challenge from modern views.

(b) Examine and evaluate traditional and modern views with reference to one of the issues discussed in part (a).

(a) In modern times many philosophical and ethical issues which have great significance to religious believers have come under fierce scrutiny from the challenges posed by new developments in philosophy and science. The conflict between the traditional and the new is a fertile breeding ground for the proliferation of many ideologies, some of which attempt to combine old and new, while some preserve the old and others discard it completely. For religious believers, who seek to hold on to what they consider to be of ultimate value, the challenge is a rigorous one. One question which has dominated religious scholarship since the enlightenment is that of the authority of scripture and its status as an inspired work.

The concept of the authority of scripture has been held to be of paramount importance to religious believers since the early church was evaluating the Jewish scriptures.

It can be understood in one of two ways. If the Bible has causative authority, it is understood to be an inspired text through which the Holy Spirit produces the faith necessary to believe what it says. It is self-authenticating and has the power to lead to salvation. Canonical authority views scripture as the norm for knowledge of God and is both directive (a guide) and corrective (a judge). It is fixed, invariable and is inerrant in all matters, including those of history, geography and chronology. This view immediately faces significant challenges from modern views: an *a priori* acceptance of scripture's truth in all things became increasingly difficult to maintain as science gained greater force. Protestant scholasticism, which supported the model of inerrant inspiration, itself paved the way for source criticism.

The growth of biblical criticism and interpretative methods has led to the rise of many ways of deconstructing the biblical text and offering interpretations which are coloured by the preconceptions of the critics, but which also offer important insights into the way the Bible has been interpreted over the centuries and the way in which the original writers handled the material available to them. Biblical criticism need not be automatically associated with the rationalist and sceptical movements, which have had the effect of dethroning the Bible. For many critics, the value of biblical interpretation lies in satisfying intellectual curiosity and making valuable use of a wider awareness of literary style. Wellhausen, for example, was concerned to reveal the Bible's vital role as a source of historical evidence, and said that academic objectivity was not an attack on the authority of scripture. Rather, it was quite independent of it.

The rationalist schools of criticism, however, which have their roots in the belief that the Bible should be read like any other book, could be seen to pose a serious challenge to the Bible's authoritative status. If the Bible can be read like any other book, then it is taken as if it were an entirely human creation, in which inaccuracies can be detected and whose authors were affected by their own time-bound assumptions. That there are inconsistencies in the text is not a matter of dispute — it is how significant they are which is a subject of debate. On the one hand, biblical authority can be abandoned altogether, since personal interpretation of the text is no less reliable. However, it is still possible to allow that biblical literature is valid because it is culturally relative and the texts can be read productively and interpreted as finished wholes, taking into account the authors' circumstances. Furthermore, as Rudolph Bultmann observed, salvation is obtained through faith in Jesus and not by the accuracy of the biblical text, and it is the Christian's right to ask radical questions about it.

Related to this issue is that of Christian ethics, which emerged in the eighteenth century as a distinct subject alongside other academic disciplines in Christianity. For the New Testament writers, ethical teaching was clearly part of their total outlook, not an independent subject, although key issues can be clearly identified. As the early church developed, it drew its ethical teaching initially from Jewish traditions, interpreting rather than rejecting the Jewish law, and focused upon the character of Jesus, who established moral norms — such as humility — which were not previously highly regarded. Later, ethical teaching was affected by the increase in non-Jewish congregations and a decline in the expectation of an imminent parousia. Above all, the ethical teaching of the New and Old Testaments is dominated by the sense that God's authority in matters of conduct is supreme.

Modern views on biblical interpretation and on the relationship between modern moral codes and the rules apparently laid down in scripture raise issues of particular concern, most especially, perhaps, the question of how the evangelists chose to arrange their material. Although Paul's teaching appears to be direct, the only access we have to the ethical teaching of Jesus is via the evangelists' portrayal of him, which was inevitably influenced by their own time and community. A difficulty invariably arises when we try to translate the ethical teaching of the New Testament to the present day. As Houlden observed: *'Students should recognise that in making judgments about present-day applications of New Testament ethics, writers are inevitably conditioned by their more general doctrinal standpoint about the role of scripture in Christian judgment.... These may themselves be affected by non-theological factors, such as the degree to which a writer... has come to feel the force of the relativism of moral judgments in relation to their specific contexts'* (Coggins and Houlden, 1990). Houlden's point seems to be that both writer and reader are affected by their particular perspectives. If we maintain that scripture is authoritative and binding for all times, and that there is no room to accommodate the writers' cultural and situational norms, or the readers' current perspective, then we are obliged to consider the ethical teaching of the Bible quite independently of the circumstances in which it was written and those in which it is read. For many modern thinkers this is not acceptable or practical, since it will lead genuine seekers of the truth to abandon its principles as anachronistic and irrelevant, rather than encourage them to testify to its continuing direct and unchallenged relevance.

Religious believers today face a great many moral dilemmas which compel them to extrapolate from the biblical text if they are to find an answer which has some relationship to scriptural teaching. The biblical writers were not affected by the ready availability of abortion on demand, of companies offering assisted suicide to 'death tourists', by issues of gay and lesbian rights, genetic engineering and animal experimentation, to single out just a few of the myriad ethical dilemmas which face the modern-day religious believer. The freedom of choice which humankind expects to be able to exercise would have not been an issue for a society which lived under God's sovereign rulership. While some ethical norms may have remained the same — the sanctity of life, for example — their application has changed. The call to take up arms against the enemy, to which the people of Israel readily respond in the Old Testament, is not always matched today by a ready willingness to go to war. On the other hand, while it would be naïve to argue that abortion was unheard of in first-century Palestine, the reason for which a woman might seek an abortion would not be because she felt that pregnancy would threaten her chances of promotion. Times have changed, and with them people's situations, and modern thinkers are compelled to address the question of whether biblical teaching can continue to have any validity at all.

(b) An issue that clearly emerges from these debates is that of the relationship between God and morality. The traditional view of this relationship is that the twofold principles of creation and covenant lay the foundation for God's authority to enforce and demand, to reward obedience and punish disobedience. The concepts of the authority of scripture and of how we interpret the ethical teachings of the Bible face serious challenges from modern views, but this need not entail their complete destruction. Rather, modern interpretative approaches can offer new and relevant insights into biblical teaching, and the essentially unchanging nature of humankind offers a strong argument for the continuing validity of moral teachings grounded in fundamental realities.

Millar Burrows observed that the Bible writers present a picture of God who commands things because they are good. He wrote (1946): *'What is right is not so because God commands it; he commands it because it is right, and it is right because it is good for man. This may be true even of what we may call strictly religious rather than moral requirements such as the observance of the Sabbath.'* However, he maintained that this does not force us into acknowledging that there must be some impersonal goodness that is higher than God. Rather, God commands what is right for human beings because he has superior knowledge and knows all the implications of our actions, so humans should seek his advice as they would the advice of earthly experts. God is not subject to a higher source of authority and knowledge — he knows what is good because he made the world and all that is in it.

The view that morality is made and made known by God is open to many modern challenges, however. The issue is essentially *how* humans can tell the difference between right and wrong. We make moral judgements and — to a remarkable extent — arrive at similar conclusions, but this does not explain *why* these moral norms are the case, or whether they are relative statements, held to be authoritative only to those who claim them to be so. For the modern thinker there is a vast range of alternative explanations for morality which need not include God. For the logical positivists, and A. J. Ayer in particular, moral statements have no factual value, since they have no scientific or rational basis. Rather, they are expressions of emotion or opinion, exclamations of personal preference which we may or may not choose to be influenced by. Not only do moral statements need no divine foundation, they have no real value at all, except to identify how the speaker feels. This view is compatible with the view which maintains that factual statements cannot lead to moral statements since there can be no justification in moving from an 'is' to an 'ought'. A factual statement merely conveys information about what is objectively the case, but it cannot lead us to assume any moral value, good or bad, based on that observation alone.

Alternatively, we may believe that morality is an illusory means of controlling society, or that it is simply the herd mentality of the individual. This was the view of Nietzsche, who believed that 'herd morality' impoverishes humankind by depriving it of natural values and ethics. Looking to God for moral guidance and the hope of reward serves only to rob human beings of their authentic existence. Nietzsche advocated 'biological heroism' in the place of a God-based morality, rejecting traditional moral values which tend to preserve the weak and the helpless, who can make no contribution to the overall good of society. Humankind's goal should be the development of an *Übermensch*, or 'Superman', who would establish his own value system, rejecting and despising weakness. This is a vastly different picture from the God of both Old and New Testaments, who loves the poor and the weak and who makes laws that ensure their protection.

Further modern challenges can be made to the model of divine morality. Existentialism, advocated particularly by Sartre, maintains that humans must make their moral choices without any compass to guide them. The price of human freedom is that we must make our free choices in 'abandonment and despair', since we are free to define our existence and essence entirely by the way we choose to live. Sartre assumed that God cannot exist since if he did he would rob humans of their moral autonomy, and humans who allow themselves to be influenced by religion, as well as by politics or society, are acting in 'bad faith'. Sartre maintained that human beings are neither basically good nor evil, because there are no values other than those which they have created for themselves.

The studies of anthropology have also shed much light on the development of morality among richly diverse societies, leading to the prevalence of cultural relativism — the view that there are no universal codes of right conduct. Relativism maintains that knowledge, morals and ethics are not absolute — a view which Nietzsche argued could only be a good thing: *'The advantage of our times, nothing is true, everything is permitted.'* Such a view of morality leaves no room for a divine command theory which maintains that God-given moral laws are absolute — unchanging and relevant to all human experience.

Clearly, these modern challenges to the authority of divinely commanded morality cannot all be dismissed out of hand. We are aware that individuals have many and varied views on matters of morality, that some societies accept as morally valid behaviour that which others would reject, and that we live in a tension between freedom and conformity. However, the question of whether there is *ultimately* a divine explanation of morality is not cancelled out by these challenges. First, all challenges to religious morality assume a naturalistic world — God is dead or never existed. James Sire asked whether, in such a world, we can ever be good. Is there a reason to be good? The reason to be good must derive from getting an 'ought' from an 'is'. 'Is' simply states fact, e.g. 'Child abuse is' — that is, there are instances of it. Sire argued that to determine why it is wrong — 'You ought not to abuse children' — there needs to be an existent moral being who is the repository of goodness, or else right and wrong are merely labels we attach for emotional, pragmatic or egotistical reasons, and moral facts are just descriptions and have no reason behind them.

Furthermore, morality needs a foundation because moral disagreements are too vast and too important just to leave to chance, and we are aware that simply thinking something is right does not make it right. After all, at one time people genuinely believed the world was flat, but we would be hard pressed to find anyone today who believed that this could be proved to be the case. Rather, nihilistic and relative interpretations of ethics can be fundamentally damaging to society's moral character since they could be said to encourage a culture of moral freedom to the point of anarchy. In reality, we do not truly believe that everything is relative and that whatever you believe is just as valid and true as what I believe. If this were the case, then we would have to accept that our moral opinions carried very little weight at all. Sire maintained that ultimately we can only say whether something actually is right or wrong if we accept that there are absolutes — otherwise everything is simply opinion. Evolution does not satisfactorily explain morality as having survival value, as this itself is simply describing a factual situation and does not offer a complete explanation which must go beyond the observable facts.

As in so many issues of religious philosophy, the best explanation is claimed to rest in the existence of a divine moral commander. Sire observed that since God created the universe and made himself known to humankind, then he must be the source of all morality, because good for the world and for humans is being what God intended it to be. God does not leave it to humans to work it out, but has communicated it directly to them. Christianity therefore does not identify a problem of good — it is easily explained. Moral responsibility is only possible if there is someone to be responsible to and this cannot simply be an absolute being, but must be a person. Jesus is the supreme revelation of God's moral character and exemplifies good, and seeking to please and glorify God provides a motivation for living a good life. Sire (1994) observed: *'Since God is the all-knowing knower of everything, as beings made in his image, we can be the some-times knowing knowers of some things.'* Human knowledge is thus best explained by the notion of being made in the image of God and moral knowledge must be part of this.

In conclusion, it is interesting to note J. P. Moreland's observation: *'In recent years there has been a noticeable increase in the number of intellectuals who embrace historic Christianity as a rational worldview.... These trends do point to the fact that a number of thinkers believe that secularism is an inadequate view of the world and that a rational apologetic can be given for historic Christianity'* (cited in Sire, 1994). If this is the case, it clearly suggests that despite the prevalence of alternative explanations to those notions which were once assumed to be meaningful only within a religious framework, modern challenges to religious philosophical and ethical issues have not had the last word.

Bibliography

Atkinson, D. and Field, D. (eds) (1995) *A New Dictionary of Christian Ethics and Pastoral Theology*, IVP.

Augustine of Hippo (1998 edn) *Confessions*, Oxford Paperbacks.

Ayer, A. J. (1936) *Language, Truth and Logic*, Penguin.

Barrett, C. K. (1955) *The Gospel According to St John*, SPCK.

Berkovits, E. *Faith after the Holocaust*, Ktvan Publishing House.

Berkovits, E. (1979) *With God in Hell*, Hebrew Publishing Company.

Blaiklock, E. M. (1959) *Acts*, Tyndale.

Boff, L. (1986) *Liberation Theology: From Confrontation to Dialogue*, New York.

Bonino, J. M. (1985) *Doing Theology in a Revolutionary Situation*, Fortress.

Bonnington, M. and Fyall, B. (1996) *Homosexuality and the Bible*, Grove Books.

Bright, J. (1981) *A History of Israel*, SCM.

Bruce, F. F. (1995) *Romans*, IVP.

Burrows, M. (1946) *An Outline of Biblical Theology*, Westminster.

Chatterton, D. (2000) *Reflections on Religion*, D. Chatterton.

Coggins, R. and Houlden, L. (eds) (1990) *A Dictionary of Biblical Interpretation*, SCM.

Cole, R. A. (1990) *Mark*, W. B. Eerdmans.

Conn, J. W. (1989) *Spirituality and Personal Maturity*, Paulist Press.

Cruz, N. (1968) *Run, Baby, Run*, Hodder & Stoughton.

Drane, J. (1999) *Introducing the New Testament*, Lion.

Drane, J. (2000) *Introducing the Old Testament*, Lion.

Dumoulin, H. and Maraldo, J. C. (eds) (1977) *Buddhism in the Modern World*, Collier Mac.

Fackenheim, E. (1983) *Quest for Past and Future*, Greenwood Press.

Fletcher, J. (1966) *Situation Ethics*, SCM.

Flew, A. (1955) *Theology and Falsification*, SCM.

Flew, A. (1984) *God, Freedom and Immortality: A Critical Analysis*, Prometheus.

Frankena, W. K. (1973) *Ethics*, Prentice Hall.

Friedlander, A. (1994) *Riders Towards the Dawn*, Continuum International Publishing Group.

Fuller, R. H. (1972) *The Formation of the Resurrection Narratives*, SPCK.

Green, J., McKnight, D. and Marshall, I. M. (eds) (1992) *A Dictionary of Jesus and the Gospels*, IVP.

Griffin, D. (1976) *God, Power and Evil: A Process Theodicy*, The Westminster Press.

Gutierrez, G. (2001) *A Theology of Liberation*, SCM.

Halverson, M. and Cohen, A. (eds) (1960) *A Handbook of Christian Theology*, Fontana.

Harris, J. (1984) *The Value of Life*, Routledge.

Heaner Lancaster, S. (2002) *Women and the Authority of Scripture*, Trinity Press.

Hick, J. (ed.) (1964) *The Existence of God*, Macmillan.

Hick, J. (1966) *Faith and Knowledge*, Fount.

Hick, J. (1968) *Christianity at the Centre*, SCM.

Hick, J. (1968) *Evil and the God of Love*, Fontana.

Hick, J. (1973) *Philosophy of Religion*, Prentice Hall.

Howatch, S. (1990) *Scandalous Risks*, HarperCollins.

Hughes, S. (1983) *Marriage as God Intended*, Kingsway.

Hume, D. (1975 edn) *An Enquiry Concerning Human Understanding*, Oxford University Press.

Hume, D. (1998 edn) *Dialogues Concerning Natural Religion*, Oxford Paperbacks.

Hyatt, J. (1980) *Exodus*, Marshall, Morgan and Scott.

Mackie, J. L. (1955) *Evil and Omnipotence*, Mind.

Mackie, J. L. (1982) *The Miracle of Theism*, Oxford University Press.

Magee, B. (1997) *Confessions of a Philosopher*, Phoenix.

Marshall, I. H. (1980) *Acts*, IVP.

Mitchell, B. (ed.) (1971) *The Philosophy of Religion*, Oxford University Press.

Moltmann, J. (2001 edn) *The Crucified God*, SCM.

Moore, G. E. (1993 edn) *Principia Ethica*, Cambridge University Press.

Nagel, T. (1987) *What Does it all Mean?*, Oxford University Press.

Noth, M. (1996) *The History of Israel*, XPRESS Reprints.

Parsons, S. F. (2002) *The Cambridge Companion to Feminist Theology*, Cambridge University Press.

Porter, J. (1995) *Moral Action and Christian Ethics*, Cambridge University Press.

Rahula, W. (1986) *What the Buddha Taught*, Atlantic Books.

Ripper, A. (2000) *Muslims: Their Religious Beliefs and Practices*, Routledge.

Robinson, J. A. T. (1963) *Honest to God*, SCM.

Rubenstein, R. (1992) *After Auschwitz*, Johns Hopkins University Press.

Ruether, R. R. (1983) *Sexism and God-Talk*, SCM.

Shereshevsky, E. (1996) *Rashi, the Man and his World*, Jason Aronson.

Sire, J. (1994) *Why Should Anyone Believe Anything at All?*, IVP.

Sobrino, J. (1978) *Christology at the Crossroads*, Orbis.

Storr, A. (1964) *Sexual Deviation*, Penguin.

Swinburne, R. (1971) *The Concept of Miracle*, Macmillan.

Swinburne, R. (1979) *The Existence of God*, Oxford University Press.

Swinburne, R. (ed.) (1989) *Miracles*, Macmillan.

Swinburne, R. (1996) *Is There a God?*, Oxford University Press.

Thompson, M. (1996) *The Philosophy of Religion*, Hodder & Stoughton.

Vardy, P. (1996 edn) *The Puzzle of God*, Fount.

Warfield, B. B. (1950) *The Person and Work of Christ*, Presbyterian and Reformed Publishing Company.

Whale, J. S. (1957) *Christian Doctrine*, Fontana.

Wiles, M. (1986) *God's Action in the World*, SCM.

Wilson, A. N. (1998) *Paul: The Mind of an Apostle*, Pimlico.

Wolters, C. (ed.) (1998 edn) *Revelations of Divine Love*, Penguin.